IN DEEP

ALSO BY DAVID ROHDE

Beyond War: Reimagining America's Role and Ambitions in a New Middle East

A Rope and a Prayer: The Story of a Kidnapping (with Kristen Mulvihill)

Endgame: The Betrayal and Fall of Srebrenica, Europe's Worst Massacre Since World War II

IN
DEEP

THE FBI, THE CIA, AND THE TRUTH
ABOUT AMERICA'S "DEEP STATE"

David Rohde

W. W. NORTON & COMPANY
Independent Publishers Since 1923

Portions of *In Deep* appeared in different form in *The New Yorker*

For information about special discounts for bulk purchases, please contact
W. W. Norton Special Sales at specialsales@wwnorton.com or 800-233-4830

Manufacturing by Lake Book
Book design by Lisa Buckley
Production manager: Anna Oler

ISBN 978-1-324-00354-0

W. W. Norton & Company, Inc., 500 Fifth Avenue, New York, N.Y. 10110
www.wwnorton.com

W. W. Norton & Company Ltd., 15 Carlisle Street, London W1D 3BS

1 2 3 4 5 6 7 8 9 0

For my daughters Ella and Julia
and my wife Kristen

As an instrument for practical action, law is responsive to the wisdom of its time, which may be wrong, but it carries forward, sometimes in opposition to this wisdom or passion, a memory of received values.

—*Edward Levi, United States Attorney General, 1975–1977*

CONTENTS

PROLOGUE: WHISTLEBLOWERS

The government source who leaked the story to me about the first phone call between President Trump and Vladimir Putin seemed genuinely frightened. Published by Reuters several weeks after Trump took office in 2017, the piece contained no bombshell disclosures about coordination between the 2016 Trump campaign and Russia. Instead, it exposed politically embarrassing details regarding how the new American president had conducted himself. During the hour-long conversation, Trump had denounced the primary nuclear arms agreement between the United States and Russia as one of many bad deals negotiated by the Obama administration. When Putin raised the possibility of extending the treaty, known as New START, Trump paused and asked his aides what the treaty was, according to my source and an official who had spoken with my colleague Jonathan Landay. When we asked the White House for comment, spokesman Sean Spicer said Trump knew what the New START treaty was but had turned to his aides for an opinion. Throughout the call, Trump also ceaselessly bragged to Putin about his own popularity.

Other, more damaging accounts of Trump's first calls with foreign leaders—of Mexico and Australia—had already leaked to news outlets and drawn more attention. Officials in the White House were furious about the multiple leaks involving presidential phone calls. They vowed to launch formal criminal investigations and prosecute the perpetrators. To help protect the source, we agreed to cut off contact with each other. In a final conversation, I promised that I would go to prison to protect the source's identity. We both knew that the whistleblower was more likely to be prosecuted than me.

Two and a half years later, in the fall of 2019, a whistleblower complaint filed by a CIA official about a phone call between Trump and another foreign leader—the president of Ukraine—sparked an impeachment inquiry. I wanted to know what my source on the Trump-Putin call thought of the whistleblower and the firestorm then unspooling. We met in a restaurant in the Washington area. The source did not mince words: Career government officials had a duty to report waste, fraud, and misconduct by government officials, including the president. The whistleblower, whose identity Trump was demanding be made public, should be protected and the state of divisiveness in Washington was lamentable: "When doing your job as a policy expert means you are physically in danger, not from an international adversary, but from people in your own government, it's confounding."

To President Trump, my source, as well as the Ukraine whistleblower, are part of a conspiracy by a group of unelected government officials to force a duly elected president from power. They are members of the "deep state"—an ill-defined term that Trump uses to refer to people ranging from senior FBI and CIA officials to the Pentagon, to career civil servants across the federal government. Those officials, Trump and his allies argue, have mounted a concerted effort to delegitimize his presidency. Trump has vowed to make the "deep state" a cornerstone of his reelection effort. Democrats say Trump is spreading conspiracy theories for political gain. They defend the civil service, which was created after the Civil War to prevent politicians from turning the federal government into a patronage mill where supporters receive jobs based on political loyalty, not merit.

Every modern American president has expressed distrust of career government officials in Washington. They view themselves, correctly, as carrying a democratic mandate from voters to implement the policy platform that they promised voters. Jimmy Carter feared that members of the CIA would refuse to implement reforms designed to end decades of agency abuses. Ronald Reagan thought liberals in the State Department opposed his effort to confront Communism. George H. W. Bush distrusted independent counsels. Bill Clinton believed the FBI had gone rogue. George W. Bush's administration searched intensively for the intelligence officials who they thought leaked the existence of his post-9/11 warrantless eavesdropping program. Barack Obama feared that Pentagon officials had tried to box him into deploying large numbers of troops to Afghanistan. But no president had attacked the motives of career government officials as publicly or angrily as Trump. No president has so openly trafficked in conspiracy theories for political gain.

On June 16, 2017, Trump became the first American president to apply the term "deep state" to the United States government. Trump retweeted to his 60 million followers a post from Fox News host Sean Hannity promoting his program that evening. Hannity began his show with footage of the shooting that week of three people, including Republican House Majority Whip Steve Scalise, at a Republican practice session for Congress's annual charity baseball game in Alexandria, Virginia. A left-wing activist angered by Trump's election had fired 62 rounds from a semiautomatic rifle at the Republicans. It was a miracle that no one, apart from the gunman, had been killed. Gabrielle Giffords, a Democratic congresswoman shot in the head by a mentally ill man in 2011, condemned the politically motivated attack. For a moment, there was bipartisan fear that the country's polarization could spark wide-scale political violence.

Hannity, though, dismissed Democratic condemnations of the shootings as "a farce to hide the left's true intentions." In a twelve-minute monologue, he condemned the investigation of Special Counsel Robert Mueller and warned viewers that the "deep state" was trying to reverse the result of the 2016 election. "This deep state, this fourth branch of government, as we're calling it, doesn't care about getting the truth to you, the American people. And of course, the media—they're the willing accomplices. Their goal is the exact opposite here," he said. "They are selectively leaking information, intelligence information that is meant to damage, in this case, the president of the United States of America." Hannity concluded his monologue with a warning. He said "hatred" was part of the left's DNA, and predicted more violent attacks against "the president, conservatives, Republicans in this country."

Three years into the Trump presidency, "deep state" has become part of the Trumpian lexicon, along with "witch hunt" and "fake news." President Trump himself increasingly invokes the term. In 2019, Trump used it at least 23 times, twice the number he did in 2018. The president and his supporters blame the "deep state" for leaks, including the one I wrote about for Reuters, that disparage him. They blame it for Trump's impeachment. Mike Rogers, a Republican congressman from Alabama, decried it on the floor of the House during the final impeachment debate: "This is a sad day for our nation when one political party, along with their cohorts in the deep state and the mainstream media, try to hijack our Constitution."

.   .   .

This book is an effort to answer the question of whether a "deep state" exists in America. To conservatives, the "deep state" is an ever-growing government bureaucracy, an administrative state that they think relentlessly encroaches on the individual rights of Americans and whose highest loyalty is to its own preservation and power. Liberals are less apt to use the term "deep state," but they fear the "military-industrial complex"—a cabal of generals and defense contractors who they believe routinely push the country into endless wars, operate a vast surveillance state, and enrich themselves in the process. Voters of all ideologies increasingly disdain the politicians, lobbyists, and journalists who they feel unilaterally set the country's political agenda and are increasingly out of touch with ordinary Americans.

The feverish debate surrounding the term "deep state" raises central questions about American democracy. Is it possible for civil servants, law enforcement officials, and journalists to be politically neutral? Have the FBI, CIA, and other intelligence agencies grown too powerful? Are politicians spreading conspiracy theories for their own political gain? How vast should a president's power be?

Belief in a "deep state" is pervasive and increasingly partisan in the United States. In a 2018 Monmouth University poll, 74 percent of Americans said they believed that "a group of unelected government and military officials" is either definitely or probably "secretly manipulating or directing" national policy. Eight in ten believed that the federal government currently monitors or spies on the activities of American citizens. Racial minorities and NRA members are even more likely to believe in the "deep state" than other Americans. A 2019 YouGov poll found that among Republicans who have heard of the term "deep state," 83 percent believed it was trying to undermine Trump. Among Democrats, only 10 percent did.

For decades, "deep state" was a designation primarily used by political scientists to describe Turkey's military, which repeatedly tried to undermine the emergence of democratic rule in that country. The term "deep state" was also occasionally applied to Egypt's military, which blocked democratic reforms in that nation as well. In 2007, Peter Dale Scott, a retired University of California, Berkeley, English professor, published *The Road to 9/11*, which, for the first time, explicitly applied the term "deep state" to the United States. Scott accused the US military of having fueled conflict both inside and outside the country from the Cold War to 9/11. After that book's publication, Scott became an occasional guest on Alex Jones's far-right conspiratorial radio program. Trump has praised Jones, who appeared with him during the 2016 presidential campaign.

In an interview, Scott told me that he regretted appearing on the show and was angered by how Jones and his audience have used the concept of a "deep state." "They have vulgarized the term," he said. "They have made it a less useful term."

On December 16, 2016, an anonymous author, writing under the pseudonym "Virgil," published a 4,000-word article in Breitbart

News, then under the leadership of Steve Bannon. Entitled "The Deep State vs. Donald Trump," the piece introduced the term "deep state" to a broader conservative audience. The author defined the "Deep State" as all federal employees as well as their political supporters, the policy elite (the "chattering class"), and the mainstream media ("MSM").

> It stretches across the whole of the federal government—indeed, the entirety of the country. And it includes not only bureaucrats, but also a galaxy of contractors, profiteers, and others in the nominal private sector. And it includes not only Democrats, but also Republicans. And oh yes, the MSM and the chattering class.

The tendentious essay concluded by declaring that a "great power struggle" was under way between Trump and the "Deep State," fed by over $4 trillion a year in federal spending. "Who's likely to prevail?" Virgil asked, asserting that "We can answer by observing that Trump has done well so far, and yet we can also observe that the Deep State hasn't given up, and probably never will."

Declarations of a "deep state" conspiracy by Trump have created a potent political narrative that taps into Americans' long-standing suspicions of government, particularly among conservatives. After decades of being the party of law and order, Republican support for the FBI has dropped under Trump. In a 2018 poll, 73 percent of Republicans agreed with the statement that "members of the FBI and Department of Justice are working to delegitimize Trump through politically motivated investigations." According to other polls, the number of Republicans who have a positive view of the bureau has declined from 59 percent in 2014 to 48 percent in 2019. Trust in the CIA has fallen as well, with Republicans who say they trust the agency decreasing from 66 percent in 2017 to 60 percent in 2019. In another reversal of traditional party roles, more Democrats than Republicans said they trust the CIA. Today, the FBI, CIA, and civil servants as a whole face their greatest crisis of public confidence since Watergate.

.   .   .

There are, in fact, millions of Americans who spend their lives working for the federal government. Some are health workers, some are park rangers. Others are covert CIA operatives. Because the vast majority of these people are unelected, their personal political views regularly conflict with those of elected officials. But by statute, they are required to implement all lawful policies of elected officials. Since 1939, the Hatch Act had barred federal workers from engaging in political activity while performing government duties.

Like the president and members of the military, civil servants take an oath of office. "I do solemnly swear that I will support and defend the Constitution of the United States against all enemies, foreign and domestic," the oath reads; "that I will bear true faith and allegiance to the same; that I take this obligation freely, without any mental reservation or purpose of evasion; and that I will well and faithfully discharge the duties of the office on which I am about to enter. So help me God."

Career civil servants said that they implement the policies of elected officials, regardless of party, and roundly dismissed the idea of a "deep state." In private, they warn elected officials of the potential pitfalls of a proposed policy, whether it has been attempted in the past, and if it violates existing laws. They contend that a healthy tension exists between elected officials who often rush to implement policies and civil servants who often prefer caution. The result, they argue, is better policies. Some experts argue that career civil servants, like the press, represent an additional "check and balance" that helps prevent abuses by the executive, legislative, and judicial branches.

Civil servants, like members of any profession, are not uniformly professional. Some government workers cut corners, are incompetent, or have clear political biases that distort their work. Some obstruct policy implementation rather than aid it. As in any profession, a percentage steal or otherwise abuse their positions. In general, the loyalties of most civil servants tend to lie with their respective institutions, which they defend, try to grow, and strengthen. They fight other government agencies for turf, budget, and influence. Civil servants are part of what I will call the "institutional government," a term chosen for its relative neutrality. Americans use many terms—some derogatory, some complimentary—to describe government workers. As the chart below illustrates, one's semantic choices reflect where one stands on the political spectrum:

BAD

Military Industrial Complex   Deep State

Generals   Shadow   Administrative State
                                  Government
CEOs   The Swamp

Corporate Shill   Mass   Regulators
                                  Surveillance
Wall Street Tool   Unelected Bureaucrats

Bankers   Politician

                                          Pencil Pusher

LIBERAL ←——————————————————————————————→ **CONSERVATIVE**

Lawmaker

Public Servant

Civil Servant   Entrepreneur

Government Expert   Small Government

Regulators   The Market

Nonpartisan Watchdog   Generals

Good Government   Jack Ryan

GOOD

An EPA worker may be a "watchdog" to a Democrat but a "job-killer" to a Republican; a conservative may see a national-security contractor as a "patriot," while a liberal may deride them as a "war profiteer." A federal government worker can be seen as a trustworthy "expert," or an obstructionist "pencil-pusher." Terms like "deep state" and "good government" are political rhetoric—ways of declaring whether we find the institutional government objectionable. But whether we like it or not, the institutional government is real and, at least in some areas, such as law enforcement and national security, necessary.

All told, nine million Americans work for the federal government as contractors, full-time employees, or members of the military. These people make up roughly five percent of the country's 160 million–person workforce. The largest group are the 3.3 million people who serve in the military or work as defense contractors. (About 1.3 million Americans are active-duty service members, a decline from roughly two million during the Cold War.) These military personnel are supported by hundreds of thousands of defense contractors, a number that surged after September 11, 2001, and has in recent years abated.

About two million people are civilian workers for the federal government—a figure that has remained largely constant since the 1950s. They vary from public-health experts at the Centers for Disease Control and Prevention, to TSA agents who screen passengers in airports; Social Security Administration workers who issue payments to retirees; diplomats who serve worldwide; FBI agents who work in 56 field offices across the country.

All countries have permanent governments—but not all countries supervise them in the same ways, or to the same extent. After taking office, an American president installs more than three thousand political appointees. A British prime minister appoints only a few hundred. In the American federal government, presidential appointees often work at the top and, in some cases, throughout government agencies. In Britain, the prime minister appoints a member of Parliament to head each government ministry; virtually all of a ministry's other positions are filled by permanent government employees. Two popular 1980s BBC comedy series, *Yes Minister* and *Yes, Prime Minister*, were centered on the power struggles between a newly appointed minister and the "permanent secretary," or career civil servant, who runs the agency day to day. Usually, the minister tries to enact a new political agenda, while the permanent secretary's primary goal is to protect the institution. The system is more or less similar in France and Germany. In general, American elected officials have more power over permanent government workers than their counterparts in other liberal democracies.

Since the late 1950s, Americans' trust in government has declined dramatically. When Pew first polled Americans' views on government in 1958, roughly three-quarters of respondents said they trusted the federal government to do the right thing most of the time. In the 1960s and early 1970s, the Vietnam War and Watergate demolished trust in government. In the 1980s and 1990s, when the economy surged, trust in Washington temporarily surged as well. After the 9/11 attacks, it soared to a three-decade high of 60 percent—before quickly declining after the 2003 Iraq invasion and the 2009 financial crisis. Under Obama, roughly 20 percent of Americans said they trusted the government to do the right thing. Under Trump, the number has declined to 17 percent. The exact long-term cause is unclear, but potential explanations range from rising partisanship to soaring income inequality.

.   .   .

My goal in reporting and writing *In Deep* is to inject fact into the fierce debate surrounding a "deep state." Supporters of President Trump are right to argue that unelected officials who refuse to implement the orders of an elected president are a threat to American democracy. The FBI and CIA are enormously powerful organizations that have long and sordid histories of abusing the civil rights of Americans. Controlling spy and law enforcement agencies is one of the greatest challenges that the United States and other democracies face in the digital age. At the same time, the allegations of treason that President Trump has made against the FBI and CIA are momentous if true, but shameful if false. No other American president has accused the FBI and CIA of carrying out a "coup" in the United States. No other American president has so relentlessly sowed public doubt in government.

Part I of *In Deep* chronicles the CIA and FBI scandals of the past forty years—from the Church Committee's exposure of Cold War abuses, to Iran-Contra, to false intelligence about Iraq's weapons of mass destruction, to the NSA mass surveillance revealed by Edward Snowden. It also examines the bitter power struggles that have unfolded between presidents and Congress, from Ford to Obama.

Part II of the book investigates the claims and counterclaims of the Trump era, and the relentless spread of conspiracy theories online and on air. It scrutinizes the work of William Barr, who, like no attorney general since Watergate, has acted as the president's political shield and sword. Barr is the most feared, criticized, and effective member of Trump's cabinet. Democrats accuse him of using deceptive statements, religious invocations, and criminal investigations to benefit the president politically, charges he flatly denies.

It also introduces readers to two purported leaders of the "deep state": former director of national intelligence James Clapper and former FBI general counsel James Baker. It profiles Joan Dempsey, one of the highest ranking intelligence officers of her generation, who is an ardent defender of the civil service, to Richard Blee, a covert CIA operative who led the hunt for Osama bin Laden, and Tom O'Connor, an FBI agent who spent his career prosecuting extremists, from white supremacists to Al Qaeda members. And it examines the experiences, views, and political calculus of Will Hurd, a retiring Republican congressman from Texas and former undercover CIA operative, who must decide whether or not to vote for Trump's impeachment.

By examining the history of America's efforts to control its powerful law enforcement and intelligence agencies, *In Deep* traces our nation's journey from an era of bipartisan consensus about reining in the powers of government to its current state of hyper-partisanship. It also finds reasons for optimism. In 2019, 70 percent of Americans agreed that low trust in government—and in their fellow citizens—made it harder to solve the country's problems. Roughly two-thirds of Americans believed it was very important to increase Americans' trust in government and in each other. Based on dozens of interviews with CIA operatives and FBI agents, *In Deep* answers the question of whether the nation's intelligence agencies and its politicians are abusing or protecting the public trust.

PART I

PRESIDENTIAL POWER FROM FORD TO OBAMA

I know the capacity that is there to make tyranny total in America, and we must see to it that this agency and all agencies that possess this technology operate within the law and under proper supervision, so that we never cross over that abyss. That is the abyss from which there is no return.

—Senator Frank Church of Idaho

ONE

The Church Committee

On April 29, 1976, a select investigative committee of the US Senate, led by Frank Church of Idaho and John Tower of Texas, released a six-volume report that detailed decades of illegal FBI and CIA spying on American citizens. Formed after *New York Times* journalist Seymour M. Hersh reported allegations of secret government spying on domestic targets, the committee discovered abuses more widespread than those committed during Watergate. From the 1940s to the 1970s, American intelligence and law enforcement agencies had investigated more than half a million Americans who were engaged not in crimes but in constitutionally protected political activities. The misconduct spanned the tenures of six presidents—from FDR to Nixon—and implicated both Democrats and Republicans.

In a society that declared itself exceptional, democratic, and free, the violations of privacy and liberty were stunning. The CIA secretly opened and photographed nearly a half-million letters mailed between private citizens in the United States, including the personal correspondence of John Steinbeck, Hubert Humphrey, and Richard Nixon. Agency operatives had secretly funded or infiltrated student groups, university centers, and foundations across the United States. The FBI broke into the offices of hundreds of political groups, tapped their phones, and opened their mail to obtain information agents could use to disrupt and discredit movements the bureau had unilaterally deemed threats to domestic security. Without obtaining court orders, agents investigated 500,000 people whom they declared "subversives" and infiltrated grassroots political groups that spanned the ideological spectrum—from the far-right John Birch Society to the far-left Students for a Democratic Society. All told, the FBI had kept files on more than one million Americans.

The heads of the CIA and FBI lied to presidents about their activities; in 1970, for instance, they assured Richard Nixon that they were no longer opening citizens' mail, when, in fact, the practice continued. At one point, FBI Director J. Edgar Hoover created a list of 26,000 Americans to be rounded up and detained in the case of "national emergency." They consisted of "influential" individuals deemed likely to "aid subversive elements" because of their "subversive associations and ideology." The list included lawyers, doctors, scientists, professors, labor union organizers, journalists, and the writer Norman Mailer.

The National Security Agency, an organization few Americans knew existed at the time, had secretly collected millions of international telegrams sent to, from, or transiting the United States. By the 1970s, the NSA had opened intelligence files on at least 75,000 Americans, including prominent businesspeople, artists, and athletes, and politicians such as Tennessee senator Howard Baker, a Republican member of the committee, and Church himself, its chair. The IRS was also implicated, launching investigations "on the basis of political rather than tax criteria," and opening intelligence files on 11,000 Americans.

Military-intelligence agents maintained files on and surveilled Senator Adlai Stevenson III and Representative Abner Mikva, both of Illinois, because they participated in anti–Vietnam War political meetings. State and local officials were monitored as well. FBI agents compiled a 2,076-page investigative file on US Supreme Court justices and used court employees as informants.

Hoover fed presidents dirt on their political rivals. Chief executives from both parties received it. Franklin Delano Roosevelt asked the FBI to compile the names of citizens who sent telegrams to the White House opposing his pre–World War II support for Britain. Truman obtained inside information from the FBI on labor union negotiation plans and journalists' publishing schedules. Eisenhower received FBI reports on the political and social contacts of Eleanor Roosevelt and Supreme Court Justice William O. Douglas with foreign officials.

The Kennedy administration had the FBI wiretap three officials of the executive branch, a congressional staffer, and a Washington law firm. Attorney General Robert F. Kennedy received "information of a political nature" from FBI wiretaps of Martin Luther King Jr. and a member of congress. Johnson had the FBI conduct background checks of the staff of his 1964 election opponent, Republican senator Barry Goldwater. He had FBI agents compare senators' anti–Vietnam War statements to the Communist party line. Johnson also obtained purely political intelligence from FBI wiretaps of fellow Democrats during the 1964 Democratic National Convention.

Nixon engaged in the most extensive abuses. He authorized a wiretapping program that produced purely political and personal information for the White House, including information about a Supreme Court justice. His administration wiretapped sixteen executive branch officials, one of their relatives, and four journalists. Nixon attorney general John Mitchell secretly targeted opponents of the Vietnam War, black nationalist groups, and officials suspected of leaking politically damaging information. While serving as attorney general, Mitchell controlled a secret slush fund used for smear campaigns against Nixon's Democratic political rivals. In one bizarre "dirty tricks" operation, Mitchell approved the payment of $10,000 to a faction of the American Nazi Party to carry out a failed effort to remove Governor George Wallace from the presidential primary ballot in California. Judges later ruled that Mitchell's actions violated the Constitution.

After Mitchell resigned as attorney general, he became chairman of Nixon's 1972 reelection campaign. In a series of scandals that became known as "Watergate," political operatives and former CIA and FBI officials broke into Democratic National Committee's campaign offices in the Watergate complex, followed members of Democratic candidates' families, assembled dossiers on candidates' personal lives, forged letters on the candidates' letterhead and distributed them, seized confidential campaign files, investigated the lives of dozens of Democratic campaign workers, and leaked false stories to the press. Facing impeachment after lying about his role in Watergate for years, Nixon resigned. Mitchell was convicted of conspiracy, obstruction of justice, and perjury. He is the nation's only former attorney general to be sent to prison.

In 1973, a year prior to Nixon's resignation, the historian Arthur Schlesinger Jr. warned the American presidency had grown out of control and exceeded its constitutional limits. In the influential book *The Imperial Presidency*, he described its symptoms: "The all-purpose invocation of 'national security,' the insistence on executive secrecy, the withholding of information from Congress, the refusal to spend funds appropriated by Congress, the attempted intimidation of the press, the use of the White House as a base for espionage and sabotage directed against the political opposition."

Nixon, Hoover, and their aides illustrated the dangers of paranoia, conspiracy theories, and bias. Hoover singled out African-American civil rights groups for infiltration, wiretapping, and disruption. Suspecting that Martin Luther King Jr. was a Communist sympathizer, agents planted negative stories about King in the press, bugged his hotel rooms, and sent him and his wife a tape recording which, they claimed, was evidence that King conducted extramarital affairs. Shortly before he traveled to Oslo to accept the 1964 Nobel Peace Prize, agents sent King an anonymous letter suggesting he commit suicide.

Under the bureau's counterintelligence program, known as COINTELPRO, agents carried out "black bag jobs" where they broke into Americans' homes without warrants, stole incriminating material, or planted false information. In one case, an agent broke into a home and left behind a forged letter addressed to the husband of a white woman working at a civil rights organization. The letter falsely accused the woman of having affairs with her black male colleagues. In crude, cartoonish language, an FBI agent tried to mimic what he thought was the voice of an African-American woman. "Look man, I guess your old lady doesn't get enough at home, or she wouldn't be shucking and jiving with our Black men, in action, you dig?" the FBI agent wrote. "Like all she wants to integrate is the bedroom and us Black Sisters ain't gonna take no second best from our men. So lay it on her, man, or get her the hell out." The letter was signed "a soul sister."

When asked by a committee investigator if he found any of the bureau's actions illegal or immoral, William Sullivan, the FBI's number-three official, replied, "Never once did I hear anybody, including myself, raise the question, 'Is this course of action, which we have agreed upon, lawful? Is it legal? Is it ethical or moral?' We never gave any thought to this line of reasoning because we were just naturally pragmatic."

The Church Committee's findings showed that the problem went beyond presidents and their loyalists. The country's most powerful law enforcement and intelligence agencies—the FBI and the CIA— had secretly and, in some cases, unilaterally broke the law. Vastly more powerful mechanisms for controlling both organizations were needed.

. . .

In the fall of 1975, Church and Tower co-chaired nationally televised hearings that outlined the abuses. In a model for future investigations, the two senators created a politically powerful narrative that shifted American public opinion. Democrats and Republicans alike declared certain FBI and CIA practices abhorrent, immoral, and criminal. Tower assailed FBI agents for illegally inspecting Americans' bank records, viewing their tax returns, and burglarizing their homes solely because of their political views. "The impact of those abuses on individuals and on legitimate political, social, religious and philosophical interests represents a dangerous erosion of our Constitutional guarantees," Tower warned. Church chastised presidents and members of Congress for pressuring the bureau to defend the country but neglecting to lead it. "If fault is to be found, it does not rest in the bureau alone," Church said. "It is to be found also in the long line of attorneys general, Presidents and Congresses" who "failed to give it adequate guidance, direction and control."

In a remarkable example of bipartisanship, Church, Tower, and several moderate Republican senators convinced, after much resistance, President Gerald Ford and CIA Director William Colby to give the committee a document known as the "Family Jewels." The top-secret internal CIA history chronicled wrongdoing dating back to the agency's creation in 1947. The report confirmed that CIA operatives administered LSD to unwitting Americans as part of a series of covert medical tests and plotted assassination attempts against foreign leaders such as Cuba's Fidel Castro and the Congo's Patrice Lumumba. It also revealed Operation CHAOS, a spy program conducted inside the United States in which CIA operatives opened files on, and sometimes tracked, nearly 10,000 anti–Vietnam War activists and groups, including four members of Congress and John Lennon. To this day, some CIA veterans consider the release of this file a betrayal of the agency.

Career CIA and FBI officials acknowledged that, in a handful of cases, J. Edgar Hoover's use of the bureau for political point-scoring grew so toxic that it distracted agents from their mission. One FBI official complained that the bureau spent more time chasing Hoover's enemies than catching thieves. The CIA's head of counterintelligence, James Angleton, grew so paranoid about the influence of potential Soviet disinformation within the agency that he treated all Soviet defectors as likely double agents, detained some of them for years, and stopped reading the CIA's own cables. During his twenty-year tenure, Angleton and his aides also ruined the careers of some CIA officers by declaring them suspected double agents, while declining to explain why they had fallen under suspicion. Colby, who removed Angleton from his post and implemented other changes, came to believe that the agency had to confess to its sins in order to gain the trust of Congress, the press, and the public. "The agency's survival," he wrote in his memoir, "could only come from understanding, not hostility, built on knowledge, not faith."

The committee's success stemmed, in part, from its size, structure, and makeup. It had six Democrats and five Republicans, creating a single-vote margin that encouraged consensus. Its members included future vice president Walter Mondale, future Senate majority leader Howard Baker, and Democratic and Republican presidential candidates Gary Hart and Barry Goldwater. Most importantly, the committee was given 150 staffers, far more than were allotted to most congressional investigations.

Fritz Schwarz, the Church Committee's chief counsel, interviewed dozens of FBI and CIA officials who had operated for decades in the shadows of American society. Speaking with them in public testimony and private interviews, Schwarz was surprised by his personal reaction to the agents and operatives. A scion of the family that founded New York's fabled F.A.O. Schwarz toy store, Schwarz had grown up in Manhattan, attended private schools, and received undergraduate and law degrees from Harvard. As a white Anglo-Saxon Protestant, he expected to identify more with CIA officials, who, at the time, were often privileged Ivy Leaguers like himself. FBI officials tended to be working-class Catholics. "The CIA people were culturally and educationally like me," Schwarz recalled in an interview. "The FBI people were not."

Schwarz felt more anger toward the FBI as an organization. He considered its suppression of constitutionally protected political activity a graver threat to the legitimacy of American democracy than the CIA's misconduct. "The FBI's wrongdoing was to undermine our democracy," Schwarz said. "The CIA's wrongdoing was to undermine our reputation overseas. Undermining our democracy was far more dangerous to the country." On a personal level, Schwarz was most disgusted by senior CIA officials. They were "amoral rather than immoral," and shockingly duplicitous, he said. Schwarz watched in dismay as Richard Helms, who served as CIA director from 1966 to 1973, told lie after lie during committee interviews. "He was the best liar I have ever seen," Schwarz recalled. "He was extremely skillful. You couldn't catch him in a lie."

Over the course of fifteen months, the Church Committee met 126 times, interviewed 800 witnesses, and reviewed 110,000 documents. Its six-volume final report spanned 2,695 pages. The committee found that the abuses were not the "product of any single party, administration, or man." The abuses were institutional and the product of a fevered period of American history: the Cold War. The fear of Communists and other foreign rivals and ideologies infiltrating American government and society led intelligence and law-enforcement officials to conclude that existing laws and tactics were insufficient. "It was my assumption that what we were doing was justified by what we had to do," an anonymous FBI official testified, for the "greater good, the national security."

In a prescient interview on *Meet the Press*, Church warned of a future in which technological advances "could be turned around on the American people" and used to facilitate a system of government surveillance. "No American would have any privacy left, such is the capability to monitor everything: telephone conversations, telegrams, it doesn't matter. There would be no place to hide," Church said. "I know the capacity that is there to make tyranny total in America, and we must see to it that this agency and all agencies that possess this technology operate within the law and under proper supervision so that we never cross over that abyss. That is the abyss from which there is no return."

The Church Committee issued 96 recommendations designed to prevent future abuses. It took years to fully enact them, but over time Congress, with the support of Presidents Ford and Carter, created new Senate and House intelligence committees to monitor the work of the CIA, NSA, and other intelligence agencies. Ford and Carter issued executive orders barring the CIA from operating inside the United States and from carrying out political assassinations abroad. They ordered intelligence chiefs to inform congressional leaders of all covert CIA action programs.

Other reforms were enacted to curtail FBI and NSA abuses in the name of national security. The Foreign Intelligence Surveillance Act of 1978 created a new Foreign Intelligence Surveillance Court to review all national security–related eavesdropping requests inside the United States. The law made explicit that the agencies could only wiretap an American citizen or resident as part of a national security investigation with the approval of a federal judge. Finally, citing the forty-eight-year tenure of J. Edgar Hoover and reports that he had collected damaging information about John F. Kennedy and other officials, Congress passed a law setting a ten-year term for future FBI directors.

The committee's work brought national prominence to Church, who ran for president in 1976 but lost the Democratic nomination to Jimmy Carter. In the 1980 Ronald Reagan–led electoral wave, Church lost his Idaho Senate seat to a conservative Republican challenger. In 1984, at the age of 59, Church died of pancreatic cancer. Supporters declared the committee's work his greatest legacy. Opponents said he had endangered the nation by tying the hands of its spies.

TWO

Ford, Cheney, and Rumsfeld

A s the reforms were enacted, resentment of the Church Committee simmered in the intelligence community and White House. Some Ford administration officials saw its reforms and recommendation as a congressional power grab. Supporters of executive branch power felt that, in the wake of Watergate, the Democratic-controlled Congress was unduly impinging on the president's power to protect national security and conduct foreign affairs. The Church reforms were seen as an extension of the War Powers Act, which Congress passed in 1973, overriding Nixon's veto. A Vietnam-related effort to prevent presidents from unilaterally entering the country into wars, the law required presidents to inform Congress within 48 hours of deploying American military forces into hostilities.

Antonin Scalia, a staunch conservative running the Justice Department's Office of Legal Counsel, issued legal memos outlining the administration's views on presidential power. The son of an Italian immigrant, Scalia grew up in Queens and attended Georgetown University and Harvard Law School. After teaching law for several years, he joined the Nixon administration. Scalia, who, a decade later, would be appointed by Ronald Reagan to the Supreme Court, championed the view that presidents had sweeping powers and should aggressively combat legislative and judicial branch encroachment.

Scalia's allies included Donald Rumsfeld, Ford's 42-year-old chief of staff and later defense secretary, and Rumsfeld's deputy, 34-year-old Dick Cheney. To Scalia, Rumsfeld, and Cheney, invasive congressional and judicial oversight of the CIA and FBI was a perversion of what they saw as the constitutional order. While liberals hailed the Church reforms, Scalia and his allies viewed them as an infringement of presidential power under their interpretation of the Constitution. Supporters of expansive of presidential power cited the writings of Alexander Hamilton, who warned in the Federalist Papers that a strong chief executive was needed to defend the country in war or a moment of crisis. "A feeble executive implies a feeble execution of the government," Hamilton wrote. "A feeble execution is but another phrase for a bad execution: And a government ill executed, whatever it may be in theory, must be in practice a bad government."

After Nixon's August 1974 resignation, Ford took office promising to restore public trust. A genial Michigan Republican who had served in the House for twenty-five years, Ford saw healing the nation as his charge. In a surprise decision a month into his tenure, Ford unconditionally pardoned Nixon, enraging many voters. The decision would doom Ford's election effort and his presidency. His approval rating plummeted from 71 percent to 37 percent in five months. In yet another assertion of congressional power, the House Judiciary Committee launched an investigation into whether Ford had secretly promised Nixon the pardon in exchange for the presidency.

In response, Ford took a step that supporters of presidential power and prerogative bemoan to this day. On October 17, 1974, Ford voluntarily testified before the House Judiciary Committee's Criminal Justice Subcommittee. He was only the third sitting president, after Abraham Lincoln and Woodrow Wilson, to testify before Congress. To backers of executive branch power, a president answering questions from members of the legislative branch demeaned the presidency. To members of Congress, it was the embodiment of the founders' vision of three coequal branches of government acting as checks and balances on one another.

Ford's gambit failed to ease public anger at the pardon. Three weeks after his testimony before Congress, Democrats won a landslide victory in the November 5, 1974, midterm elections, gaining a veto-proof two-thirds majority in the House and sixty seats in the Senate. Emboldened by what they saw as a historic electoral mandate, the Democratic-controlled Congress passed measures to further curb the power of the presidency. Urged on by Rumsfeld, Cheney, and Scalia, Ford fought back. He vetoed a bill that strengthened the Freedom of Information Act, giving the public greater access to government documents. Scalia argued that the amendments infringed on the secrecy of the FBI and other intelligence agencies. In the wake of Watergate and Vietnam, though, most Americans remained distrustful of sweeping presidential powers. Democrats in Congress overrode Ford's veto with a 65–27 vote in the Senate, and 371–31 vote in the House.

For the remainder of his presidency, Ford fought what he viewed as the erosion of presidential power. In his two and a half years in office, he issued sixty-six vetoes. With their sweeping majorities in the House and Senate, Democrats overrode his vetoes a dozen times. A new generation of lawmakers, elected in the post-Watergate era, saw unchecked presidential power as a threat to the nation, not its salvation. The Church Committee consensus that improper activities by the FBI and CIA were not acceptable and that both organizations required congressional oversight was widely embraced. The legislative branch reached the apex of its power in the post–World War II era and, arguably, in American history.

.   .   .

While battling Congress, Ford enacted other reforms designed to restore faith in the presidency. In perhaps his greatest appointment, he chose Edward Levi, the president of the University of Chicago, as the first post-Watergate attorney general. After the corruption of John Mitchell's Nixon-era tenure, Levi instituted sweeping reforms designed to make the Justice Department's enforcement of federal law as apolitical as possible. He made restoring public trust in the department—among both liberals and conservatives—the central focus of his tenure. Levi issued the first-ever "Attorney General's Guidelines" for how the FBI should conduct domestic national security investigations. The new rules required the bureau to produce evidence of a crime before conducting wiretaps or searching homes, reduced the number of investigations from 21,414 in 1973 to 4,868 in 1976. Levi worked with Clarence M. Kelley, a career law enforcement officer whom Nixon had appointed FBI director after Hoover's death in 1972, to reduce the embezzlement that had become common among agents. Levi and Kelley also improved coordination between the FBI and CIA—a practice Hoover had discouraged.

Levi so thoroughly embraced nonpartisanship that confusion surrounded his political leanings. News accounts questioned whether he was a libertarian, liberal, or conservative. Scalia, the conservative future Supreme Court justice, praised his tenure. "He brought two qualities to the job," Scalia told the *New York Times*, "a rare intellectuality and a level of integrity such as there could never be any doubt about his honesty, forthrightness or truthfulness." Liberal Massachusetts senator Ted Kennedy hailed him as well. "Levi entered office under the most difficult and trying circumstances," Kennedy said, "yet he leaves a department once again characterized by integrity, intellectual honesty and commitment to equal justice."

Lawyers and political scientists credit Levi with creating the model of a post-Watergate attorney general and restoring public trust in the Justice Department. Under Levi, the attorney general implemented the law enforcement policies the president wished, such as cracking down on organized crime. But the attorney general should not, for example, target for prosecution individuals whom the president considered political enemies, as Nixon and Mitchell had. To Levi, an attorney general should use their power as the country's top law enforcement official to enforce the law in a neutral manner, not to play political favorites or protect the president. In an essay marking the US bicentennial, Levi warned of the dangers of "cycles of bitterness" consuming the country. "There is a kind of theme which runs through the modern world that human relationships should be looked at in terms of power relationships, in terms of the manipulation of power," Levi wrote. "I really think that's one of the most wicked ways of looking at the world. It's a very incomplete way. It strips people of their humanness. It converts all the other good attributes people have into just an ability or a desire to manipulate others."

. . .

As the 1976 presidential election approached, Ford came under pressure from Rumsfeld and Henry Kissinger, the secretary of state, as well as Ronald Reagan, the then conservative governor of California, to lead the Republican Party more aggressively. The fall of Saigon in April 1975 compounded the image of the United States in retreat, and Reagan mounted a primary challenge against Ford that autumn. Conservatives called for Ford to confront the Soviets more aggressively and revive morale at the embattled CIA. In late 1975, Ford fired Colby, the agency director who had cooperated with the Church Committee, after only thirty months on the job. He nominated George H. W. Bush as his replacement. Ford hoped that Bush, who had served as a congressman from Texas, Republican National Committee chair, and UN ambassador, would be more successful in defending the agency from attacks on Capitol Hill. Church and other Democrats opposed Bush's nomination, citing his "prolonged involvement in partisan activities at the highest party level."

In his confirmation hearing, Bush vowed not to present a "political tilt" to intelligence briefings, and defended the CIA, insisting it should not be dismantled as some liberal activists demanded. Bush's performance changed the minds of few Democrats, who controlled the Senate. Eight days after Bush's hearing, a killing in Greece altered the political dynamic. Richard Welch, the CIA station chief in Athens, was shot dead by a local leftist group after returning home from a Christmas party with his wife. A foreign newspaper had identified

Welch as station chief, but White House and CIA officials, as well as supporters of the CIA in Congress, blamed the Church Committee's disclosure of CIA assassinations abroad. No clear evidence existed that the Church Committee's work had caused the assassination, but support for Bush's nomination surged among Republicans and conservative Democrats.

In January 1976, the Senate debated Bush's nomination. South Carolina Republican (and former Dixiecrat) Strom Thurmond argued that the public was more worried about the Church Committee's disclosure of national secrets than about Bush's past political work. "That is where the public concern lies, on disclosures which are tearing down the CIA," he said, "not upon the selection of this highly competent man to repair the damage of this over-exposure." With the support of conservative Democrats, Bush was confirmed in a 64–27 vote. Political support in Congress was shifting back toward the agency.

Regretting his cooperation with the Church Committee, Ford took a hard line on a House investigation of the CIA chaired by Otis Pike of New York. Pike, a bow tie–wearing moderate Democrat from Long Island and former World War II fighter pilot, struggled to control the panel and win the trust of the White House. After Ford declined to share sensitive information with the Pike Committee, its final report leaked to CBS News's Daniel Schorr, who gave a copy to the *Village Voice*, which published it. In its report, the House panel accused the White House of "foot-dragging, stone-walling, and careful deception." Ford and Bush, backed by Republicans and conservative Democrats in the Senate, defended the CIA and condemned congressional leaks.

Scalia, Cheney, and Rumsfeld continued to contend that a powerful presidency, unhindered by aggressive oversight from Congress and the courts, was necessary in order to defend the country. Post-Watergate, their maximalist view of executive power remained largely on the fringes of American politics. It would gain greater currency during the Reagan administration, after the 9/11 attacks, and, unexpectedly, when Donald Trump won the presidency in 2016—forty years after the Church Committee completed its work.

. . .

Despite the Church and Pike investigations, the CIA continued to attract new young recruits. One of them was William Barr, who would briefly work at the CIA and later serve as attorney general for both George H. W. Bush and Donald Trump. Barr, who declined to be interviewed, grew up in Manhattan, among the bookish elite of the Upper West Side.

Barr's mother, Mary, taught at Columbia, and worked as an editor at *Redbook*. His father, Donald, was the headmaster at Dalton, a progressive private school on the Upper East Side. During the Second World War, Donald had served in the Office of Strategic Services, the precursor to the CIA. As headmaster, he believed that discipline instilled morality. While birth control and feminism were reshaping conventions around sex and work, Donald insisted on traditional values. Chip Fisher, who attended Dalton at the time, remembered him as brilliant but out of place: "It was like having Jonathan Edwards at the pulpit," Fisher said. "You had a very conservative headmaster in the midst of a very dramatic change." Dalton parents saw Barr as autocratic and obsessed with adherence to rules. In the early seventies, after a protracted and ugly public fight with the school's board, he was forced out of his job.

Mary Barr, an observant Catholic, sent William and his three brothers to Corpus Christi elementary school. At a young age, Barr displayed his conservatism. In the first grade, he delivered a speech in favor of Dwight Eisenhower's presidential campaign. Later, he declared his support for Richard Nixon, and a nun promised to pray for him. In high school, at Horace Mann, an elite private school, Barr—known then as Billy—defended the Vietnam War. Barr delighted in intellectual combat: "He was virulently anti-Communist," a classmate recalled. He really liked to push people's buttons." Garrick Beck, another classmate, disliked Barr's politics but admired his integrity. Even then, he said, Barr was convinced that only a strong president could protect the country. "He always viewed it as more of a constitutional republic than a direct democracy." Beck said. "He believes the presidency needs to be more powerful in order to oppose the threats that America faces."

For college, Barr attended Columbia. While his classmates marched against the war in Vietnam, he studied government. He told a high school counselor that he hoped one day to lead the CIA, and, during breaks from school, he spent two summers as an intern there. In 1973, he received a master's degree in government and Chinese studies from Columbia and then joined the CIA as an intelligence analyst. At the time, the Church Committee was uncovering decades of abuses by the CIA, and laws were being passed to curtail its activities. But Barr embraced its mission and questioned the aggressiveness of the congressional oversight, later saying that the Church Committee delivered "body blows" to the agency.

Barr spent two years as an analyst, but he was also considering a career in law. He started taking night classes at George Washington University Law School, and, in 1975, he transferred to the agency's Office of Legislative Counsel. The following year, George H. W. Bush became the CIA director, and Barr helped prepare him for testimony on Capitol Hill. One hearing involved a bill that would require the CIA to send a written notification to Americans whose mail the agency had secretly opened. Among the bill's sponsors was Bella Abzug, a liberal Democrat who represented Barr's old neighborhood in New York. As a defense attorney, Abzug had won a stay of execution for Willie McGee, a black man convicted of raping a white woman in Mississippi; she had also represented several Americans accused by Senator Joseph McCarthy of being Communists. The CIA spied on her for twenty years, surveiling anti-war rallies where she spoke and opening her mail.

As Abzug and her colleagues grilled Bush about the CIA's activities, Barr tried to help the new director. "I went up and sat in the seat that's behind the witness," he recalled in a 2001 oral history of the Bush administration. "Someone asked him a question, and he leaned back and said, 'How the hell do I answer this one?' I whispered the answer in his ear, and he gave it, and I thought, 'Who is this guy? He listens to legal advice when it's given.'"

Barr's work in the agency's legislative affairs office helped him develop a personal relationship with Bush. It also cemented his views of congressional oversight, which he saw as excessive, inappropriate, and, at times, comical. He told friends that he was appalled by the mediocrity of some members of Congress and the stupidity of their questions. It was the first round in a lifelong war that Barr would wage against congressional oversight. For the next forty years, Barr would work to strengthen the power of the president.

· · ·

Another ambitious young member of the intelligence community shared Barr's concern regarding congressional oversight. James R. Clapper Jr., an Air Force intelligence officer with a gift for cracking codes, was also suspicious of Congress. Over the next forty years, the two men would rise rapidly in their respective fields of law and intelligence. While Barr would serve as attorney general in the Bush and Trump administrations, Clapper would serve as President Obama's director of national intelligence. In the Trump era, they would criticize each other's work.

The son of a National Security Agency official, Clapper was born in Fort Wayne, Indiana, but grew up on military bases surrounded by intelligence officers. In 1944, his father, James, was drafted into the Army and assigned to decode German and Japanese radio transmissions. After the war ended, Clapper, at the age of five, boarded a ship with his mother and sailed across the Atlantic to meet his father in Egypt. During a stopover in Italy, the ship struck a mine and nearly sank. Clapper and his family lived in Asmara, the capital of Eritrea, at a former Italian navy communications station that had been turned into an American listening post.

Two years after the family arrived, Clapper's mother got pregnant with their second child and his father, concerned about medical care, moved the family back to the United States. The journey home on US military aircraft took them through Egypt and Germany. As their plane approached the Cairo airport, Clapper saw hundreds of mothballed fighters and bombers baking in the sun. "As far as the eye can see, in all the parking areas were airplanes just sitting in the sun rotting—the arsenal of democracy," Clapper recalled in an interview. "It was just unbelievable—the equipment we turned out." When the family landed in Frankfurt, they saw a city covered in rubble where German civilians begged for handouts. During a train ride to the German coast, Clapper saw more devastation. "Just mile after mile of rolling stock that had been destroyed or damaged," he recalled. "The destruction was unbelievable. That was burned into my consciousness."

Over the next decade, Clapper's father worked for the NSA conducting surveillance around the world. Clapper lived on or near military bases in Virginia, Japan, Germany, and other locales. During a 1953 visit to his grandparents in Philadelphia, he noticed that he could listen to local police radio traffic if he held the television dial between two stations. The twelve-year-old Clapper began taking notes and tracking police code words. Deciphering communications enthralled him. "There was just enough there to really entice me," he said. "It just intrigued me."

In high school, Clapper decided to become an army intelligence officer like his father, whom he deeply admired. Rejected for admission by West Point, Clapper enrolled in an Air Force ROTC program at the University of Maryland. During the summer of 1962, he attended an ROTC summer training at Otis Air Force Base in Massachusetts. One afternoon, President Kennedy arrived for a family vacation in nearby Hyannis Port. Kennedy shook hands with the cadets, and asked Clapper which type of plane he wanted to fly. When Clapper responded that he wanted to be an intelligence officer, Kennedy paused and, according to Clapper, looked a bit skeptical. The president then told him, "Good. We need more like you."

In 1965, Clapper married his college girlfriend, Sue, in the chapel of NSA headquarters in Fort Meade, Maryland. Months later, he was sent to Vietnam, where he served as an intelligence officer on an air base outside of Saigon. Clapper watched in dismay as more senior officers ignored clear evidence that the American war effort was failing. After the war, Clapper rose quickly through the ranks. In 1975, while he was a major running the Pacific Command's signal intelligence operations in Hawaii, he watched the Church Committee hearings on television. He begrudged calls for increased congressional oversight of intelligence agencies. "To be honest, I was resentful because I had always thought, particularly in my younger days, that the intelligence community was always going to do the right thing," he said. "I thought, 'now we're going to have Congress overlooking us.'" Clapper defended the NSA's surveillance of Vietnam War protesters and black nationalist groups in the early 1970s. "There was genuine concern about an insurrection in this country," he contended. "I was genuinely frightened with what was happening in the country."

Over the course of his career, Clapper would become one of the most well-known intelligence officials in the country, and garner both praise and criticism. Clapper would play a role in the creation of the faulty intelligence assessment that was used for the 2003 invasion of Iraq. Democrats in Congress would accuse Clapper of lying to the American people about government surveillance in 2013, a charge Clapper denies. But the strangest turn would come in the Trump era. Barr, who in some ways had much in common with Clapper, would launch a criminal investigation in 2019 into whether Clapper was part of a "deep state" plot to discredit Trump's presidency.

THREE

Carter Strengthens Oversight

On July 5, 1976, Jimmy Carter, the leading Democratic presidential candidate, met privately in a Hershey, Pennsylvania, hotel room with the director of the CIA, George H. W. Bush. The day before, Carter had celebrated the country's bicentennial in Philadelphia at multiple campaign events, continuing his surprise domination of the Democratic primary field.

The meeting was not part of a "deep state" conspiracy. Carter, a foreign policy novice, had asked for a series of CIA briefings on world affairs that would help him better prepare for the upcoming presidential campaign, particularly the debates. Most major party nominees receive CIA briefings, but Carter had requested his early—before he formally secured the Democratic nomination. President Ford, displaying magnanimity toward the man he would likely face in the general election, approved a series of limited briefings by Bush and CIA experts.

That both Carter and Bush would later be elected president seemed inconceivable at that point. Carter, a little-known governor from Georgia, was leading Ford in opinion polls but was by no means a shoo-in for election. Bush, for his part, appeared to have derailed his political career by agreeing to become director of the CIA, an organization still deeply distrusted by many Americans.

Before the meeting, it was unclear if the two men would get along. They came from polar opposite backgrounds. Bush was the son of a US senator, a graduate of Phillips Academy and Yale, and a supporter of Ford's attempt to curtail Congress's post-Watergate powers. Carter, a born-again, evangelical Christian and peanut farmer, was skeptical of the CIA, and was running for president on an idealistic post-Watergate slogan: he promised to never lie to the American people.

To the surprise of both men's aides, Carter displayed a voracious appetite for intelligence, and the meeting lasted longer than expected. Carter asked pointed questions about a broad array of topics, impressing Bush and CIA analysts. "The conversation ranged over virtually the entire field of intelligence," Richard Lehman, Bush's national intelligence deputy, wrote in an internal CIA memo, "from the future of Rhodesia to morale in the Agency." Two weeks later, Carter won the Democratic nomination, capping his improbable political rise. In a rebuke of the agency, Carter cited the work of the Church Committee during his acceptance speech. "The embarrassment of the CIA revelations could have been avoided if our government had simply reflected the sound judgement and good common sense and the high moral character of the American people."

After Carter secured the nomination, Bush agreed to provide a more detailed briefing at Carter's home in Plains, Georgia. Logistical issues complicated the effort. Like other CIA directors, Bush traveled in a government-owned Gulfstream jet, but the airport in Plains—which had a population of seven hundred—consisted of a 4,400-foot sod runway, too soft and too short for the plane. CIA officials decided to fly Bush by jet to the Fort Benning, Georgia, army base and then by helicopter to "Peterson Field" in Plains. Unable to locate the site on aeronautical maps, CIA staffers eventually learned that Peterson Field was essentially a meadow on the outskirts of town owned by a farmer named Peterson. Carter warmly welcomed Bush and his staff to the two-bedroom ranch house that he had built himself and lived in with his wife Rosalynn and daughter Amy. During a briefing that spanned several hours, Carter again displayed an intense interest in intelligence and asked sharp questions. The Democratic nominee, though, kept his personal views of the CIA secret. Privately, Carter opposed its long history of funding pro-American dictators who engaged in gross human rights abuses. If elected, he intended to stop it.

In three nationally televised presidential debates, Carter came across as credible on foreign affairs, while Ford, in fact, committed a major gaffe, claiming that Poland was not dominated by the Soviet Union. Most importantly, Ford's standing among voters never fully recovered from his deeply unpopular surprise pardon of Nixon. On November 2, 1976, Carter narrowly won the presidency, garnering 50 percent of the vote to Ford's 48 percent. Democrats retained a two-thirds majority in the House and a 61-seat majority in the Senate.

Carter would serve only a single term as president, but in that time he embraced measures designed to prevent a repeat of Nixon-like abuses by a president and Hoover-like abuses by the FBI and CIA. First, Carter set a tone that was the opposite of the all-powerful imperial presidency embraced by Nixon. Carter carried his own luggage, enrolled his daughter Amy in public school, and famously walked to the White House after being inaugurated as president. Carter initially shunned the playing of "Hail to the Chief," dismissing it as too much pageantry.

More importantly, he enacted sweeping new laws and reforms, including several recommended by the Church Committee, that altered the balance of power in Washington. Carter signed into law strict new ethics legislation that empowered independent counsels and inspectors general to investigate executive branch waste, fraud, and abuse. He empowered Congress's new intelligence oversight committees, created a new Foreign Intelligence Surveillance Court to curtail improper government surveillance, and prosecuted FBI officials for breaking into the homes of Americans without warrants.

Supporters of executive branch power, such as Scalia, Cheney, and Barr, bemoaned the changes, which they said crippled the presidency. But for the next forty years, presidents—Republicans and Democrats alike—publicly embraced the system. Privately, they may have questioned it, but they all appeared to make the same political calculation:

namely, that if they engaged in Nixon-like abuses of executive power or suggested the president was above the law, they would rapidly lose public support and potentially be driven from office. That would begin to change after the 9/11 attacks and change entirely with the 2016 election of Donald Trump.

. . .

Carter received his first CIA briefing as the president-elect in his home in Georgia. At the outset of the meeting, Bush offered to continue to serve as CIA director in Carter's new administration. Bush conceded, though, that Carter might want a new director. The president-elect grew uncharacteristically quiet, according to a memo Bush wrote summarizing the conversation. "No discussion, no questions about any of the points I had made," Bush wrote. "Carter was very cold or cool, no editorializing, no niceties, very business-like." In a subsequent interview, Carter said he considered Bush's past work in partisan politics as disqualifying. "The job of DCI must be depoliticized," he said, using the acronym for Director of Central Intelligence. "Bush was too political."

After the awkward exchange regarding Bush's future, the CIA director revealed to President-elect Carter a dozen top-secret, covert action programs the CIA was conducting around the world. Carter listened quietly as Bush described the CIA's funding of various dictators long seen as bulwarks against Communism. Bush later recalled that Carter "seemed to be a little turned off. He tended to moralize." Bush was right. The president-elect was determined to limit Washington's support of authoritarian leaders and to mount a new, human rights–based strategy to counter Soviet expansionism.

A month before taking office, Carter committed the kind of unforced political error that would hamper his presidency. Without consulting a wide circle of advisors, Carter chose a nominee for CIA director that baffled members of his own party—former Kennedy administration aide Ted Sorensen. A gifted speechwriter who had been called JFK's "chief of staff for ideas," Sorensen was a member of JFK's brain trust, but he had no experience in intelligence and had never run a large organization. Joe Biden, at the time an ambitious young member of the newly created Senate Intelligence Committee, made a discovery that deeply embarrassed Carter. In 1965, Sorensen had removed 67 boxes of letters, documents, and other material from the White House, including seven boxes that had contained classified information. First, Sorensen used the material to write a book about Kennedy. Then, when he donated the papers to the National Archives, he claimed a $231,923 tax deduction. After Biden and other Democrats accused Sorensen of mishandling classified information, he withdrew his nomination.

Sorensen's downfall showed the power of the newly created Senate Intelligence Committee. Senate Majority Leader Mike Mansfield, a Democrat from Montana known for his bipartisanship, chose Daniel Inouye, a Democratic senator from Hawaii and World War II war hero, as chairman of the new committee. As a Japanese-American, Inouye was initially barred from enlisting in the US military by the Roosevelt administration. He later received the Medal of Honor after he was shot five times and lost his right arm while attacking three German machine gun positions. Inouye's popularity—he had an 84 percent favorable rating among Americans after he played a central role in the Senate Watergate hearings—burnished the new intelligence panel's credibility.

In an effort to encourage bipartisanship, the new panel had the same structure as the Church Committee, with the majority party receiving one more seat than the minority. Its Republican vice chair was Barry Goldwater, the Arizona conservative who had served on the Church Committee. The committee also had a single unified staff, not a majority and a minority one, in another effort to foster unity. In an effort to show intelligence officials that information would not leak, secure facilities were built in the US Capitol to hold closed hearings and store classified documents. Finally, as a "select" committee, its members were selected by party leaders, not party caucuses, theoretically boosting their quality. Inouye promised that the committee could "restore responsibility and accountability to U.S. intelligence activities," without compromising the country's national security.

In a pattern that would continue for decades, the new House Intelligence Committee was far more partisan, a reflection of the differences between the two chambers. Unlike the Senate panel's one-seat differential between majority and minority parties, the number of seats on the House committee matched the proportion of seats held by party in the House overall. Because of the Democrats' two-thirds majority in the House, they held nine committee seats while Republicans held four, creating little incentive for bipartisanship. The House committee had a staff of twenty, less than half as many staffers as the Senate panel. House Speaker Tip O'Neill appointed a close friend, Massachusetts Democrat Edward Boland, as the first chairman of the permanent House committee. Bob Wilson, a California Republican, was appointed its first ranking member. Echoing the tone set by Inouye, Boland declared that "this will not be an inquisition like the Church and Pike committees."

Agency officials remained skeptical, particularly of the House panel. For decades, it would struggle to win the trust of intelligence officials, who complained that the House committee leaked intelligence for political gain far more often than the Senate panel. The creation of the new committees further lowered morale within the CIA. No other Western democracy had given their legislatures such sweeping—and potentially intrusive—oversight powers, particularly the power to subpoena documents and testimony. Veteran intelligence officers feared that their sources and methods would leak to the press. At the same time, liberals dismissed the committees as toothless.

·   ·   ·

As Congress asserted its new powers over the CIA, a college student named Richard Blee agonized over whether to follow in the footsteps of his father and join the agency. The Church Committee had investigated the work of his father, David Blee, the CIA's chief of counterintelligence. The elder Blee emerged from the inquiry unscathed, but officers from his generation felt that the committee had unfairly maligned the CIA as a whole.

Blee's father, a Harvard-educated lawyer, had served in the Office of Strategic Services (OSS), the precursor to the CIA, during World War II. After being dropped off on an island near Thailand to monitor the communications and movements of the Japanese fleet, David Blee fell in love with espionage. After the war, he joined the CIA and served as station chief in Karachi. The elder Blee won accolades for decisiveness in one of the most bizarre episodes of the Cold War. On March 6, 1967, Svetlana Alliluyeva, the daughter of former Soviet dictator Joseph Stalin, appeared without warning at the American Embassy in New Delhi and requested political asylum. While officials in Washington debated how to respond, Blee, working with the US ambassador to India Chester Bowles, took Svetlana to the airport, put her on a plane to Europe, and flew her out of the country.

Soon after, Blee was promoted. He returned to Washington and became head of all espionage conducted in the Middle East. In 1971, he took over the Soviet Division, working to end the climate of paranoia that had paralyzed CIA operations under James Angleton, who believed that virtually every Soviet defector was a double agent. In the final years of his career, Blee had served as the CIA's head of counterintelligence, Angleton's former position. A new generation of clandestine officers praised him for reversing Angleton's approach, welcoming defectors, and revitalizing American covert operations.

Richard Blee had grown up believing that his father was an American diplomat. He lived with his parents and siblings overseas, moving from Karachi to New Delhi to Washington, thinking his father worked for the State Department. As a teenager, he learned the truth about his father's work. The CIA abuses exposed by the Church Committee, particularly CIA spying on Americans, troubled the younger Blee. But he feared that the agency was being scapegoated by Church and other politicians for political gain. Veteran intelligence operatives complained to him that elected officials approved covert operations—and then blamed the agency when things went wrong. "The Church Committee was a huge body blow," Richard Blee told me in an interview. "A lot of people said it was unfair."

With his father's blessing, Richard Blee joined the agency in 1979. Following the path of other recruits, he was trained at The Farm, the secret agency facility that teaches covert officers CIA tradecraft. He then worked in the agency's Office of Security, which safeguarded agency facilities, screened applicants, and conducted counterintelligence investigations. Blee's goal was to serve—like his father—as a station chief in Central Africa, South Asia, or the Middle East. "I wanted the more challenging environments," Richard Blee said. "I was 24 years old and I wanted to take on this challenge. My goal wasn't to take the offer in Paris, I wanted to go to the jungle."

As the younger Blee adjusted to life in the CIA, older intelligence officers told him morale was at an all-time low. They said Carter administration staffing cuts and other changes had gutted covert operations. Echoing his father, they warned that politicians would attack the agency for political gain. In his own career in the Clandestine Service, Blee would excel, becoming a station chief and spymaster, like his father. He would warn elected officials of a grave new threat to the country. And he would be ignored.

. . .

As part of his drive to reform the agency, Carter chose a second nominee for CIA director: Stansfield Turner, a Rhodes Scholar and Navy admiral. Turner had been in Carter's class at Annapolis, but the two young men did not know one another. (Turner and Carter both ranked in the top ten percent.) After graduation, Carter served on American submarines for seven years and returned to Georgia. Turner remained in the Navy, serving in Korea and Vietnam, running the Naval War College, and commanding the US Second Fleet and NATO forces in southern Europe. Turner had not lobbied for the position, but Carter passionately believed in the fellow naval officer's integrity and insisted that he take it. Like Carter, Turner, a practicing Christian Scientist, was religious. During his Senate confirmation hearing, Turner promised to conduct intelligence operations "strictly in accordance with the law and American values" while protecting the identities of the agency's sources. "People's lives are at stake," he said. The following day, the Senate unanimously confirmed Turner as CIA director.

Following Carter's instructions, Turner enacted broad reforms designed to modernize the agency and remove poor performers. The layoffs infuriated members of the Directorate of Operations. All told, Turner dismissed 825 CIA officers, beginning with the bottom five percent based on performance reviews. "We were aware that some of the unqualified and incompetent personnel whom he discharged were deeply resentful, but I fully approved," Carter said in a 2007 interview.

While cutting staff, Turner increased spending on spy satellites and other technologies that provided new ways of gathering intelligence. Veteran covert operatives argued that adversaries would learn to mask their communications and that human sources were still needed to learn valuable secrets. Turner proceeded as planned. Over time, his relationship with the clandestine service became so poisonous that Turner accused CIA operatives of mounting disinformation campaigns to discredit him.

Carter remained a voracious consumer of intelligence. He received the President's Daily Brief and read it carefully, scribbling notes or questions in the margins of each page, which allowed CIA analysts to see which topics most engaged the president. Turner said the administration's goal was to improve the agency, not dismantle it. "Lots of people think President Carter called me in and said, 'Clean the place up and straighten it out.' He never did that," Turner told the *New York Times* after his retirement. "From the very beginning, he was intensely interested in having good intelligence."

Carter approved a new covert action campaign backed by his

national security advisor, Zbigniew Brzezinski, that distributed cassette tapes, fax machines, and magazines across Eastern Europe. In the Soviet Union itself, the CIA disseminated the work of dissident writers. The goal of the operation was to foment dissent and undermine the Soviet control of information. The covert program was part of Carter's broader strategy to promote human rights as a way to delegitimize the Soviets.

Strengthening the Church reforms, Carter signed an executive order that broadened Ford's ban on assassinations and required intelligence chiefs to regularly update congressional intelligence committees on their work. It also banned the CIA from conducting electronic surveillance inside the United States, and authorized only the FBI to conduct physical searches inside the country. Carter's approach, though, was inconsistent and did not always prioritize human rights. He continued to support certain dictators, such as the shah of Iran, a policy that would prove disastrous.

.   .   .

As with the CIA, Carter initially struggled to find a new leader of the FBI. After taking office, Carter had quickly appointed as attorney general Griffin Bell, a personal friend from Georgia and former federal appellate judge. But when Clarence Kelley, the career law enforcement officer running the FBI, told the new administration he wanted to retire, Carter and Bell spent a year trying to find a replacement. They created a blue-ribbon commission to recruit an apolitical candidate who would reform the bureau, boost morale, and serve the full ten-year term Congress had mandated as part of the Church reforms. After other candidates turned down the job for health and family reasons, Carter and Bell made a surprise choice that critics initially questioned.

William Webster, a 53-year-old St. Louis federal appeals court judge and former federal prosecutor, was unknown in Washington. But Bell believed that Webster's experience as a federal judge and his status as a registered Republican would boost Carter's claim that he was trying to depoliticize the bureau. Carter, for his part, believed that Webster, a practicing Christian Scientist like Turner, had integrity. Webster agreed to serve the full ten-year term for $57,500 a year, the same amount as his judge's salary.

In an effort to highlight the bureau's independence, Webster asked that his swearing-in ceremony be held at the FBI headquarters, not the White House. In a show of bipartisan support, Carter, Mondale, Supreme Court Chief Justice Warren Burger, Attorney General Bell, and the chairmen and ranking members of the House and Senate judiciary committees attended the ceremony. (Mondale, a former member of the Church Committee, gave Webster a copy of the panel's report and told him to read it.) Sharing a motto that he would use throughout his nine-year tenure, Webster told agents that the bureau could "do the work that the American people expected of us in the way that the Constitution demanded of us." The reaction among rank-and-file agents was mixed. Some Hoover loyalists—known internally as "Hoover hard hats"—initially resisted Webster's efforts to rein in the bureau's tactics and diversify its 8,000 agents, who were overwhelmingly white males.

Webster and the new administration, though, were intent on reforming the bureau. Two months after Webster took office, Bell indicted three former FBI executives for illegally spying on Americans—acting FBI director L. Patrick Gray; the bureau's number-two official, Mark Felt; and former head of intelligence Edward Miller. In the early 1970s, the three FBI executives had ordered 58 FBI agents to break into the homes without court orders, open the mail, and tap the phones of relatives and friends of fugitive members of the Weather Underground, a radical anti-war group. The indictments infuriated agents, hundreds of whom held a silent protest in Washington on the day the charges were announced. Felt and Miller argued that foreign intelligence services were aiding the Weather Underground and that the FBI's searches were therefore legal. (Unknown to the public and everyone involved in the case was the fact that Felt was "Deep Throat"—the anonymous source who had helped *Washington Post* reporters Bob Woodward and Carl Bernstein break the Watergate scandal. Even though this revelation might have helped him avoid prosecution, Felt asked the reporters to continue to keep his role as a key Watergate source secret.)

In November 1980, four years after the Church Committee revealed systematic FBI abuses, Felt and Miller were convicted of conspiring to violate the constitutional rights of Americans. Neither man was sentenced to prison, and the charges against Gray were dropped due to a lack of evidence. But the convictions of two former senior FBI officials was, to many at the bureau and in the public, a powerful symbol of the Carter administration's efforts to rein in the FBI.

Bell and Webster would prove to be two of Carter's finest appointments. Over his nine years as FBI director, Webster restored credibility to the bureau and was lauded by both liberals in the Carter administration and conservatives in the Reagan administrations. Bell, working with Webster, led the effort in Congress to pass the Foreign Intelligence Surveillance Act, which established the new FISA Court where federal judges approved applications to surveil Americans for national security reasons.

In a move that further strengthened Edward Levi's model of an independent attorney general, Bell criminally investigated Carter's relatives and aides. Bell filed suit against Carter's brother Billy, accusing him of working for the Qaddafi regime in Libya without registering as an agent of a foreign government. (Billy Carter settled the lawsuit.) And he indicted Bert Lance, a longtime Carter friend and the head of the Office of Management and Budget, on fraud charges in Georgia. (Lance was acquitted of all charges.)

In October 1978, Carter also signed into law three statutes designed to prevent waste, fraud, and abuse in the executive branch. The Civil Service Reform Act was the first major reform of the federal government workforce since 1883. It created a cadre of experienced, apolitical managers—known as the Senior Executive Service—tasked with improving efficiency and accountability across the government, working with political appointees to implement the president's policies. Carter also signed the Ethics in Government Act, which required federal officials to disclose their financial histories and created the Office of Independent Counsel, tasked with investigating potentially illegal acts by the president and other senior officials. Lastly, Carter signed the Inspector General Act, which established a dozen independent inspectors general in federal departments who could investigate reports from whistleblowers of fraud and abuse. In an effort to create a more open and transparent presidency, Carter made White House records subject to release under freedom of information laws and invoked "executive privilege" only once, declining to release to Congress documents regarding a proposed oil import tax.

During the second half of Carter's term, the seizure of 52 American hostages in Iran, the president's political missteps, and a weak economy drove down his popularity. White House aides blamed the CIA for failing to warn Carter of the dangers of supporting the shah of Iran. CIA officials said Carter marginalized them. In November 1980, Reagan defeated Carter in one of the most lopsided presidential elections in US history. Economic malaise and the hostage crisis, more than other factors, had doomed his presidency.

While Carter failed in other areas of his presidency, he played a leading role in establishing mechanisms to police American presidents, monitor intelligence and law enforcement agencies, and prevent the emergence of a "deep state." Scalia, Cheney, and other advocates of expansive presidential power assailed Carter's reforms. But there was broad public support for "good government" laws designed to prevent crimes. The raft of reforms enacted by Carter set a post-Watergate standard for disclosure, behavior, and investigation in Washington. In the short term, they would be questioned, tested, and altered by Reagan, as well as other presidents, but over time the need for them would be embraced by Republicans and Democrats.

FOUR

Reagan, Meese, and Iran-Contra

Reagan and his senior aides arrived in Washington determined to reverse the reforms of the 1970s that had empowered Congress, special prosecutors, and inspectors general, and, in their view, had weakened the presidency. During his eight years in office, Reagan used defense spending and tax cuts to promote economic growth. He filled Americans with a sense of national optimism not experienced since before Vietnam. And he struck historic nuclear arms agreements with the Soviet Union.

But Reagan's presidency ushered in two scandals that reinforced concerns regarding an all-powerful presidency. Early in his first term, an undercover FBI sting operation known as Abscam, which had ensnared members of Congress, ignited fears of a return to the outrages of the Hoover era. And, in his second term, the CIA and White House were caught breaking multiple laws and flagrantly lying to Congress about covert CIA operations, US arms sales, and secret hostage negotiations, in what became known as the Iran-Contra scandal. The Reagan administration's actions would test popular support for increased presidential power, but in the end, the post-Watergate reforms and the constitutional checks and balances that have divided power and restrained all three branches of government since the country's founding would stand.

. . .

In the 1970s, Melvin Weinberg, a shrewd New York grifter, came up with a seemingly foolproof hustle. Clad in a three-piece suit and sunglasses, Weinberg traveled the New York area in a chauffeur-driven limousine pretending to be a high-ranking executive of an obscure foreign bank. On some days, Weinberg would say the bank was based in the Middle East. On others, it was in Switzerland or England. After showing off his illusory wealth and connections, Weinberg made a seemingly generous offer to people with credit problems. For several thousand dollars, he promised to process their loan applications and put in a good word for the applicant at his fictional foreign bank. After collecting his fee, Weinberg would inform his mark that the bank had, unfortunately, declined their application. Then he would disappear.

It was a classic con. No foreign bank existed. No loan application was submitted for review. After Weinberg turned his scam into a cross-country operation that ensnared celebrities, he drew the attention of the FBI, which eventually arrested him and recruited him as an informant. In a sting operation code-named "Abscam," Weinberg helped send a half-dozen members of Congress to prison for accepting bribes. The biggest public corruption scandal of the 1980s, Abscam was the basis for the 2013 David O. Russell film *American Hustle*, with a portly, toupéed Christian Bale playing Weinberg, and Amy Adams playing his mistress and co-conspirator.

Born and raised in the Bronx, Weinberg was the son of a homemaker and a shop owner who sold plate glass windows. In one of his earliest scams, Weinberg boosted his father's sales by smashing store windows in the neighborhood. In another, he traveled to Mexico and tried to swindle Yaqui Indians into selling him their gold-mining rights.

Weinberg's foreign bank loan ruse was his most sophisticated. His British-born mistress, Evelyn Knight, posed as his business partner.

Her accent gave him a sheen of sophistication. In truth, she worked as a housekeeper. Weinberg described Knight as "the salad dressing, the schmaltz" of the con. After initially defrauding people in the New York area, Weinberg expanded geographically, defrauding loan applicants in Pennsylvania, Tennessee, California, and Nevada. Offering "celebrity discounts," he duped the singer Wayne Newton and the comedian Joey Bishop into applying for loans as well. In an interview with the *New York Times Magazine,* Weinberg defended the caper as a kind of dream fulfillment operation. "When a guy is in a jam and lookin' for money, it's my philosophy to give hope," he said. "If you say you can't do nothin', you're killin' his hope. Everybody has to have hope. That's why most people don't turn us in to the cops. They keep hopin' we're for real."

In 1977, FBI agents arrested Weinberg and charged him with fraud and conspiracy. Initially, he refused to reveal the whereabouts of Knight. Then he handed her over to the bureau in the hopes of reducing his own three-year prison sentence. "I told them: 'let's make a deal,'" Weinberg recalled in a 2013 interview. "You feel like a real f——ing heel." To avoid jail time, Weinberg agreed to become an FBI informant and work with John Good, an ambitious FBI agent based on Long Island. Their first case involved solving a decade-old mystery: the theft of two missing seventeenth-century paintings—a Ter Borch and a Rubens. In an attempt to recover them, agents created a fictitious company called "Abdul Enterprises," and posed as wealthy Arab sheiks with millions in cash. Weinberg spread the word to cons and criminals that he had befriended deep-pocketed Saudis. (For his work, Weinberg received a $3,000 monthly stipend.) The "Abscam" ruse worked flawlessly. Criminals who tried to sell the missing paintings to the undercover agents were arrested.

Impressed by Weinberg's skills and connections, Good, the FBI agent, set his sights higher. He and his fellow agents designed a scheme to ensnare public officials on the take. Weinberg arranged a series of meetings with Angelo Errichetti, the Democratic mayor of Camden,

New Jersey. As he was being recorded, Errichetti offered FBI agents posing as rich Saudis entree to Atlantic City, which had recently legalized gambling, in exchange for kickbacks. "Without me," Errichetti told them, "you do nothing." Errichetti eventually set up meetings between the undercover agents and members of Congress. As hidden cameras recorded their conversations, FBI agents dressed as sheikhs offered senators and representatives bags of cash in exchange for investment advice, green cards, and government contracts.

Despite the stakes, Abscam, at times, was slapdash and amateurish. During one conversation with an elected official, a tape recorder attached to the underside of a coffee table fell to the floor. Weinberg, thinking quickly, kicked it out of sight with his foot. Weinberg complained that the FBI failed to properly fund the operation. For a front company to be credible, "It's got to look like it's got money." Instead, undercover agents purchased their Saudi headscarves and robes for $37 from a costume shop. They bought a dagger at a flea market for $2.75 and gave it to a public official as a traditional Saudi gift. At one dinner, kosher corned beef was accidentally served. "It was a farce," Weinberg recalled in a 2013 interview. "Here was an Arab eating kosher food in a headdress made for a kid. The thing came down to his shoulders where it should have come down to his knees. It was stupidity."

All told, five House members, one senator, an immigration official, a state legislator, and a mayor were convicted of taking bribes. After news of the probe leaked in 1980, videotapes of congressmen accepting the bribes aired on national television. Good, the FBI agent, credited Weinberg with the investigation's success. "Mel was a fabulous con man," he told the *Newark Star-Ledger*. "Without him, it's unlikely we ever would have had a case."

Not every member of Congress proved to be corrupt—John Murtha, a Pennsylvania Democrat, turned down a bribe—but other congressmen gleefully accepted payoffs. Richard Kelly, a Republican from central Florida, stuffed $25,000 in cash in his pockets and asked one of the agents, "Does it show?" John W. Jenrette Jr., a Democrat from South Carolina, told the agents after accepting a bribe, "I've got larceny in my blood." Michael "Ozzie" Myers, a Democrat from Philadelphia, pocketed $50,000 and told an FBI agent, "Money talks in this business and bullshit walks." The investigation's biggest catch was a US senator, Harrison "Pete" Williams Jr., a Democrat from New Jersey. A liberal stalwart, Williams claimed that he was entrapped by FBI agents, and accused the bureau of misconduct. "It is not only Pete Williams that stands accused or indicted," Williams said, referring to himself in a speech on the Senate floor. "It is all of us, the entire Senate, that stands accused and intimidated by another branch of government."

Abscam was the first test of the system that the Church reforms had created to prevent the FBI from committing Hoover-like abuses. In a repeat of the Watergate and Church investigations, the Senate created a select committee to investigate the operation. James Neal, a former Watergate prosecutor, served as its special counsel, and Daniel Inouye, the head of the Senate Intelligence Committee, was one of the committee members. Critics questioned the bureau's methods and called for the passage of new laws requiring a judge to pre-approve FBI undercover operations. The American Civil Liberties Union accused agents of luring the officials into carrying out crimes that they were not predisposed to commit. Two federal prosecutors claimed that Weinberg coached officials into saying the exact words needed for a conviction, and that he selectively taped parts of conversations.

Justice Department officials defended Good and Weinberg. The number-three official in the department at the time, Rudolph Giuliani, argued that informants often aided investigations. Giuliani, who would go on to become New York's mayor and President's Trump's personal lawyer, said the FBI had a right to investigate public officials. "There is no constitutional right not to be investigated," Giuliani told the *New York Times* in 1982. "You need someone who can get the confidence of the crook, and that will generally be a crooked person. Bishops and rabbis don't get the confidence of crooks."

William Webster, in his third year as FBI director, chose to fully cooperate with the investigation rather than trying to stonewall it. Webster testified in public and private, offered full access to FBI records, and assured lawmakers that the FBI of J. Edgar Hoover had not returned. He assured lawmakers that the sting operation was properly conducted and that the defendants were not entrapped. During each videotaped meeting, Webster testified, a federal prosecutor monitored the conversations and called agents if they appeared to engage in entrapment. Webster ordered agents to let public officials leave if they were uninterested. "I said, 'if they're corrupt, they'll come back,'" Webster recalled in a 2002 interview.

After months of hearings, the select committee recommended changes in FBI undercover operations but found no systematic misconduct by agents. James Neal, the former Watergate prosecutor, said, "We have not found a smoking gun in Abscam." Most importantly, the judicial branch, in the form of jury trials, validated the FBI's work. Judges and juries rejected the claims of entrapment and convicted the officials of accepting bribes. Webster and the bureau survived the scandal.

Skeptics contended that Webster, and other FBI and CIA directors, learned, over time, how to manage congressional oversight, co-opted members with public promises of disclosure, and gave private briefings in which directors said they needed flexibility to fight crime and protect the American people. Several massive intelligence failures were, in fact, missed by the FBI, the CIA, and the oversight committees as well. During Webster's tenure, Robert Hanssen, an FBI counterintelligence agent, began a twenty-two-year run of spying for the Soviets without being detected. In exchange for $1.4 million in cash and diamonds, Hanssen revealed the names of ten Soviet informants who were subsequently executed. Webster himself later described the Hanssen case as "possibly the worst intelligence disaster in U.S. history."

After Abscam, Mel Weinberg continued to be accused of fraud. His estranged wife, Cynthia Marie Weinberg, insisted that he had accepted a payoff from one of the Abscam defendants, a claim Weinberg denied. Before committing suicide in 1982, she accused Weinberg of mounting a campaign to discredit her. "I haven't the strength to fight him anymore," she wrote in her suicide note, and then asked for forgiveness. "What I am about to do is cowardly." The couple's son was sixteen years old at the time. Weinberg married Knight, his longtime British mistress, that same year; their marriage, his third, ended in divorce. Before retiring, Weinberg worked as an investigator who tried to shut down factories that manufactured fake designer handbags and clothing. He died in Florida in 2018.

During the making of *American Hustle*, Weinberg was paid $250,000 for his life story and was flown to Los Angeles to meet with Christian Bale. Weinberg said that had the operation continued, he could have sent "at least a third of the whole Congress" to jail. "I'm a swindler," he said. "There's only one difference between me and the congressmen I met on this case. The public pays them a salary for stealing."

. . .

While the Senate Select Committee questioned the conduct of the FBI, the Reagan White House defended the bureau's work. Ed Meese, the counselor to the president, held that the constraints placed on the bureau by the Carter administration and Congress were excessive. At Meese's urging, Reagan pardoned the two former senior FBI officials, Mark Felt and Edward Miller, whom the Carter administration had successfully prosecuted for ordering break-ins that violated Americans' civil rights. In a rebuke of the Church Committee's findings and Carter, Reagan issued a pardon statement that said the two men had "served the country with distinction" and "acted on high principle to bring an end to the terrorism that was threatening our nation." FBI agents hailed the pardons as vindication for the bureau. Meese, a supporter of sweeping executive branch power, praised them as well.

In a separate effort to ease the constraints placed on the bureau by Carter and Congress, Reagan's new attorney general, William French Smith, asked Webster if he wanted any other restrictions enacted by the previous administration removed. Webster declined. In the 2002 interview, Webster reflected on the difference between the two administrations. "The Carter administration would have people like Senator, then Vice President Mondale, who because of their experiences, were trying to tighten down on things without necessarily thinking through the consequences," Webster said. "The Reagan administration came with a different attitude. They were always talking about loosening up, loosening up, because they are doing their duty."

In a 1983 interview, former president Ford called for a balance of power between the presidency and congress. "I think that at times in our country in recent years we have had both an imperial presidency and an imperiled presidency. I think that at times the Congress had tended to encroach on the prerogatives of the presidency. On the other hand, there have been times in our memories when the president tended to disregard the Congress," Ford said. "So you probably can never define with precision where that line of demarcation should come. But we must be conscious that our country doesn't work well when one branch of the government tries to be too dominant."

Reagan, Meese, and other officials, though, pushed for a reassertion of the power of the presidency. In another reversal of Carter's policies, Reagan fought to block access to executive branch deliberations and attempted to enforce secrecy oaths for officials with access to sensitive intelligence information. Reagan administration officials did not use the term "deep state," but they contended that federal government was filled with left-leaning civil servants who resisted Reagan's cuts in the size of federal departments. In an innovation, Meese and other aides quickly filled nearly 3,000 positions across the government with experienced conservative appointees. After those officials were in place, the administration was able to implement its policies.

One such appointee was William Barr, the former CIA legislative affairs aide who had advised George H. W. Bush when he testified before Bella Abzug and other House members. After obtaining his law degree from George Washington University in 1977, Barr left the CIA to work as a clerk for Malcolm Wilkey, a pro–presidential power federal appeals court judge who had been heavily criticized for a dissenting appeals court opinion he issued at the height of the Watergate scandal. In 1973, the appeals court had ruled that Nixon had to turn over Oval Office tapes that had been subpoenaed by a federal criminal court. In a 5–2 ruling, Wilkey wrote a dissenting opinion that argued a president has an "absolute" privilege to refuse the other two branches of government. Nine months later, the Supreme Court, in a historic 8–0 ruling, flatly rejected that argument and ordered the White House to hand over the tapes. The ruling was a massive blow to Wilkey and other supporters of executive branch power. Barr's time working as a clerk for Wilkey, according to friends, bolstered his belief in a more powerful presidency.

In 1982, the Reagan White House hired Barr as a deputy assistant director for legal policy. Barr met a group of like-minded young conservative lawyers, including Ted Olson and Chuck Cooper, who began to devise legal theories that would allow the executive branch to regain the power they felt it had lost during Watergate. In 1982, Olson founded "The Federalist Society" with other conservative lawyers. In a bid to reverse *Roe v. Wade* and other court rulings of the 1960s and 1970s that conservatives viewed as misguided liberal judicial activism, the organization promoted conservative "originalist" interpretations of the Constitution and a reassertion of presidential power. Barr joined the society as well. Over time, it grew to be one of the most influential legal organizations in the country. In 2019, thirty-seven years after its founding, five of the nine justices on the US Supreme Court would be current or former Federalist Society members.

After working for the Reagan administration for a year, Barr left the White House in 1983 to work for a law firm but remained close to Olson and Cooper and committed to their cause. In 1986, Meese, then serving as attorney general, received a report from aides that recommended steps to enhance the power of the presidency. It called for Reagan to veto more legislation, for the White House to decline to enforce laws that "unconstitutionally encroach upon the executive branch," and it outlined the legal theory that the president had complete control of all executive branch functions. In a subsequent speech, Meese argued that Supreme Court rulings did not establish the " 'supreme law of the land' that is binding on all persons and parts of government, henceforth and forevermore." He urged local officials to make their own interpretations of the Constitution. The report and speech were a direct attack on the judicial branch's power and the post-Watergate consensus that coequal branches of government were needed to constrain presidential overreach and preserve American democracy.

In another assertion of presidential power, the Reagan administration backed a lawsuit Ted Olson filed that challenged the constitutionality of independent counsels after one was named to investigate him. Members of Congress had accused Olson, who was then running the Justice Department's Office of Legal Counsel, of lying to Congress about the willingness of EPA officials to hand over documents to House investigators. Olson challenged the constitutionality of independent counsels, which he, Meese, and other conservatives argued were infringements on the power of the presidency. Olson argued that presidents—and presidents alone—had the authority to conduct criminal investigations, even of members of their own administration.

Conservatives also viewed independent counsels as both unaccountable and costly, and accused Democrats of using them as political weapons to smear Republican administrations. Democrats in Congress insisted that independent counsels were needed to prevent Watergate-like abuses, and renewed the law when it expired in 1983 and 1987. (Reagan, fearing a political backlash if he issued a veto, reluctantly signed both bills.) In the fourteen years since Carter had signed the law, myriad independent counsels had been named. One targeted alleged drug use by Carter's chief of staff, Hamilton Jordan— and ultimately pressed no charges. Six others investigated various Reagan administration officials but found no criminal wrongdoing.

The 1988 Supreme Court ruling in the case *Morrison v. Olson* devastated Olson, Meese, Cheney, Barr, and other supporters of executive power. In a 7–1 vote, the justices upheld the constitutionality of independent counsels. The majority found that independent counsels do not interfere "unduly" or "impermissibly" with the powers of the executive branch. The one dissenting justice was Antonin Scalia. In a blistering thirty-page opinion, Scalia argued that the Constitution granted executive powers of investigation and prosecution solely to the president. In his opinion, Scalia warned that a politically biased independent prosecutor could endlessly carry out "debilitating criminal investigations" for minor crimes. "Nothing is so politically effective," Scalia wrote, "as the ability to charge that one's opponent and his associates are not merely wrongheaded, naive, ineffective, but, in all probability, 'crooks.'" Ultimately, prosecutors declined to charge Olson.

.   .   .

While Barr and other young Republican lawyers advanced conservative legal theories, another young American began her career as an intelligence officer with an internship in the Office of Naval Intelligence. Joan Dempsey had no idea that she would rise to become one of the highest-ranking intelligence officers of her generation. Over a forty-five-year career, Dempsey would eventually serve as deputy director for intelligence at the Defense Intelligence Agency and deputy director for intelligence community management at the CIA—the third-highest ranking official in the US intelligence community at the time. Throughout her career, she found civil servants to be apolitical professionals who worked with both Republican and Democratic administrations to implement their policies.

Dempsey had grown up in a farming town in southern Arkansas. Her father, James, often talked at dinner about how serving in the Navy had exposed him to the world and opened up opportunities for him. "He convinced me it would be a great life," Dempsey recalled. In 1974, after her first year in college, she followed her father's advice and enlisted in the Navy. Almost immediately, Dempsey realized that despite her father's good intentions, he had failed to consider how male sailors would behave toward her. "He didn't tell me what it would be like as a woman," she said, "because he didn't serve with women and couldn't know."

At the time, women were barred from deploying on ships, airplanes, and submarines. Unable to serve at sea, Dempsey excelled in training courses on shore. As she rose through the ranks, male sailors resented her. "I was treated badly by my counterparts," she said. For reasons she still doesn't understand, she was able to memorize and master Morse code in a matter of days. She heard Morse differently than other sailors. Even when coded messages were played at high speed, she was able to decipher them. "I could intercept thirty to forty groups of code in a minute," she said. "It was music to me."

Despite her skills as a cryptologist, Dempsey's continued rise "generated a lot of hate and discord" from male sailors, she said. Her first overseas deployment was as a Morse code intercept operator on a secret American base installation in Asia. Dempsey spent months monitoring Soviet radio traffic. Although she was gathering intelligence for the US government, she did not yet view her actions that way. "At the time, I didn't think of myself as a member of the intelligence community," she said. "I was a Navy cryptologist."

After three years of service, Dempsey left the Navy, returned to Arkansas, and obtained a political science degree from Southern Arkansas University and a master's degree from the University of Arkansas. She applied to a program the Carter administration had created, the Presidential Management Fellows Program, to attract top graduate students to work as civil servants. To her surprise, Dempsey was accepted.

After an internship at the Office of Naval Intelligence, Dempsey was hired as a staff officer. The sense of mission and the apolitical nature of the work appealed to her. At the time, groups of anti-war protesters were gathering in Washington to denounce Reagan, who they feared could spark a nuclear war with the Soviet Union. Privately, Dempsey worried that nuclear war was possible, but she felt that her work might play a role in limiting the risk.

Over time, the career civil servants who toiled daily in the intelligence agencies and Defense Department impressed her. They seemed professional, highly educated, and apolitical. They seemed to respect the political mandate that elected officials brought to Washington after each election. Some civil servants resisted change, Dempsey saw, but the overwhelming majority were "very competent do-gooders" who tried to help elected officials to implement their policy goals. "Yes, there were some that were a waste of oxygen," she said. "Most of them are very competent, very dedicated individuals who want to make things better." She was convinced that career civil servants were, on balance, a blessing to the country.

. . .

Under Reagan, the CIA experienced the most radical change of any government agency. While William Webster had embraced congressional oversight of the FBI, Reagan's new CIA director, William Casey, did the opposite. Over the course of his six-year tenure, Casey repeatedly instructed his subordinates to lie to Congress. Reagan, meanwhile, delegated near-absolute authority to Casey and paid little attention to day-to-day CIA operations. That decision nearly cost Reagan his presidency.

Casey, who had served in the OSS during World War II, was a multimillionaire Wall Street lawyer known for being a ruthless political operative. During the 1980 campaign, Casey had worked as Reagan's campaign manager. After his landslide victory, rumors circulated that Reagan would name Casey CIA director, and the president-elect received his first full CIA briefing. Douglas Diamond, a CIA expert on the Soviet economy who had briefed Carter after his 1976 election victory, recalled the striking differences between the two men. While Reagan was engaged, friendly, and raised largely factual questions, he kept the briefings short.

"The sun certainly didn't go down on this briefing like it had in Plains," Diamond recalled in a 1993 interview, a reference to Carter's long briefings in Georgia.

President-elect Reagan spent several weeks in Washington, then returned home to California. At the urging of Vice President–elect Bush, Reagan received the President's Daily Brief each day, usually in the morning. Frequently dressed in a bathrobe, he greeted CIA aides warmly and then proved to be a "thorough and very intent reader" of the daily briefing, a process that usually took about twenty minutes. Peter Dixon Davis, one of his briefers, recalled in a 1993 interview that Reagan's views on many subjects seemed already set, particularly regarding Israel. "The problem with Ronald Reagan was that his ideas were all fixed. He knew what he thought about everything—he was an old dog," said Davis. In one briefing, CIA analysts produced a three- or four-page memorandum on the backgrounds, personalities, ideologies, tactics, and strategies that divided the Palestinian movement. Reagan read the memorandum "very slowly and thoughtfully— he must have taken 10 minutes," Davis recalled. "At the end he said, 'But they are all terrorists, aren't they?'—My heart just sank."

Once Reagan moved into the White House, his one-on-one contact with CIA officers declined dramatically. A written version of the President's Daily Brief was given to Reagan's national security advisor, who then passed the briefing book to Reagan himself. Unlike Carter, Reagan did not scribble notes or questions in the PDB. And unlike other presidents, he read the PDB alone, with no CIA staffers present. Instead, he asked questions to Casey, his CIA director.

Inside the CIA, Casey set about revamping an agency that he believed had been hollowed out by the Church reforms and the Carter administration. In a signal to frustrated members of the CIA's Directorate of Operations, Casey hung a portrait in his office of the founder of the OSS, Major General William "Wild Bill" Donovan. Donovan, who had won the Medal of Honor for capturing a German machine gun nest in World War I, was famed for embracing risk. He considered virtually nothing off-limits in intelligence, from the assassination of foreign leaders to plotting coups d'état to sowing confusion by spreading lies. In a 1944 letter to Roosevelt, Donovan declared that "in a global and totalitarian war, intelligence must be global and totalitarian."

Inside the Reagan administration, Casey was famous for his rumpled appearance, intense ambition, and looseness with the facts. Tall and bald, he wore thick glasses, and had a habit of mumbling in meetings. Nancy Reagan had reportedly blocked him from becoming secretary of state because she was horrified by his manners. Reagan's senior advisors distrusted Casey as well. "I was absolutely surprised when President Reagan selected Casey," former president Ford said in a 1998 interview. "He was not qualified to be the head of the CIA." Vice President Bush said Casey was too partisan for the position. "Casey was an inappropriate choice," Bush said in a 1993 interview.

From the outset, Casey politicized the intelligence flowing to Reagan to fit his own views. He drove out analysts who didn't share his politics. Richard Lehman, who had created the first-ever President's Daily Brief in 1961 for John F. Kennedy and served as an agency analyst for 33 years, said that Casey marginalized him because he was "insufficiently hard" on the Soviet Union. "Working for Casey was a trial for everybody, partly because of his growing erraticism and partly because of his own rightwing tendencies," Lehman said in a 2007 interview. Secretary of State George Shultz was even more blunt. During the Casey era, he said, "the CIA's intelligence was in many cases simply Bill Casey's ideology."

In his first two months in office, Casey expanded the covert operations that Carter had initiated in Afghanistan and Eastern Europe, and created sweeping new covert operations in Nicaragua, Cuba, northern Africa, and South Africa as well. Citing the Soviet threat, Congress gave Casey hundreds of millions of dollars in funding that he used to hire nearly 2,000 new members of the Directorate of Operations, the clandestine service's first expansion since Nixon.

It was unclear, though, if the agency could carry out multiple covert action programs simultaneously and effectively. Robert Gates, who served as Casey's first chief of staff and later as CIA director, found the organization to be hidebound. "Burdened by years of bureaucratic encrustation and the lessons of the investigations of the 1970s, the D.O. set was hard-pressed for resources, unimaginative, and a blindered fraternity living on the legends and achievements of their forebears of the 1950s and 1960s," Gates recalled in his memoir. Some individual agents performed well, but Casey found that the CIA was "a pale reflection of its past. Even Carter Administration officials had been disappointed by the lack of imagination and boldness."

After Gates sent Casey a blistering memo recommending a top-to-bottom overhaul, Casey named him deputy director. "The agency had an advanced case of bureaucratic arteriosclerosis," Gates, who was just 38, wrote in his memo. He said CIA analysts were "close-minded, smug, arrogant" people whose work was "irrelevant, uninteresting, too late to be of value, too narrow, too unimaginative, and too often just flat out wrong."

Casey's obsession—and ultimate downfall—was Central America. He was convinced that the administration had to confront Soviet expansionism in Nicaragua and El Salvador before it reached the United States. Cuban operatives were arming and funding the Sandinista regime in Nicaragua and sending weaponry to leftist rebels in El Salvador. In December 1981, Reagan signed a covert finding that authorized the CIA to provide $19 million in arms to anti-Sandinista guerrillas, known as the Contras, who were trying to topple the country's leftist government. CIA analysts predicted that the strategy would fail because Nicaraguans, who had been brutalized by the dictatorial regime of Anastasio Somoza for more than a decade, supported the Sandinistas more than they did the Contras. Casey blocked their reports from reaching the White House.

Reagan also issued Executive Order 12333, which loosened some of the restrictions Carter had placed on the CIA, NSA, and other intelligence agencies on collecting information inside the United States. At the same time, Casey stonewalled the House and Senate intelligence committees, sharing minimal information with them and arguing that Congress was trying to micromanage foreign policy, the purview of the executive branch.

Congress fought back. In the spring of 1982, Edward Boland, the Democratic chair of the House Intelligence Committee, demanded a CIA briefing on how the agency's new covert action program was being conducted in Central America. Casey instructed three CIA staffers to tell the committee that the CIA had contacted all forces that might promote pluralism in Nicaragua. "Beyond that, I don't think details should be provided," Casey wrote. The limited briefings failed to mollify Boland and other Democrats. Six months later, Congress passed the Boland Amendment, which barred the CIA and Defense Department from spending funds on military activity inside Nicaragua. Called to testify before the House Intelligence Committee, Casey obfuscated. "Casey was guilty of contempt of Congress from the day he was sworn in," Gates later wrote in his memoir. After CIA-backed operatives mined Nicaragua's harbors in the spring of 1984, Senator Barry Goldwater of Arizona, who had served on the Church Committee and now was chairman of the Senate Intelligence Committee, angrily accused the CIA of failing to inform the committee of the covert operation as required by law. Casey insisted he had informed the committee in veiled terms.

That summer, Casey committed the most brazen act of a CIA director since the Church reforms. Violating multiple laws and executive orders, Casey and National Security Advisor Robert McFarlane began a secret program to arm the Contras without telling members of Congress. Using money from private donors and Saudi Arabia, they had National Security Council aide Oliver North secretly buy weapons and supply them to the Contras. In November 1984, as the covert arms shipments continued, Reagan, buoyed by a strong economy, won reelection in a landslide, defeating Walter Mondale in 49 of 50 states.

In the summer of 1985, Casey and McFarlane's scheme began to unravel. News reports of unexplained arms shipments to the Contras appeared in the American press. Called before Congress, McFarlane misled lawmakers, denying that arms shipments were occurring. Then in August, in a separate illegal weapons program, McFarlane and North began selling weapons to Iranian officials in the hopes they would help free American hostages in Lebanon. Reagan signed a retroactive presidential covert action finding that authorized the arms sales, but ordered his aides to withhold it from Congress, yet another violation of law. In the spring of 1986, Reagan's new national security advisor, John Poindexter, approved the diversion of $12 million from the Iran arms sales to the Contras. In testimony before eleven members of the House Intelligence Committee that summer, North misled lawmakers as well, and denied raising money for the Contras.

The significance of the actions of Casey, Poindexter, McFarlane, and North was staggering. Unable to win congressional support for funding and arming the Contras, they had carried it out anyway, violating the Constitution and the law. In the process, they repeatedly lied to Congress, the courts, and the American public. A decade after Nixon's aides broke the law to try to win a presidential election, Reagan's aides had broken the law to carry out a shadow foreign policy.

On November 25, 1986, the Lebanese magazine *Al Shiraa* broke news of the secret American arms shipments to Iran. In their White House offices, North and his secretary began frantically shredding documents. Outraged members of Congress demanded immediate answers and Casey agreed to testify under oath. The day before he was scheduled to appear, Casey suffered a massive seizure in his CIA office. Rushed to a nearby hospital, he was diagnosed with a malignant brain tumor. For the next five months, Casey drifted in and out of consciousness. In May 6, 1987, Casey died in a New York hospital. Exactly what Reagan and Bush knew of Casey's illegal diversion of funds would remain one of the mysteries of the Reagan presidency.

. . .

Four weeks after news of what became known as the "Iran-Contra" affair broke, Attorney General Meese, under intense political pressure, appointed an independent counsel to investigate potential criminal misconduct. Meese chose Lawrence Walsh, a lifelong Republican and former judge and deputy attorney general, was appointed independent counsel to investigate potential criminal misconduct. FBI agents arrived at CIA headquarters with subpoenas and began collecting documents to prevent them from being destroyed, as had occurred in the White House. Morale at the agency plummeted again. Casey had empowered the agency and then driven it off a political cliff.

In a nationally televised address in March 1987, Reagan denied any knowledge of the illegal diversion of funds and apologized to the American people. "As angry as I may be about activities undertaken without my knowledge, I am still accountable for those activities," he said from the Oval Office. "As disappointed as I may be in some who served me, I'm still the one who must answer to the American people for this behavior."

Reagan appointed Webster, the by-the-book FBI director, as Casey's successor at the CIA. Like past presidents, he promised to clean up the agency. A select congressional committee, co-chaired by Democratic senator Daniel Inouye of Hawaii and Representative Lee Hamilton of Indiana, held Watergate-style hearings through the summer of 1987 regarding Iran-Contra. Senator Warren Rudman of New Hampshire and Representative Dick Cheney of Wyoming, Ford's former White House chief of staff, were the ranking Republicans. Guided by Inouye, these hearings produced overwhelming evidence that McFarlane, Poindexter, North, and CIA officials had flagrantly violated the congressional ban on the United States providing support to the Contras. Meese was accused of orchestrating a cover-up.

But the televised hearings failed to follow a Watergate script when North—dressed in his Marine uniform—defiantly defended his actions, saying they were necessary to battle Communism and terrorism. Instantly, the Marine officer became a folk hero of conservative talk radio. Poindexter, though, played the most important role. In an act that saved Reagan from potential impeachment, Poindexter testified that he acted on his own and never informed the president of the illegal diversion of funds. "The buck stops here with me," Poindexter told the committee.

In his final remarks at the conclusion of the hearings, Senator Inouye cautioned that a "cabal" of officials who believed they had a "monopoly on truth" was a recipe for "autocracy." The officials had operated "a shadowy government with its own air force, its own navy, its own fundraising mechanism, and the ability to pursue its own ideas of the national interest, free from all checks and balances, and from the law itself. It is an elitist vision of government that trusts no one, not the people, not the Congress and not the Cabinet. . . . I believe these hearings will be remembered longest not for the facts they elicited, but for the extraordinary and the extraordinarily frightening views of government that they exposed."

In November 1987, the committee's majority released a final report that concluded that the administration had engaged in "secrecy, deception, and disdain for the law." It held Reagan responsible for the scandal. "If the President did not know what his national security advisors were doing, he should have," the lawmakers concluded. "The President set the U.S. policy towards Nicaragua, with few if any ambiguities, and then left subordinates more or less free to implement it."

Rudman and two other Republican senators backed the majority report and agreed that the affair was a grave constitutional breach. But Cheney, two Republican senators, and all five other Republican House members on the committee issued a minority report that dismissed the majority report as "hysterical." Cheney argued that the Reagan administration had done nothing improper because foreign policy and national security were solely controlled by the executive branch. Cheney attacked the War Powers Act and Church reforms as brazen attempts to create "all but unlimited Congressional power." He argued that the legislative branch did not have the power to bar the President from funding the Contras. "The power of the purse," Cheney wrote, "is not and was never intended to be a license for Congress to usurp Presidential powers and functions." The minority report even attacked the Reagan administration, saying it should have argued that it had a constitutional right to flout Congress's ban on funding the Contras. At the time, the minority report attracted little attention because its views were considered outside the political mainstream. That would change after 9/11.

After the issuing of the reports, Democrats tried to make the abuse of presidential power a political issue. With the 1988 presidential election approaching, Democrats noted the similarities between the Watergate and Iran-Contra scandals. A cabal of White House loyalists had broken the law—and then flagrantly lied to the American people about it. Attention shifted from Reagan to Bush, his vice president and would-be successor. In a series of interviews, Bush emphatically denied any knowledge of the diversion, claiming he was "out of the loop." Walsh, the independent counsel, pressed his investigation of Bush and the administration.

For the first time in modern American political history, the executive branch's defiance of Congress—and of the constitutional order—threatened to become the deciding issue in a presidential campaign. American voters would have a say in how much a president should respect the powers of Congress. The widespread assumption that any president who defied Congress would be forced from power like Nixon would be tested. As would the ability of a president to escape accountability with half-truths.

FIVE

Bush, Barr, and the Power of the Presidency

T hroughout George H. W. Bush's political career, he was rarely seen as an ideologue. He supported a restoration of the presidential power that had existed before Watergate, but he favored methodical, not radical, steps to the rolling back of congressional authority. In fact, some conservatives saw his moderation as a political liability. In his final days in office, a frustrated Bush would deliver two crippling blows to the legislative branch's ability to curtail the executive. And William Barr would play a central role in both of those decisions.

As Reagan prepared to leave office and the 1988 presidential race approached, it was unclear if George H. W. Bush would ever occupy the Oval Office. Before Iran-Contra, he was thought to be in a powerful position to win the Republican nomination and the presidency. But the scandal had damaged Reagan's popularity, driving his approval rating from 60 percent to 48 percent. Remembered today as a popular president who was the face of optimism after the Carter era, Reagan's average approval rating in office, 53 percent, was higher than that of Nixon, Ford, Carter, George W. Bush, and Obama, but lower than that of Eisenhower, Kennedy, Johnson, George H. W. Bush, and Clinton.

In an apparent effort to put questions about Iran-Contra to rest, Bush published a carefully vetted autobiography, *Looking Forward*, in the summer of 1987, that was designed to showcase his deep experience in government, and his commitment to family and American values. Bush devoted a few pages of his book to the scandal. The vice president repeated his long-running claim that he knew little about the arms shipments to Iran and nothing about the illegal diversion of cash to the Contras. He reinforced the narrative that Poindexter and North had kept senior members of the administration in the dark. "At no point along the way, from its beginning to its end," was the full National Security Council membership "formally brought together to discuss the Iran initiative," Bush wrote. "Not one meeting of the National Security Council was ever held to consider all phases of the operation." Bush's account was misleading.

Weeks after the vice president published his book, the Iran-Contra Committee's majority report contradicted parts of Bush's narrative. Bush, the report found, had attended a "full NSC meeting" on January 7, 1986, where Weinberger and Shultz both argued against the arms-for-hostages deal. The report also disclosed that North arranged for Amiram Nir, an Israeli counterterrorism expert who was deeply involved in the arms-for-hostage deal, to brief Bush on the operation when Bush visited Israel in 1986.

Iran-Contra complicated his campaign in other ways. On the trail, Bush touted his experience heading the "Vice President's Task Force on Combating Terrorism." When Bush unveiled the group's final report on March 6, 1986, he was uncompromising. "Our policy is clear, concise, unequivocal," he said. "We will offer no concession to terrorists, because that only leads to more terrorism." Yet, as Bush spoke, he knew that the Reagan administration was secretly selling tens of millions of dollars' worth of sophisticated anti-tank missiles to Iran in exchange for its help in gaining the release of American hostages in Lebanon. After news of the arms shipments became public, members of the task force said that Bush had never informed them of the clandestine arms shipments during their work.

While Shultz and Weinberger vocally opposed the secret program in White House meetings, no clear evidence emerged that

Bush—a former CIA director—had aggressively argued against them as well. Bush said that he personally had "reservations" about the sales but never publicly criticized Reagan's ten-month delay in sharing with Congress the retroactive Presidential Covert Action finding he signed.

In the first Republican primary debate of the 1988 race, former secretary of state Alexander Haig demanded to know whether Bush had advised Reagan to carry out the arms-for-hostages deal. Bush gave a vague answer, running down the debate clock. "You haven't answered my question," Haig interjected. Bush replied: "Time's up." Several days later, Senator Bob Dole of Kansas, Bush's primary rival at that point, called for Bush to release all notes, records, or memos that he had kept regarding Iran-Contra. "Lay it out there," Dole said. "Let the American people see it."

A live, nationally televised interview on *CBS Evening News* between Bush and anchor Dan Rather ended acrimoniously after CBS reported that Bush was more involved in the affair than he had publicly acknowledged. "You know what I'm hiding?" Bush retorted. "What I told the President. That's the only thing. And I've answered every question put before me."

Two weeks later, in a humiliation for Bush, Dole decisively won the Iowa caucuses, with Pat Robertson, the televangelist, coming in second, and Bush relegated to third. After hesitating for months, Bush followed the advice of his two most aggressive advisors—campaign manager Lee Atwater and communications advisor Roger Ailes—and went on the attack in New Hampshire. Atwater and Ailes aired television ads that portrayed Iran-Contra as a strength for Bush. They attacked Dole for not defending Reagan during the scandal, correctly betting that registered Republicans were less troubled by the issue than Democrats. Bush won the New Hampshire primary and then swept the South on Super Tuesday, regaining momentum. Bush's fundraising and organizational advantages allowed him to lock up the nomination before the Republican National Convention in New Orleans that

August. The presumption that any president who defied Congress would be punished by voters had been proven hollow.

When Bush arrived in New Orleans to accept the nomination, a sprawling network of campaign advisors awaited him. One of them was William Barr, who had advised Bush when he testified before Congress as CIA director. After leaving the Reagan White House, Barr had maintained his close relationship with some of Bush's aides. Bush delivered an acceptance speech that exhibited his political contradictions. In a sign of his moderation, Bush declared the country's myriad community service organizations "a thousand points of light." In an appeal to conservatives, he vowed, "Read my lips: no new taxes"—a promise that would haunt him politically.

Guided again by Atwater and Ailes, Bush went on the offensive against Massachusetts governor Mike Dukakis, declaring the Democratic nominee a tax-and-spend liberal. In an infamous campaign ad, Atwater and Ailes portrayed Dukakis as weak on crime, smearing him with the case of Willie Horton, an African-American felon who had raped a white woman and stabbed her partner while on furlough from prison in Massachusetts. Dukakis fought back and cited Iran-Contra as evidence of Bush being weak on terrorism. "You cannot make concessions to terrorists, ever, ever," Dukakis said in their first debate. "That's the tragedy of the Iran-Contra scandal." The issue, though, never gained traction. Aided by a strong economy, Bush easily defeated Dukakis.

The vice president appeared to have paid little if any political price for his contradictory answers regarding Iran-Contra. In the absence of Oval Office recordings proving complicity, plausible deniability was enough for voters to give a candidate they liked the benefit of the doubt. Nixon was the exception, not the norm. In the wake of Bush's victory, the specter of another Watergate would have less of an impact on future presidents. The reforms from the 1970s remained in place, but the presidency had regained much of the political power it had lost to Congress.

. . .

After Bush's win, C. Boyden Gray, Bush's future White House counsel, asked Barr to run the Justice Department's Office of Legal Counsel. One of Washington's most coveted legal positions, the office provides advice to the president and all federal agencies. It is also considered a launching pad for more senior positions. Past directors had included Scalia and Supreme Court Chief Justice William Rehnquist and multiple solicitors general.

Barr, who was only 39, hesitated to take the job because he worried that it would not be valued in the private sector. "I, in some ways, wanted a more commercial job with a little bit more application to private practice," Barr recalled in his 2001 oral history interview on the Bush presidency. After Gray assured Barr that his legal views on expansive executive power would be welcomed, he accepted. "Boyden Gray thought that that was a very important job, and was intent on getting someone in that position who believed in executive authority," Barr said. During the Bush administration, Gray, Barr, and other conservatives would continue Meese's drive to reverse what they saw as post-Watergate encroachments on presidential power.

Several months after Barr accepted the position, he produced an unsolicited memo warning other administration officials to resist attempts by Congress to undermine President Bush's power as president. Barr listed ten recent examples of what he described as the legislative branch seizing power from presidents, from "Micromanagement of the Executive Branch" to "Attempts to Restrict the President's Foreign Affairs Powers." The memo was a legal call-to-arms. "It is important that all of us be familiar with each of these forms of encroachment," Barr wrote. "Only by consistently and forcefully resisting such congressional incursions can executive branch prerogatives be preserved."

With Bush and Gray's full support, Barr chaired meetings where the general counsels of executive branch departments drafted a joint strategy for how the administration would combat Congress. "We set up some things because of Boyden's and my own interest in the powers of the Presidency and President Bush's, too," Barr recalled. "I think Bush felt that the powers of the Presidency had been severely eroded since Watergate and the tactics of the Hill Democrats over an extended period of time when they were in power."

In private, Bush opposed the aggressive tactics embraced by some Republicans regarding executive power. At one meeting, Bush praised Barr for advising him to resist demands from conservatives that he become the first president to use a line-item veto. Barr said the legal case for line-item vetoes was weak and he feared that testing the issue could lead to a court ruling against the presidency. Barr recalled Bush saying, "My view is that you weaken the Presidency by asserting powers that aren't given, and then getting defeated. Unless you feel that we have a good claim here—I don't want you stretching—I think the way to advance executive power is to wait and see, move gradually. Certain prerogatives are clearly ours, and we should not reach for something that's beyond our grasp."

Bush also abided by post-Watergate norms and avoided taking any steps that could be seen as politicizing the Justice Department. "Watergate made Republican administrations very wary of the Justice Department," Barr said in the 2001 interview. "And I think Republican administrations—including the Reagan administration, and certainly the Bush administration—took the view that the Attorney General–Justice Department was special and different, and you didn't mess around with it, didn't intervene, you didn't interfere."

In foreign affairs, Bush was bolder. In 1989, he ordered 21,000 US troops to invade Panama, the largest American military deployment since Vietnam. The country's military leader, General Manuel Noriega, had been indicted on drug trafficking charges by federal prosecutors in Miami. After a coup by pro-American Panamanian forces failed to dislodge Noriega, Bush cited protecting the 35,000 Americans citizens who lived in Panama and combating the narcotics trade as justifications for the invasion. (Bush did not disclose that Noriega had worked as a CIA informant since 1967, including the years when Bush served as CIA director.) Twenty-three American soldiers and at least 516 Panamanians died in the invasion, but 80 percent of Americans approved of it in opinion polls. The UN General Assembly decried the invasion, calling it a "flagrant violation of international law."

Barr had played a small but secret legal role in the invasion. As the head of the Office of Legal Counsel, he issued a legal opinion that an American president has "inherent constitutional authority" to order the FBI to take people into custody in foreign countries. The opinion reversed an earlier Justice Department policy that the president lacked such authority and expanded executive branch power. After seeking refuge in the Vatican diplomatic mission in Panama, Noriega was arrested by FBI agents and later tried and imprisoned in the United States. After 9/11, the seizure of foreign nationals overseas by the United States would be vastly expanded.

In 1990, Bush backed military action again after Iraqi president Saddam Hussein invaded Kuwait. Barr, who had by this time been promoted to deputy attorney general, participated in a White House meeting at which Bush asked if he needed the approval of Congress to use force in Kuwait and Iraq. Citing executive power and dismissing the War Powers Act, Barr said the president had the power to go to war without congressional approval. Barr recalled: "I said, 'Mr. President, there's no doubt that you have the authority to launch an attack.' I explained why I thought he did under the Constitution as commander-in-chief, and I gave him some different theories."

Barr then took two even more unusual steps. First, he advised Bush that the president had the power to launch a "preemptive" attack on Iraqi forces, if Bush felt they were preparing to launch a chemical weapons attack on American troops. Then, he gave Bush political advice. Barr, a 40-year-old deputy attorney general, counseled Bush that he should try to gain the support of Congress even though, in Barr's view, he didn't need it legally. He told Bush that congressional approval would put the administration in a stronger political position. According to Barr, Secretary of Defense Dick Cheney objected to Barr giving Bush political advice. "Cheney said, 'You're giving him political advice, not legal advice,'" Barr recalled. "I said, 'No, I'm giving him both political and legal advice. They're really sort of together when you get to this level.'" Barr exhibited traits he would show again when he served in the Trump administration—boldness and a willingness to mix politics with legal opinions.

After Bush and his aides convinced Congress to pass a bipartisan resolution supporting military action, more than 500,000 American troops led a February ground attack that drove Iraqi forces out of Kuwait in one hundred hours. In a lopsided victory that seemed to banish the ghosts of Vietnam, 300 soldiers from the US-led coalition perished and an estimated 8,000 to 10,000 Iraqis died. Bush's approval ratings soared to over 80 percent, the highest of any modern American president. Eighteen months away from reelection, Bush seemed destined for a second term.

. . .

Nine months after the liberation of Kuwait, Barr was promoted to attorney general to replace Richard Thornburgh, who had left the post to run for US Senate in Pennsylvania. At 41, he was one of the youngest people ever appointed attorney general. Allies and adversaries described Barr as a formidable thinker who relished debating issues of Roman history, Christian theology, and modern morality. As attorney general, he earned the nickname Rage and Cave: when he felt that his principles had been violated, he tended to protest, then gradually accept the situation. Colleagues described him as both supportive and self-regarding, happy to delegate but impatient with incompetence. A self-styled polymath, Barr had strong opinions on issues ranging from legal arcana to the proper mustard to apply to a sandwich. During a trip to Scotland with a friend, he quizzed the owner of a local inn about whether the paint on the wall was "Card Room Green or Green Smoke, by Farrow & Ball." The innkeeper had no idea what he was talking about.

During his fourteen-month tenure as attorney general, Barr redoubled his efforts to expand the authority of the presidency. He also carried out tough-on-crime policies, increased drug-related prison sentences, and cracked down on illegal immigration. His approach reflected the views he held before, during, and after his time as the country's chief law enforcement officer. In a 1995 symposium on violent crime, he argued that the root cause was not poverty but immorality. "Violent crime is caused not by physical factors, such as not enough food stamps in the stamp program, but ultimately by moral factors," he said. "Spending more money on these material social programs is not going to have an impact on crime, and, if anything, it will exacerbate the problem." Barr also dismissed the idea of excessive sentences and wrongful convictions. "The notion that there are sympathetic people out there who become hapless victims of the criminal-justice system and are locked away in federal prison beyond the time they deserve is simply a myth," he wrote. "The people who have been given mandatory minimums generally deserve them—richly."

When rioting erupted in Los Angeles after the 1992 acquittal of four police officers who were videotaped beating motorist Rodney King, Barr deployed 2,000 federal law enforcement agents to the city on military planes. He argued that federal civil rights charges should have been brought against both the rioters and the police officers who assaulted King. "We could have cleaned that place up," he lamented. "Unfortunately, we just brought the federal case against the cops and never pursued the gangsters."

A devout Catholic, Barr won praise from social conservatives for his staunch opposition to *Roe v. Wade*. In a July 4, 1992, interview on *Larry King Live*, he predicted that the Supreme Court would eventually overturn the landmark ruling. "I think it will fall of its own weight. It does not have any constitutional underpinnings."

Barr also won praise from backers of presidential power for his opposition to the appointment of independent counsels. In his 2001 oral history interview, Barr warned that politically ambitious prosecutors would be tempted to investigate innocent individuals to make a name for themselves. "There's no other power like it in government—the prosecutive power destroys lives." Barr said.

Barr took pride in the fact that, as attorney general, he turned down multiple requests for independent counsels. "At some point the public integrity section told me that I had received more requests for independent counsel in eighteen months than all my predecessors combined," Barr recalled. "It was a joke."

The most politically sensitive independent counsel request concerned "Iraqgate"—a 1992 investigation into whether Bush administration officials played an improper role in a criminal scheme involving an Italian bank, Banca Nazionale del Lavoro. Investigators said that US government–backed agricultural loans to Saddam Hussein were illicitly used for weapons purchases. Barr rejected calls to appoint an independent counsel, drawing the ire of William Safire, a conservative columnist at the *New York Times*, who mockingly referring to him as "Coverup-General Barr." (A subsequent investigation by the Clinton Justice Department found no wrongdoing by Barr or any Bush Administration officials.)

As the 1992 presidential election approached, the attention of Bush, Barr, and other conservatives was focused on an existing independent counsel: Iran-Contra prosecutor Lawrence Walsh, who was still probing the scandal five years after he was appointed. To Barr, Walsh was an example of post-Watergate congressional overreach, someone who, as Scalia had warned, could endlessly carry out "debilitating criminal investigations" of the executive branch.

Barr was disdainful of Walsh and said his continuing investigation had hung over the Bush presidency. "It was very difficult because of the constant pendency of the Iran-Contra case and Lawrence Walsh, who I thought was a—I don't know what to say in polite company," Barr recalled in 2001. "He was certainly a headhunter and had completely lost perspective, and was out there flailing about on Iran-Contra with a lot of headhunters working for him. The whole tenor of the administration was affected by that." Nearly twenty years later, while serving as Trump's attorney general, Barr himself would be accused of using his authority as a prosecutor for political gain.

. . .

While Barr cracked down on crime and criticized independent counsels, Bush experienced the most dramatic drop in popularity of an incumbent president in modern American history. After the triumph of the first Gulf War, his approval rating plummeted from over 80 percent in the spring of 1991 to 31 percent in the summer of 1992. The primary reasons were a punishing economic recession and Bush's violation of his "no new taxes" pledge as part of a bipartisan deficit reduction deal.

Throughout the 1992 presidential race, Bush's Democratic opponent, Bill Clinton, overcame reports of extramarital affairs, and led Bush in the polls. The most damaging dynamic for Bush was the independent candidacy of billionaire businessman Ross Perot, who drew conservative and independent voters away from Bush. In the final weeks of the general election, Bush closed the gap, but it proved not enough. Clinton, promising to focus on the economy and bring change to Washington, won the presidency, garnering 43 percent of the vote to Bush's 37 percent. Perot captured 18 percent of the vote, a record for a third-party candidate.

Supporters of Bush also blamed Independent Counsel Walsh. Four days before the election, Walsh had filed a new criminal charge against former defense secretary Caspar Weinberger, and revealed an entry from Weinberger's diary that cast doubt on Bush's long-running claim that he had opposed trading arms for hostages. The diary entry from Weinberger said that during a January 7, 1986, White House meeting Bush had, in fact, approved of the scheme. Clinton took political advantage of the diary entry, saying the disclosure showed that Bush could not tell the truth. His running mate, Al Gore, called the diary entry a "smoking gun."

White House officials accused Walsh of timing the new charge so that it would sway the election. Walsh's office said they had filed the charge to meet a judge's deadline. Conservative anger at Walsh, which dated back to Oliver North's defiant 1987 congressional testimony, had built as his investigation dragged on for five years. Poindexter and North were convicted of lying to Congress, but their convictions were overturned on appeal (due to mistakes made by congressional investigators, not Walsh). Four other figures pleaded guilty. Weinberger awaited trial.

After losing the election, Bush became convinced that the Weinberger charge had cost him the presidency, according to Barr. Bush believed "that the gap was closing, and he had momentum going into that last weekend," Barr said. "He did say to me that he felt that that indictment had cost him the election. He was very infuriated by it."

On Christmas Eve, 1992, Bush pardoned four former officials whom Walsh had prosecuted for lying to Congress—Robert McFarlane, Elliott Abrams, Alan Fiers, and Clair George—and two who were awaiting trial—Weinberger and Duane "Dewey" Clarridge. Bush declined to pardon North, Poindexter, and several businessmen who said their goal was to simply profit financially from arms shipments.

In a statement accompanying the pardons, Bush embraced the position argued by Cheney in the Iran-Contra committee's minority report. In four years, Cheney's view had gone from the fringe of the Republican party to the center of it. "The prosecutions of the individuals I am pardoning represent what I believe is a profoundly troubling development in the political and legal climate of our country: the criminalization of policy differences," Bush wrote. "These differences should be addressed in the political arena, without the Damocles sword of criminality hanging over the heads of some of the combatants. The proper target is the President, not his subordinates; the proper forum is the voting booth, not the courtroom."

Barr enthusiastically supported the pardons. When some aides suggested that only Weinberger be pardoned, Barr urged Bush to pardon as many people as possible. "I favored the broadest," Barr said in the 2001 interview, referring to the number of pardons. "There were some people arguing just for Weinberger, and I said, No, in for a penny, in for a pound."

In addition to the pardons, Bush and Republicans in Congress allowed the independent counsel law enacted by Carter to lapse on December 15, 1992. Bush, a lame duck, did not fear the political repercussions.

The pardons infuriated Walsh, who said for the first time that he believed that Reagan and Bush had engaged in a cover-up. "What set Iran-Contra apart from previous political scandals," Walsh later wrote in his memoir, "was the fact that a cover-up engineered in the White House of one president and completed by his successor prevented the rule of law from being applied to the perpetrators of criminal activity of constitutional dimension."

To Democrats and supporters of congressional oversight, the Iran-Contra pardons were an enormous blow to Congress's ability to act as a check on the president and ensure that executive branch officials did not lie to legislators. Executive branch officials had blatantly lied to oversight committees while carrying out an illegal covert operation that involved the clandestine sale of American weaponry, the diversions of millions of dollars in cash, and the violation of a congressional ban on support to the Contras. The core goal of the Church reforms—public oversight of secretive intelligence agencies by elected representatives—had been thwarted.

Yet, to Barr and other supporters of presidential power, Walsh and other independent counsels were themselves the unaccountable, anti-democratic force. Barr said that independent counsel probes like Walsh's reinforced his belief that the post-Watergate reforms had gone too far in shifting prosecutorial power away from presidents and other elected officials. "The other big problem is this notion that has gained currency that there's something wrong about political officials reviewing cases," Barr recalled in the 2001 interview. "Actually, this has largely been precipitated by the liberal critics of the Department of Justice and by the Democrats on the Hill. It's very destructive to personal liberty because what they're trying to do is to say that political-level people shouldn't be reviewing cases."

Barr was espousing a view that was the polar opposite of the apolitical approach established by Gerald Ford's attorney general Edward Levi. Barr argued that having political leaders review whether individuals should be criminally prosecuted would lead to more equitable outcomes. He argued that if elected leaders abused prosecutorial powers, they could be voted out of office. "The second-guessing is not for political reasons," Barr said. "It's really because someone is exercising some maturity of judgment, and putting things in perspective and saying, 'Why would you indict this person over this?'"

Skeptics argued that political leaders do not always show maturity of judgment. Intense pressure to win the next election can distort an elected official's thinking. Prosecuting one's political rivals as criminals can prove effective at the ballot box. As Donald Trump would show in his dealings with Ukraine, the desire to have criminal investigations launched against one's political opponents can cause an elected leader to act corruptly.

SIX

Clinton, Reno, and Impeachment

O n January 20, 1993, Clinton took the oath of office, promising to bring generational change to Washington, strengthen the American economy, and, above all, refocus Washington on domestic concerns after decades of military brinksmanship with the Soviets. In his inaugural address, Clinton also called for the devolution of power in America. "And so I say to all of us here, let us resolve to reform our politics, so that power and privilege no longer shout down the voice of the people," he said. "Let us give this capital back to the people to whom it belongs."

Clinton would, though, end up defending executive branch power as Republican presidents had. He would engage in the same power struggles with Congress as his predecessors. During his two terms in office, anti-government militia movements would form that viewed Clinton as a dictator who used federal law enforcement agencies to oppress Americans. Republicans in Congress would accuse him of thwarting investigations. He would be impeached and acquitted. The presidency would be battered but would retain its strength.

. . .

In one of his first major decisions as president, Clinton struggled to identify a viable candidate to replace William Barr as attorney general. His first two nominees, Zoë Baird and Kimba Wood, withdrew their nominations after leaks to the press revealed that they had employed undocumented immigrants to care for their children. (The prolonged episode, which became known as "Nannygate," deeply frustrated the administration.) On March 11, 1993, Clinton's third choice—a relatively obscure Miami prosecutor named Janet Reno—was sworn in as the country's first-ever female attorney general.

The choice was a departure from the practice of past presidents, who chose nationally known figures or close advisors for the powerful position. Clinton said he initially heard of Reno from his brother-in-law Hugh Rodham, who worked as a public defender in a drug court Reno had established in Miami. Initially, Clinton had dismissed the idea of appointing Reno because she had no experience in federal law enforcement, but he eventually chose her after determining that her fifteen years of experience in Miami gave her "enormous exposure to a wide range of issues that the Justice Department deals with."

Reno would serve in the position for all eight years of Clinton's presidency. Under her leadership, the Justice Department sued Microsoft for violating antitrust laws, and aggressively supported the 1994 Crime Bill that reduced crime but fueled mass incarceration. Reno strengthened the post-Watergate tradition of keeping the attorney general's office apolitical, repeatedly appointing independent counsels over the objections of the president. At the same time, a raid involving federal law enforcement officers and children in Waco, Texas, marred Reno's tenure and forever associated her in the eyes of conservatives with a callous, overreaching, and deadly federal government.

Reno inherited the Waco crisis—an ongoing standoff between federal agents and members of a religious cult in Texas—when she took office. Two weeks before Reno was sworn in, eighty armed agents of the Bureau of Alcohol, Tobacco, and Firearms (ATF) had raided the Branch Davidian religious community's compound about 90 miles south of Dallas. David Koresh, a 33-year-old preacher who claimed to be the son of Christ and have the gift of prophecy, led the community. ATF agents who had been told that the Davidians were illegally stockpiling weapons planned to serve search and arrest warrants on Koresh. Instead of the pastor surrendering, a five-hour gun battle followed that left four ATF agents and six Davidians dead.

The clash was the second lethal confrontation between federal agents and heavily armed civilians in seven months. During the final year of the Bush administration, in August 1992, federal marshals had tried to serve an arrest warrant on Randy Weaver. A white supremacist living with his family in a remote cabin on Ruby Ridge in northern Idaho, Weaver was wanted for selling two illegal sawed-off shotguns to an undercover agent. A shootout erupted, and two people—federal marshal William Francis Degan, and Weaver's fourteen-year-old son, Sammy—were shot dead. A standoff ensued and members of the FBI's elite Hostage Recovery Team joined the marshals. The following day, an FBI sniper fired at a Weaver family friend, Kevin Harris, as he stood on the cabin's front porch holding a rifle. The bullet struck and injured Harris, and then traveled through the cabin's front door and killed Weaver's wife Vicki as she held their baby daughter in her arms. A subsequent Justice Department review harshly criticized the procedures the FBI used in the incident, including rules of engagement for when snipers could fire.

Eager to avoid turning Waco into another Ruby Ridge, Reno ordered federal agents to surround the compound, begin negotiations, and end the standoff peacefully. A total of 123 people—including 43 children—remained inside the two-story wooden complex where Koresh lived with his followers, including women and girls he had been accused of physically and sexually abusing. As in Ruby Ridge, the FBI's Hostage Recovery Unit took over the operation. Seven weeks of negotiations ensued, as dozens of television crews and journalists covered the standoff. Daily updates from FBI officials were broadcast live on CNN, which had learned it could draw large numbers of viewers when it covered prolonged crises and natural disasters.

The standoff reflected a growing political and culture divide in the country. Many liberals dismissed the group as a "cult" and generally accepted the government's argument that children were in danger. They also viewed the group's large cache of weapons as a threat to public safety. Conservatives criticized Koresh but saw the raid as unlawful government overreach. They argued that the Branch Davidians were exercising their right to religious freedom and had defended themselves when attacked by federal agents.

On Sunday, April 18, 1993, Reno went to the White House for a secret meeting with Clinton. After a month of fruitless negotiations, the FBI had developed a plan to storm the compound, arrest Koresh, and apprehend any Branch Davidian members involved in killing the four federal agents. Reno expressed her concern to Clinton that Koresh might be sexually abusing the children in the compound or planning a mass suicide. She was also under pressure from FBI officials, who said they could no longer keep so many resources tied up in one location.

The following morning, federal agents drove tanks and armored vehicles up to the sprawling complex, knocked holes in its walls, and fired more than 300 tear-gas canisters inside it. FBI officials hoped that the tear gas would cause Koresh and his followers to surrender. Instead, four hours after the operations began, fires broke out at three locations inside the structure. On live national television, as the prairie wind stoked the flames, the complex burned to the ground.

Federal agents said they had started no fires and fired no shots. They blamed the Davidians for setting the blaze. Survivors later claimed that one of the tanks knocked over a lantern and ignited the inferno. All told, 76 Branch Davidians—including children ages ten or younger—died in the fire. Autopsies showed that twenty Branch Davidian members, including Koresh and several children, died of gunshot wounds to the head. One toddler died of a stab wound to the chest. Critics later blamed Reno for giving Koresh what he wanted: a final cataclysmic battle that matched his prophecies of an apocalypse and mass suicide.

Reno immediately apologized for the raid, publicly calling the decision to confront the group "obviously wrong." "I'm responsible," Reno said in a press conference. "The buck stops with me." In a live television interview, she offered to resign, a stance that initially won her plaudits.

Two weeks after the fire, the House and Senate held hearings on Waco. Representative John Conyers, a liberal Democrat from Michigan, angrily accused Reno of treating the standoff as a military operation and condemned her decision to order the tear-gas assault. "This is a profound disgrace to law enforcement in the United States of America, and you did the right thing in offering to resign," Conyers said, adding, "I'd like you to know that there is at least one member in the Congress that isn't going to rationalize the deaths of two dozen children that weren't cultists. They weren't nuts, they weren't criminals. They were innocently trapped in there." As Conyers spoke, Reno grew visibly angry. "I haven't tried to rationalize the death of children, Congressman," she replied, her voice rising. "I feel more strongly about it than you will ever know."

The hearing showed how congressional oversight was evolving. The dramatic exchange between Reno and Conyers dominated television coverage, as had Reno's offer to resign during a live interview the previous night. A more sedate Senate hearing garnered less attention. For politicians trying to make a name for themselves, dramatic moments of public conflict generated publicity.

In the fall of 1993, the Justice and Treasury departments issued reports on the standoff that sharply criticized the ATF's decision to carry out the initial raid. The head of the agency was fired after it was revealed that some ATF officials lied about the information the organization received before the raid. An undercover agent warned his superiors that Koresh was armed and ready for the raid, but the ATF proceeded anyway. The Justice Department disclosed that the FBI had found no evidence that Koresh was molesting children in the compound during the standoff, contradicting Reno's claims.

In June of 1994, in a seeming end to the controversy, juries convicted five surviving members of the Davidians of participating in the killing of the four ATF agents during the initial confrontation, and each was sentenced to forty years in prison. The hearings, reports, and trial all found that the fires had been set by Branch Davidians, not the FBI. News media reports concluded that the fires had been set by Koresh and his followers.

Yct, as time passed, conspiracy theories regarding Waco began to spread. The National Rifle Association, which had been taken over by a more hardline leadership group in 1991, began calling the ATF "armed terrorists" who used "Gestapo" tactics on "honest citizens."

Steve Stockman, a Republican congressman from Texas, wrote in an article in *Guns & Ammo* magazine that the Clinton administration had staged the Waco standoff to create popular support for the 1994 assault weapons ban—ignoring the fact that former presidents Ford, Carter, and Reagan also supported the ban. Stockman later retracted the claim, but it helped fuel conspiracy theories. (In 2018 Stockman would be sentenced to ten years in federal prison for using $1.2 million in funds from political donors to cover his own personal expenses.)

In the Midwest and the western United States, militia groups whosc members believed that federal agents had intentionally murdered children in Waco began receiving new members. Many of the groups began stockpiling arms to defend themselves from what they viewed as a tyrannical federal government. Linda Thompson, a militia member and Clinton critic, created a 1993 video entitled *Waco, The Big Lie.* Based on doctored footage, it purported to show FBI armored vehicles attacking the compound with flamethrowers. Thompson later claimed that the four ATF guards killed in the initial raids were former bodyguards of Clinton whom the president had ordered assassinated.

Twenty years after the Church reforms, the oversight mechanisms designed to create public trust and transparency in government—congressional hearings, criminal trials by juries, and news media reporting—were increasingly dismissed by large parts of the American public. In part, the suspicion was fueled by the way ATF and FBI officials covered up mistakes made during the Waco and Ruby Ridge standoffs. The primary force driving the distrust, however, was rising partisanship between Democrats and Republicans. Trafficking in conspiracy theories and portraying one's political opponents as extremists produce political benefits.

Changes in the news media impacted politics as well. The Reagan administration had ordered the FCC to revoke the "Fairness Doctrine," which required radio license holders to present controversial issues of public importance in balanced ways. Rush Limbaugh and other hosts demonstrated in the 1990s that supporting one's political party and attacking the opposition could be a popular form of entertainment that attracted large numbers of listeners nationwide. Partisan talk radio vastly expanded its audience and influence.

. . .

A year after taking office, Clinton, who had vowed to run the most ethical administration in American history, was himself the focus of multiple criminal and civil investigations. During and after his first presidential campaign, a political dynamic took hold that would surround Clinton and his wife Hillary for decades to come. Republicans cited reports of misconduct by the Clintons—from financial improprieties to marital infidelity—as evidence of endemic corruption. The Clintons denied wrongdoing, but sometimes told half-truths, or failed to fully release records, extending the controversy. Democratic operatives dismissed the investigations as "out of control" and a "witch hunt." Republicans, in turn, saw each scandal as further proof of the Clintons' criminality and Democrats' duplicity. The view of one's political opponents as illegitimate, immoral, and, in some cases, criminal, would steadily grow, and explode in the Trump era.

In an effort to ease political pressure, Clinton asked Reno to appoint a special counsel in January 1994 to investigate multiple scandals plaguing the administration—a failed Arkansas real estate deal known as Whitewater, the dismissal of personnel from the White House travel office, and the suicide of Deputy White House Counsel Vince Foster. Clinton and his aides hoped that his welcoming of an independent counsel investigation would forestall a congressional investigation and bring coverage of the scandal to a close.

Within weeks, Reno chose Robert Fiske, a registered Republican and respected former federal prosecutor in New York. After several months of investigation, Fiske found that Foster's death involved no foul play and was, in fact, a suicide, rebutting conspiracy theories that Foster had been killed because he knew damaging secrets about the Clintons.

In a further effort to promote transparency, Clinton signed a bill in July 1994 that recreated the Office of Independent Counsel. Dismissing arguments that independent counsels had become tools for partisan attack, Clinton said the statute "has been in the past and is today a force for Government integrity and public confidence." He immediately regretted the decision. In August 1994, a federal judge ruled that Fiske should be removed as independent counsel because the new law required a panel of judges, not the attorney general, to choose independent prosecutors. A judicial panel then chose Ken Starr, a former solicitor general in the George H. W. Bush administration and a more partisan figure, as Whitewater independent prosecutor. Adding to Clinton's political problems, Reno appointed a second independent prosecutor to examine whether Agriculture Secretary Mike Espy had improperly accepted gifts from companies regulated by his department. Clinton, echoing Bush and Reagan, now bemoaned the power of post-Watergate independent prosecutors.

In one of the worst midterm drubbings suffered by a president, Republicans gained 54 seats in the House in the 1994 elections, taking control of the chamber for the first time since 1952. Newt

Gingrich, the new Speaker of the House, vowed more aggressive congressional oversight of Clinton and an aggressive conservative agenda. As Scalia had predicted, accusing one's opponent of being not simply wrong on policy but also a criminal produced political dividends. Even when a Republican or Democrat was absolved of wrongdoing by a congressional investigation or court, partisans dismissed the results as a whitewash.

.   .   .

For Americans deeply distrustful of government, Waco confirmed the conspiracy theories that had first emerged in Ruby Ridge. Federal law enforcement officials killed women and children. Federal law enforcement officials were bent on seizing citizens' constitutionally protected firearms. A dramatic attack would rally others to join the fight.

On April 19, 1995, Timothy McVeigh, a militia sympathizer and former US army soldier, detonated a truck bomb outside the Alfred P. Murrah Federal Building in Oklahoma City. McVeigh carried out the attack on the two-year anniversary of the FBI assault on the Branch Davidian compound in Waco. The truck bomb, constructed of 4,800 pounds of ammonium nitrate, killed 168 people, including nineteen children in a day care center on the second floor of the building. Most of the deaths were from injuries suffered in the collapse of the building, not the explosion itself. Only eight of the victims were federal law enforcement agents, McVeigh's intended target, and none of them worked for the ATF or FBI, the agencies he blamed for Waco.

Ninety minutes after the bombing, a highway patrolman arrested McVeigh for driving a car without license plates. His co-conspirator, Terry Nichols, was arrested as well. McVeigh, who had visited Waco during the 1993 standoff and watched Thompson's documentary *Waco, The Big Lie*, declared the bombing revenge for the FBI's actions. He hoped the attack would spark an uprising. "Women and kids were killed at Waco and Ruby Ridge," McVeigh later said. "You put back in [the government's] faces exactly what they're giving out."

Initially, the bombing undercut support for militias and Waco conspiracy theorists. Republican leaders criticized right-wing groups that trafficked in conspiracy theories. After the National Rifle Association refused to rescind a fundraising letter sent out before the Oklahoma City bombing thatt called federal agents "jack-booted thugs," former president George H. W. Bush resigned from the group. In his resignation letter, Bush said he had known an ATF agent killed in Waco and a secret service agent killed in Oklahoma City. "To attack Secret Service agents or A.T.F. people or any government law enforcement people as 'wearing Nazi bucket helmets and black storm trooper uniforms' wanting to 'attack law abiding citizens' is a vicious slander on good people," Bush wrote. "Al Whicher, who served on my [Secret Service] detail when I was Vice President and President, was killed in Oklahoma City. He was no Nazi. He was a kind man, a loving parent, a man dedicated to serving his country—and serve it well he did." Bush then defended the concept of public service: "your broadside against Federal agents deeply offends my own sense of decency and honor; and it offends my concept of service to country."

Bush's stance briefly made headlines, but the atmosphere in Congress grew steadily more divided and vitriolic. Republicans insisted that Clinton and Reno were engaged in a cover-up. Clinton and Reno insisted that they had launched the Waco raid to save children from abuse. In August 1995, another Waco hearing was held.

Republicans argued that Clinton had secretly ordered the tear gas assault on the compound. Reno, appearing as the final and pivotal witness, insisted before a standing-room-only crowd that Clinton left the final decision with her. "This was the hardest decision I have ever had to make, probably one of the hardest decisions that anybody could have to make," she testified. "I will live with it for the rest of my life." Democrats lauded Reno's performance. Republicans continued to accuse her of covering up for Clinton.

. . .

As Reno struggled to counter Republican attacks, the FBI experienced turmoil of its own. At the end of the Reagan administration, William Sessions had replaced William Webster as director of the FBI. Five years later, as Clinton took office, Sessions had alienated FBI agents and members of the Bush and Clinton administrations. A lawyer and federal judge from Texas, Sessions was known for having an aloof and ineffective management style. Privately, low-ranking FBI agents complained that Sessions pulled agents away from their law enforcement duties to run errands for his wife, Alice. In FBI vehicles, agents ferried her to get her nails done, shop, and pick up firewood. Agents who refused to cooperate were demoted.

Further damaging his standing, Sessions took a step in the midst of Bush and Clinton's heated 1992 presidential campaign that violated a long-standing Justice Department practice of not releasing information about criminal investigations that could influence the outcome of an election. A month before the vote, the FBI director announced that the bureau was opening its own investigation of a potential CIA role in the scandal surrounding the Banca Nazionale del Lavoro (BNL). The move gave Clinton a fresh line of attack in the presidential campaign. It also infuriated Barr and other Bush administration officials. Forty-eight hours after Sessions announced the FBI's BNL probe, news leaked that the Justice Department had launched an internal review of potential ethics violations by Sessions, his wife, and a top aide.

After Clinton beat Bush, the outgoing president decided that Clinton should decide Sessions's fate. Barr, still angry at Sessions, released the results of the Justice Department ethics inquiry a week before the Bush administration left office. The findings were damning. In addition to having agents drive his wife on errands, investigators found that Sessions took trips on FBI jets with his wife to visit their daughter and other relatives. They also discovered that Sessions was claiming a tax exemption for his chauffeur-driven FBI limousine by declaring it a "tactical police vehicle." To support that claim, Sessions kept an unloaded handgun in the trunk. In a blistering memo released with the report, Barr called the tax exemption a "sham" that "does not even pass the red face test."

Within weeks of taking office, Clinton and his aides decided to fire Sessions, but he rebuffed repeated requests from Reno to resign. Finally, on Reno's recommendation, Clinton telephoned Sessions and dismissed him on July 19, 1993. It was the first time in the bureau's seventy-year history that a president had dismissed an FBI director. Sessions held an impromptu news conference, at which he dismissed the "scurrilous attacks" against his wife and him. After few members of Congress rallied to his defense, Sessions left office.

Two months later, Clinton appointed Louis J. Freeh as FBI director. Freeh, a highly regarded former FBI agent, federal prosecutor, and federal judge, impressed Clinton at his job interview. Clinton impressed Freeh as well. In a two-hour conversation, Clinton said that he valued the FBI's independence. He also assured Freeh, a father of six, that he himself was a family man who understood the need for time at home. When Clinton asked Freeh what he thought of the contention of some FBI officials that the Waco compound needed to be stormed to free up FBI resources, Freeh scoffed, replying, "They get paid to wait." Later, a former FBI agent called Clinton and described Freeh as too political and self-serving for the increasingly fractious environment in Washington. The call gave Clinton pause—but at that point, Freeh had already accepted the position.

Both men were in their mid-forties at the time of the appointment and both were self-made, having risen from working-class families. Initially, Clinton called Freeh one of his best appointees. Likewise, Freeh at first praised Clinton as the most talented politician of their generation. Over time, however, the two men would come to loathe one another. Two leaders who were supposed to work together to protect the country would speak in person only a half-dozen times in Clinton's eight years in office. Washington's intensifying rancor was endangering the country.

Freeh's limited communication with the Clinton White House left the bureau isolated from key national security initiatives. Clinton and senior White House officials learned from news reports about major FBI investigations that they believed had national security implications. Clinton aides viewed Freeh's belief in the FBI's independence as sincere, but criticized the director as sanctimonious and, at times, so in love with his own rectitude that he failed to communicate properly with the president.

Freeh turned in his White House pass, which forced him to sign in every time he entered the building, creating a record he planned to use if ever questioned about his independence from the president. A former Eagle Scout and a devout Catholic, Freeh would come to see Clinton's various scandals, from Whitewater to his affair with Monica Lewinsky, as evidence of the president's duplicity. He feared that Clinton, who had been accused of using the Arkansas State Police to ferry women to rendezvous, would demand the same of the FBI.

The president and his aides expressed growing frustration with Reno's continued naming of independent counsels to investigate Clinton and his cabinet. After appointing independent counsels to look into Whitewater and Agriculture Secretary Mike Espy, Reno appointed independent counsels to investigate HUD Secretary Henry Cisneros's payments to a former mistress and Commerce Secretary Ron Brown's financial dealings. Another independent counsel investigated how the White House's director of personnel security, a mid-level official, obtained the FBI background files of hundreds of former White House officials, including senior Republicans. White House officials blamed a "bureaucratic snafu."

In 1997 and 1998, independent counsels investigated AmeriCorps head Eli Segal, Interior Secretary Bruce Babbitt, and Labor Secretary Alexis Herman for various financial improprieties. As occurred in the Reagan administration, they resulted in few criminal convictions. Espy was acquitted at trial. Cisneros pleaded guilty to a misdemeanor. The

Brown inquiry ended when he died in a plane crash. No charges were filed regarding the FBI background files. And Segal, Babbitt, and Herman were all cleared of wrongdoing. All told, the investigations cost taxpayers $90 million.

As Clinton's 1996 reelection campaign approached, he faced a new type of scandal. Republicans accused Clinton of accepting donations from individuals associated with the Chinese government. They called for Reno to appoint an independent counsel to investigate these donations. In the end, several Chinese-American donors to the Clinton campaign and DNC pleaded guilty to violating campaign finance laws, the donations were returned, and Clinton was not implicated in specific wrongdoing. Many Democrats dismissed the investigations as another Republican effort to smear Clinton.

Despite being surrounded by scandals, Clinton survived politically, aided by a growing economy, a focus on domestic affairs, and his centrist policies. In the 1996 presidential election, he easily defeated Bob Dole, making Clinton the first Democratic president since FDR to win reelection. Republicans, though, retained control of the House and Senate.

A new cable news network, Fox News, began broadcasting on October 7, 1996, bringing the message of conservative talk radio hosts to a far larger audience. Founders Roger Ailes and Rupert Murdoch viewed it as a long overdue antidote to liberal bias at CNN and in other parts of the mainstream media. Gingrich, the House Speaker, continued accusing the president of misconduct. One tool for removing Clinton from office remained, the ultimate form of power for the legislative branch: impeachment.

. . .

As Washington grew more partisan, Tom O'Connor, a police detective from western Massachusetts, arrived at the FBI Academy in Quantico, Virginia, on February 19, 1997. O'Connor was achieving something that he never dreamed possible: becoming an FBI agent. Over the next twenty years, he would thrive in the bureau, investigating terrorist attacks around the world and serving as president of the FBI Agents Association.

Born and raised in Northampton, Massachusetts, O'Connor worked as a policeman and detective in his hometown for a decade. Charismatic and with the gift of gab, he was a primary character in Tracy Kidder's book about the community, *Home Town*. "I had a great gig," O'Connor recalled. While working with FBI agents on a joint investigation of a local motorcycle gang, a senior agent asked O'Connor if he wanted to join the bureau. O'Connor's wife Jeanne, a bank auditor, urged him to apply, and said she had considered joining the FBI herself after graduating from college. His father Bill, a local Irish-American politician who had served as county treasurer, approved as well. O'Connor and his wife both became special agents in the FBI's Washington field office and joined its Joint Terrorism Task Force.

On August 7, 1998, Al Qaeda bombed the US embassies in Nairobi, Kenya, and Dar es Salaam, Tanzania. The bureau dispatched 300 agents, including O'Connor, to collect evidence of the attacks, which killed 224 people, including twelve Americans. Twenty-four hours after the attack, O'Connor found himself in Nairobi. "I remember . . . clear as a bell, pulling up in a white van in front of the embassy building," O'Connor said. "I remember when I first saw that bank building . . . completely gutted . . . I said to myself then, 'This is what I'm going to work for the rest of my career.'"

Two years later, on October 12, 2000, Al Qaeda attacked an American destroyer, the USS *Cole*, as it was being refueled in Aden, Yemen. A suicide bomber rammed a small boat laden with explosives into the side of the American ship, killing seventeen sailors. Within hours, O'Connor was dispatched with a team of FBI agents to Yemen. When they arrived on the *Cole*, they had difficulty reaching the bodies of twelve of the sailors. "The blast just twisted and tore the metal," O'Connor recalled. "The sailors were trapped in behind it." Navy welders cut holes in bulkheads so that O'Connor and the other agents could reach the corpses. Collecting what remained of the sailors was grisly and wrenching, but he hoped that it would give their families closure. "Could be you, could be your nephew," he said. "Each one of these things takes a little bit away." A year later, O'Connor would respond to a far larger attack, and recover the remains of far more victims.

. . .

During Clinton's second term, Freeh faced intensifying criticism after a series of glaring mistakes by the FBI. The bureau leaked the name of Richard Jewell, an innocent man, in connection with the Olympic Games bombing in Atlanta. It falsely accused Taiwanese-American scientist Wen Ho Lee of espionage on behalf of Beijing. And it was slow to respond to warnings that terrorism posed a growing threat to the United States. Freeh testified to Congress that he had reorganized the FBI, with counterterrorism efforts being a top priority. But the changes were, in fact, limited. Counterterrorism officials called for the hiring of 1,900 new agents, linguists, and analysts to focus on terrorism. In the end, they received enough funding to hire only 76 people.

In his memoir, Freeh admitted that his constant battles with Clinton took a toll on the FBI as an institution. "He came to believe that I was trying to undo his presidency," Freeh wrote, conceding that "The lost resources and lost time alone were monumental. So much that should have been straightforward became problematic in the extreme." Eventually, Freeh regretted taking the appointment, but he feared that if he left his post Clinton would politicize the FBI.

For their part, Clinton administration officials complained that

Freeh's performance as director escaped scrutiny from Congress because of the close relationship he had developed with Republicans, who controlled the Senate and House for most of Clinton's presidency. But like Reagan and Bush, Clinton feared the political cost of firing a director of the FBI. In a *Washington Post* article assessing the vexed relationship between Clinton and Freeh, Clinton aides expressed fears of J. Edgar Hoover's excesses and warned that the FBI had grown unaccountable. They said rectitude, not corruption, had caused the FBI's failure to coordinate with the White House on important policies.

White House Chief of Staff John D. Podesta told the *Post* that he had not been informed that the FBI was developing a new surveillance system for monitoring email until he read about it in news reports. The new program raised civil liberties issues that Podesta and other White House officials felt they had the right to review. "No institution should be unaccountable," Podesta told the *Post*. "Clearly, the White House should not be, but neither should the FBI or the Justice Department or the Congress."

Podesta said the bureau should maintain independence regarding individual criminal investigations but still answer to the White House on broader criminal justice policy. "The FBI director works for the attorney general, and the attorney general works for the president," Podesta said. "To permit the bureau to operate with a total hands-off policy is to reinvite the abuses of the Hoover era."

.   .   .

After surviving multiple scandals and winning reelection, Clinton's political reckoning came in 1998. Evidence emerged that Clinton had pressured a White House intern, Monica Lewinsky, to lie to investigators about an affair they had. She was a 22-year-old intern; he was 49 and the president. Independent Counsel Kenneth Starr requested permission from Reno to investigate the new allegations. In January 1998, Reno granted it. Nine months later, on September 9, 1998,

Starr delivered a report to Congress that described eleven grounds for impeaching Clinton, including perjury and obstruction of justice. Democrats argued that his actions did not merit removal from office. They accused Gingrich of using Congress's ultimate power for partisan political gain. Gradually, popular opinion shifted against Gingrich, who had led the impeachment charge. After Republicans unexpectedly lost five House seats in the November 1998 midterm elections, Gingrich resigned as Speaker. The House impeached Clinton a month later.

The party-line vote was only the second time a president had been impeached in American history. The vote forever linked Clinton with President Andrew Johnson, who was impeached by the House in 1868 and avoided removal from office by a single Senate vote. Clinton apologized in a national television address. In January 1999, the Senate tried Clinton. With five Republicans from centrist states voting not guilty, Clinton easily avoided removal from office. Republicans expressed frustration with the outcome, but public opinion polls showed that most Americans agreed with Democrats. While disapproving of Clinton's actions, they felt these did not merit removing a president from office. Twenty years later, many Republicans would use the same argument during the impeachment of Donald Trump.

.   .   .

Overall, the investigations of presidents and of the FBI and CIA in the 1980s and 1990s by congressional committees and independent counsels produced a mixed record. The Iran-Contra investigation exposed the existence of a "secret government" and systematic lying to Congress. Republicans, though, derided Independent Counsel Lawrence Walsh and saw his $75 million investigation as a witch hunt. Democrats saw Ken Starr's investigation of Bill Clinton, which cost $57 million, as partisan as well. The Watergate investigation, by contrast, had cost $26 million.

Congressional hearings on Abscam, Ruby Ridge, and Waco were

effective in creating a sense that FBI officials were being held account-able. But a dozen other independent counsel investigations of mem-bers of the Reagan, Bush, and Clinton administrations—as well as congressional investigations on myriad topics—failed to produce evi-dence of clear wrongdoing.

The behavior of officeholders also weakened oversight. Reno's mistakes abetted right-wing conspiracy theories. FBI directors Wil-liam Sessions and Louis Freeh took their pursuit of independence to such an extreme that it hampered their work with the White House.

The lesson of the 1980s and 1990s was that oversight and investi-gatory powers should be used more carefully. Too many congressio-nal hearings and too many independent counsels diluted the impact of investigations. A public sense of investigative overkill could under-mine Congress's credibility and bolster a president, regardless of his or her conduct. The post-Watergate and post-Church reform consen-sus regarding the need to hold presidents, as well as the FBI and CIA, accountable was gradually unraveling. Over time, invoking Watergate and past FBI and CIA abuses was losing its political potency. The set of rules established in the 1970s were primarily norms, not laws. In the future, a brazen president could flout them and face few politi-cal consequences.

SEVEN

George W. Bush, 9/11, and the Return of the Imperial Presidency

O n May 29, 2001, Richard Blee arrived at the White House for a meeting with Condoleezza Rice, President George W. Bush's national security advisor. Four months after taking office, Bush and his aides were publicly promising to protect the country from terrorism. Blee hoped that they would deliver on that pledge in private. George Tenet, the director of the CIA, had invited Blee to join his weekly meeting with Rice. Cofer Black, the director of the agency's Counterterrorism Center, attended as well. At Tenet's insistence, the meeting would focus on a single topic: the growing threat posed by Al Qaeda.

For the previous two years, Blee had served as the chief of Alec Station, a CIA unit created in 1996 to track Osama bin Laden and his operatives. Prior to that, he had served as CIA station chief in Algeria as the country experienced a brutal civil war. After a decade of fighting, the Algerian army prevailed over Islamists, but 100,000 to 200,000 people had perished, most of them civilians. Blee feared that Al Qaeda and other extremist groups would gain strength and eventually threaten the United States itself. "I said this is not going to stop here," Blee recalled. "I saw the Islamic extremism spread. I knew it would be a big, huge wave."

Blee hoped to convince Rice and the new administration to support a plan of covert action against Al Qaeda that the CIA had developed in 1999 and proposed again in 2000, but that Clinton had declined to fully fund and support. The new strategy focused on tracking and capturing bin Laden, and cutting off Al Qaeda from its sources of financing. Blee believed that the leadership of Al Qaeda was determined to carry out a domestic or international attack against an American target. The cost of the ambitious five-year strategy, which involved arming anti-Taliban militia and flying drones over Afghanistan, was staggering. Fully funded, the Qaeda initiative cost more than the agency's total global counterterrorism budget.

After his return to Washington from Algeria in the mid-1990s, Al Qaeda became his obsession. He worked in various positions at CIA headquarters in Langley but tried to monitor the actions of bin Laden and other foreign jihadists. When intelligence reports arrived suggesting that bin Laden was assembling a pan-Islamic army to wage war on American interests, Blee again expressed alarm to his superiors. "I said this is a big fucking deal," Blee recalled. "The Algerians and the Saudis and the Afghans can all get together."

After Clinton named George Tenet CIA director in 1996, the new spy chief made Blee his executive assistant as part of a sweeping management overhaul. Tenet hoped to reinvigorate the agency, which was again suffering from budget cuts and low morale. (Clinton's first two CIA directors, James Woolsey and John Deutch, had struggled to develop strong relationships with Clinton and with the congressional intelligence committees, and had each lasted less than two years in office.) Tenet, who grew up working in his Greek immigrant family's diner in Queens, talked nonstop and charmed supporters and adversaries. A former staffer on the Senate Intelligence Committee and a National Security Council aide, he was able to develop strong ties with both Clinton and congressional leaders. After the 2000 election, Tenet impressed George W. Bush and the president-elect retained him as director, making Tenet one of a handful of CIA chiefs to work for both Democratic and Republican presidents.

Blee hoped that Bush would confront Al Qaeda more aggressively than Clinton had. After the August 7, 1998 Qaeda attacks on American embassies in Kenya and Tanzania, Clinton initially declined to retaliate. On August 20—three days after Clinton publicly admitted that he had an affair with Monica Lewinsky—Clinton ordered a cruise missile strike on Qaeda camps in Afghanistan and a pharmaceutical factory in Sudan. Blee suspected that Clinton had turned his attention to Al Qaeda to distract from domestic embarrassments. "Let's go distract," Blee told me. "It was the politicization and manipulation of intelligence." Clinton flatly denied that politics played any role in the decision.

After the October 2000 attack on the USS *Cole*, Blee again believed it was vital for Clinton to retaliate against bin Laden. But White House officials decided to delay acting until after the election, fearing that voters would view military strikes as an effort to bolster Gore's candidacy. In Langley, CIA analysts were instructed not to put in writing any determination of who was responsible for the attack on the *Cole*. "It was very clear to everyone who was working the problem that it was bin Laden," recalled Blee. After Gore narrowly lost to Bush, the Clinton administration decided to let Bush decide what actions to take. This failure to immediately respond to the ship attack, Blee believed, emboldened bin Laden.

When Blee, Tenet, and Black met with Condoleezza Rice in May 2001, they lobbied for the new administration to finally adopt the agency's five-year strategy for defeating Al Qaeda. When Blee spoke, he told Rice that Al Qaeda could be planning to carry out attacks inside the United States. Rice asked the officials to develop a range of options for attacking Al Qaeda but failed to follow up after their meeting. "She never pushed the bureaucracy to move forward," Blee said.

.   .   .

Four months after his meeting with Rice, Blee walked out of a morning staff meeting in CIA headquarters on September 11, 2001, and a secretary pointed at a nearby television. "Look," she said, "a plane hit the World Trade Center." Immediately, Blee knew that he had failed. "That's bin Laden," he said. "This is the attack. This is what they have talked about." Blee requested a list of the passengers on board any hijacked planes from the FAA. The agency initially refused, saying it would be illegal for it to provide information the CIA could use for domestic spying.

With one of the hijacked planes, United 93, still missing, Blee gathered Alec Station staff for an emergency meeting in their basement office. Rumors circulated that the hijackers were planning to crash the missing plane into CIA headquarters—the building they currently occupied. "It was chaos," Blee recalled. "They assumed it was coming to Langley." During the meeting, a member of Blee's team asked him if it was true that there were anti-aircraft missiles secretly installed on the roof of CIA headquarters. Blee had no idea but said, "Of course there are." Minutes later, after passengers stormed the cockpit, United 93 crashed into a field in southwestern Pennsylvania, twenty minutes away from reaching its intended target, the US Capitol.

Later that day, Blee received the passenger list from the FAA. Two Saudi men that Alec Station had been trying to track—Khalid al-Mihdhar and Nawaf al-Hazmi—were on the plane flown into the Pentagon. A sense of failure, grief, and guilt settled over Blee that he would carry for years.

· · ·

Several miles away, Tom O'Connor, the FBI agent who had investigated the bombing of the USS *Cole*, watched the attacks in New York on a television in the FBI's Washington field office. Like Blee, O'Connor and his FBI colleagues knew Al Qaeda was responsible as soon as a plane struck the World Trade Center. "Everybody thought, 'that fucker,'" O'Connor recalled, referring to bin Laden. Minutes later, an agent teaching a training course at a local Fire Department called and said smoke was rising from the Pentagon. O'Connor and another agent, Scott Stanley, sped the four miles to the iconic building in Arlington that houses the US Department of Defense. The streets were largely deserted. As they got close to the Pentagon, they saw people streaming out of the sprawling building. They drove to the site of the attack and donned blue windbreakers emblazoned with "FBI" on the back. Dozens of members of the military were trying to evacuate the injured.

Entering through a side door, O'Connor and Stanley began searching for evidence, particularly the plane's black box. They passed collapsed walls and dangling power cables. O'Connor noticed that smoke and particulates filled the air. "I remember walking down this hallway, there were lights flickering," O'Connor said. "I remember thinking, this is freaking surreal. This is the Pentagon." As more agents arrived, they began recovering bodies as part of the evidence collection effort.

For the next three weeks, O'Connor and his colleagues worked the Pentagon like a crime scene, locating the jetliner's black box, determining how far the aircraft's fuselage had penetrated the building, and seeing, day after day, how it had obliterated everything in its path. "We ran four to five teams per shift, did twelve-hour shifts, worked sixteen to seventeen hours a day, with no days off," O'Connor recalled. A leader of an evidence recovery team, O'Connor found removing the remains of the dead haunting but rewarding. "You wouldn't want to be anywhere else," he said. "It's an honor to do." O'Connor believed his work would aid the relatives of the victims. "Families want to know what happened to their loved ones," he said. "We think it's important to give them as much truth as possible." American Flight 77 had struck the Pentagon at 530 miles an hour. Sixty-four people inside the plane perished. So did one hundred twenty-five in the building. O'Connor and his colleagues collected over 2,000 separate bags of human remains.

· · ·

The deadliest terrorist attack in American history had claimed the lives of 2,977 people, mired the CIA in scandal, and sparked a decades-long "war on terror" that would kill 6,000 American soldiers and hundreds of thousands of Iraqis and Afghans. Exhaustive reviews by Congress and the 9/11 Commission found that the CIA and FBI had failed to share information that might have prevented the attacks; the Clinton and Bush administrations had failed to take the threat posed by Al Qaeda seriously enough; and American officials had failed to imagine that commercial airliners could be used to carry out mass suicide attacks.

The reviews also found that a central goal of the Church reforms—limiting the CIA's ability to collect intelligence inside the United States—had inadvertently reduced intelligence sharing between the CIA and FBI. A little-known set of 1995 Justice Department guidelines designed to separate the collection of intelligence from the collection of evidence in criminal cases compounded the problem. The procedures "were almost immediately misunderstood and misapplied," the 9/11 Commission found. "As a result, there was far less information sharing and coordination." The commission found that civil servants tended to be cautious rule-followers who jealously guarded their institutional turf. At a time when thousands of American lives depended on the ability of the FBI and CIA to coordinate in dynamic ways, both organizations failed.

On August 6, 2001, President Bush himself had been warned of a possible domestic attack by Al Qaeda in an article included in the President's Daily Brief entitled "Bin Ladin Determined to Strike in U.S." Bush later told the 9/11 panel that he remembered the article but was never informed that a Qaeda cell was active inside the United States. Tenet told the 9/11 Commission that "the system was blinking red" during the summer of 2001, but no one in the American national security community saw what was coming. "The foreign intelligence agencies were watching overseas, alert to foreign threats to US interests there," the commission found. "The domestic agencies were waiting for evidence of a domestic threat from sleeper cells within the United States. No one was looking for a foreign threat to domestic targets. The threat that was coming was not from sleeper cells. It was foreign—but from foreigners who had infiltrated into the United States."

The 9/11 Commission, like the Church and Iran-Contra committees before them, showed the continued importance and value of bipartisan investigations. Some Americans continued to believe conspiracy theories about the attacks, but the commission created a fact-based, commonly accepted narrative of events and a detailed accounting of what went wrong. Like the Church and Iran-Contra committees, the commission recommended specific reforms.

Blee argued that the best way to disrupt Al Qaeda and thwart an attack was to launch aggressive covert operations in Afghanistan—but both the Clinton and Bush administrations balked. "No one was particularly enthusiastic about getting involved in Afghanistan," Blee said. "I knew it was a quagmire, but at some point you have to do something about your enemies." Post–Cold War cuts in CIA staffing also limited the agency's ability to counter Al Qaeda, he said, which, by 2001, had an estimated three thousand members. "It was twenty or thirty people against three thousand," Blee recalled. "That was a period when the agency was firing people; the [Berlin] wall was coming down, there was no longer a need for the CIA."

In hindsight, American policymakers had become overconfident, almost serene, about the country's strength and security. A decade after the dissolution of the Soviet Union, triumphalism had taken hold in Washington. The United States, the lone superpower, could focus inward and no longer fear attack. Intelligence collection efforts had been slashed, turf wars between the CIA and FBI had been needlessly exacerbated, and politicians from both parties had promised voters a cost-free "peace dividend," along with prosperity.

.   .   .

After the attacks, public support for Bush, the CIA, and the FBI soared. Bush made waging a "war on terrorism" the defining issue of his presidency. His vice president, Dick Cheney, seized the moment and increased the power of the presidency to its greatest extent since Watergate. The administration granted vast authority and resources to the CIA, FBI, and NSA, broadened the use of secrecy, and flouted congressional oversight. In the short term, those changes were enthusiastically embraced by Americans who feared another attack. In the long term, the shift away from the traditional American division of powers between the executive, legislative, and judicial branches further undermined public trust in government on the far right and far left.

Forty-five days after 9/11, Congress overwhelmingly passed the USA PATRIOT Act—an acronym for "Uniting and Strengthening America by Providing Appropriate Tools Required to Intercept and Obstruct Terrorism." The sweeping, 343-page measure was the most dramatic change in American privacy law since the Church reforms. Section 215 of the law allowed the FBI and NSA, with the approval of a FISA Court judge, to seize or monitor the personal records of Americans held by phone companies, political groups, universities, churches, public libraries, bookstores, medical offices, and other institutions without informing those targeted. Section 505 vastly expanded the power of the FBI to issue "national security letters" that force internet service providers, financial firms, and credit companies to secretly hand over personal customer records without prior court approval and without informing the customer. Section 213 authorized "sneak and peek" searches, which allowed the FBI, with the approval of a judge, to search an individual's home or business without notifying them.

The legislation also broadened the definition of terrorism, moved to block the flow of terrorism funding worldwide, and strengthened US border security. Only one senator, Wisconsin Democrat Russ Feingold, voted against the bill, citing civil liberties concerns. Sixty-six House members voted against the law, with Texas Republican representative Richard Armey insisting that it have a sunset provision requiring that some elements expire on December 31, 2005. The vote was an early sign of the poor quality of post-9/11 congressional over-sight. Republicans in Congress, as well as many Democrats, made few efforts to challenge the executive branch.

Bush authorized the broadest and most lethal CIA covert action program in the history of the agency. Within days of the attacks, Tenet had unveiled a "Worldwide Attack Matrix" that outlined a clandestine counterterrorism campaign in 80 countries. After six weeks of American bombardment, Afghan forces backed by the CIA broke through Taliban lines north of Kabul, and advanced on the capital. To the amazement of Afghans and Americans, the Taliban withdrew from the city without a fight. Jihadist propaganda, advertisements for flight schools in the United States, and bomb-making manuals were found in houses abandoned by Al Qaeda members.

As the public cheered the early American successes in Afghani-stan, the Bush administration carried out scores of other covert pro-grams inside the United States and around the world. Some were based on the new powers the executive branch received from the PATRIOT Act. Others involved the president and his aides embrac-ing the theory of expansive presidential power promoted by Cheney. Without the approval of Congress or the courts, CIA operatives began abducting terrorism suspects from the streets of foreign coun-tries, flying them in secret to remote locations, and then brutally torturing them. Mass surveillance was conducted on Americans without their knowledge. Muslim Americans said the FBI engaged in systematic racial profiling and entrapment. A prison camp in Guantánamo Bay, Cuba, held hundreds of accused terrorists for years without trial.

The motivation of Bush and other officials was to prevent another major terrorist attack, not consolidate political power, according to former aides. But when many of the practices eventually leaked, they stoked public fears about the actions of America's spy agencies and alienated allies around the world. Bush and Cheney's massive expan-sion of executive power restored the imperial presidency in the name of national security. But they kept secret from Americans the full extent of the government's covert activities.

. . .

A month after the 9/11 attacks, an FBI official approached James Baker, a senior Justice Department lawyer, and said he needed to speak with him privately. The setting surprised Baker, who ran the office that submitted all intelligence-related requests for surveillance to the FISA Court. Instead of the two men talking in a secure conference room inside the FBI or Justice Department, the FBI official talked with Baker on the street. "There is something spooky going on," the FBI official told Baker. The National Security Agency was eavesdropping on Americans without a warrant from a FISA Court judge, the FBI official said. If true, the wiretapping was a flagrant violation of the 1978 Foreign Intelligence Surveillance Act and other Church reforms designed to protect Americans' privacy and civil liberties. Some officials in the bureau "were getting nervous" about the new surveillance, the FBI official said. He asked Baker if he knew anything about it. Baker replied that he did not.

The conversation baffled and alarmed Baker. For decades, FBI officials, including the one who had spoken with him that night, followed procedure and routed all requests through Baker's office. Formally known as the Office of Intelligence Policy and Review, the office was created in the wake of the Church reforms to ensure that FBI agents followed the law when surveilling suspected foreign spies and terrorists in the United States, and any Americans communicating with them.

Several weeks after the bureau official delivered the warning, a passage in a FISA warrant application leapt out at Baker. It contained "strange, unattributed language" and information that was not "attributed in the normal way," Baker recalled in an interview. He asked the Justice Department attorney who had submitted the application about the passage. The attorney explained that no one at the FBI would provide him with the details, and said the information was part of a "special collection." Unable to get detailed answers to his questions, Baker told the FBI that he would not forward the application to the FISA Court for approval until he learned more.

Baker then approached Daniel Levin, who, at the time, was serving as both counsel to Attorney General John Ashcroft and chief of staff to FBI Director Robert Mueller. When Baker asked Levin about the eavesdropping, Levin said he could not discuss it with him without White House approval. The conversations were unlike any Baker had experienced in a decade at the Justice Department. The Bush administration appeared to be conducting mass surveillance of Americans in flagrant violation of American law.

A Detroit native whose father worked for Chrysler, Baker had attended Notre Dame and the University of Michigan Law School. After a clerkship with a Detroit federal judge, he applied to the Attorney Generals' Honors Program, which recruits young lawyers from around the country. Baker worked as a federal prosecutor in Detroit and the Justice Department fraud division in Washington, gaining experience as a trial lawyer, traveling the world investigating cases. Baker embraced the Justice Department's culture, which, to him, prized probity, collaboration, and the strength of a legal argument, regardless of the lawyer's position. "Integrity is huge. Your reputation is huge," Baker said in an interview. "If someone really excels as a lawyer, people will listen to them."

Baker worked with FBI investigators on the 1998 US embassy attacks in East Africa and the 2000 Qaeda attack on the USS *Cole*. On 9/11, Baker, like Blee, immediately knew that Al Qaeda was behind the attack. Like Blee, he tried to rally his staff as the fourth and final hijacked plane, United 93, flew toward Washington. He asked them to continue working. "We need to stay focused because if we don't our adversaries will benefit," he recalled saying. And Baker, like Blee, felt the same sense of failure as the attack unfolded.

Three months later, in December of 2001, Baker was finally briefed on the clandestine eavesdropping program that the FBI official had warned him about on the street. Bush had personally authorized a secret program, code-named "Stellar Wind," that authorized the NSA to eavesdrop on calls between Al Qaeda members and individuals in the United States without the approval of the FISA Court. The program went beyond any of the legal measures authorized by Congress in the PATRIOT Act. The FISA Court and Congress were not notified of the program's existence. It was illegal, unconstitutional, and, in hindsight, unnecessary.

Baker was given a copy of an October 23, 2001, memo, written by John Yoo of the Justice Department's Office of Legal Counsel. Yoo, a longtime supporter of presidential power and an ally of Cheney, wrote that during wartime, the president had the power to surveil Americans without the approval of a judge. In other words, the memo asserted, the president could break the law whenever he deemed it necessary to protect the country.

Baker found Yoo's reasoning and legal research shoddy. His memorandum made no mention of *Youngstown Sheet & Tube Co. v. Sawyer*, a landmark 1952 Supreme Court decision that had limited presidential powers during wartime. "I was very angry," Baker recalled. For years, Baker had worked to be true to the legacy of the founder of his office, a former FBI agent named Allan Kornblum who helped draft the 1978 FISA law and curb improper surveillance of Americans. Baker also believed the secret program was unnecessary. Adding more lawyers to the FISA Court would allow judges to quickly review more applications. The FISA system was "scalable," Baker believed, and could work during wartime. Finally, Baker had spent years gaining the trust of FISA Court judges, and felt that they should be told about "Stellar Wind."

Baker protested to Attorney General Ashcroft, who initially ordered him in writing to keep the program secret from the FISA Court judges. After Baker received another improper application, he consulted with the head of the Justice Department's ethics office, who told him he had an affirmative duty of candor to the court, in part because its proceedings were held in secret, outside the public view.

Baker refused to sign the application and told Ashcroft and others at the department that he would block any attorney in his office from doing so. When David Addington, Cheney's chief of staff, heard of Baker's defiance, he demanded that Baker be fired for insubordination. Ashcroft refused to fire Baker, and eventually convinced the White House that the FISA Court's presiding judge should be told about "Stellar Wind." The judge was notified, and the program continued to operate for another two years.

In 2004, a far broader rebellion erupted after John Yoo, the head of the Office of Legal Counsel, left the department. Yoo's successor in the Office of Legal Counsel, Jack Goldsmith, agreed with Baker that Yoo's legal analysis was shoddy. Goldsmith declared the collection of email by "Stellar Wind" illegal, sparking a power struggle between Justice Department and White House lawyers. When Bush attempted to reauthorize the program without the approval of the Justice Department, nearly every major law enforcement official in the administration threatened to resign. Ashcroft, Comey, Baker, and FBI Director Robert Mueller all said the program violated the law. Bush backed down and modified the program.

A year later, the *New York Times* broke the story that the administration had been secretly surveilling Americans since 2001 without warrants. Critics said that Baker should have resigned, but he took pride in his role in fighting Cheney, Addington, and Yoo. He blamed these officials for devising dubious legal justifications for "Stellar Wind" and needlessly creating a secret surveillance program. "I ferreted that out," he said. "And John Yoo wanted to get me fired."

.   .   .

Bill Barr, the former attorney general, supported Cheney and Addington's effort to increase executive branch power. In op-eds and in congressional hearings after 9/11, he spoke in favor of military tribunals, the PATRIOT Act, and sweeping surveillance. "Unfortunately, in the wake of Watergate and the Vietnam War, and prompted by several sensational instances of abuse, our country embarked on a thirty-year campaign to curtail the powers of our security agencies," Barr testified to Congress. "A mindset developed during this era that all national security issues could be dealt with within the framework of our criminal justice system or pursuant to carefully-hedged, detailed procedures derived from that system."

Barr criticized the FISA Court and said the president and the executive branch agencies alone should be allowed to conduct surveillance as they pleased without the approval of a judge. "Numerous statutes were passed, such as FISA, that purported to supplant Presidential discretion with Congressionally crafted schemes whereby judges became the arbiter of national security decisions," Barr said. "I believe that many of the statutes enacted in this period were too restrictive and posed significant problems for effective counterterrorism efforts."

After leaving government, in 1993, Barr had been hired as general counsel at GTE, one of the country's largest telephone companies. In his private life, he donated to Republican political candidates, aided conservative religious organizations, and served on the boards of groups whose charitable work has been widely praised, such as the Knights of Columbus and the New York Archdiocese's Inner-City Scholarship Fund. Barr also paid the tuition of eighteen students a year at a parochial school in New York.

Barr also battled what he saw as liberal discrimination against religious Americans. In 1995, he wrote an article for a journal called *The Catholic Lawyer.* In his article, Barr complained that journalists had made "subtle efforts" to liken David Koresh's Branch Davidian cult in Waco, Texas, to the Catholic Church. "We live in an increasingly militant, secular age," he wrote. "As part of this philosophy, we see a growing hostility toward religion, particularly Catholicism." He argued that religious Americans were increasingly victimized: "It is no accident that the homosexual movement, at one or two percent of the population, gets treated with such solicitude, while the Catholic population, which is over a quarter of the country, is given the back of the hand."

His position on executive power wavered over time, depending on which party controlled the White House. When Clinton was under investigation in the Whitewater affair, a Senate committee subpoenaed documents, and Clinton's team claimed that they were protected by lawyer-client privilege. Barr called the rationale "preposterous," and later complained that Clinton had diminished his office: "I've been upset that a lot of the prerogatives of the presidency have been sacrificed for the personal interests of this particular president."

In the private sector, Barr built a reputation as a pugnacious opponent of federal regulation. As GTE's general counsel, he persuaded regulators to approve mergers that benefited his employer while arguing against those that benefited rivals. Around the office, he talked at times about such moral doctrines as natural law, but never expected secular colleagues to share his beliefs. Barr didn't socialize much with coworkers; he commuted each week to New York from Washington, where he and his wife, Christine, raised three daughters amid a Catholic community centered on a tight circle of churches, schools, and social clubs. The girls went to a Catholic school in Bethesda, where Christine worked as a librarian. (Barr's daughters later attended Catholic colleges and universities, and all became lawyers.)

The Catholic Information Center, a bookstore and chapel three blocks from the White House on K Street, was a hub for Washington's influential conservatives, staffed by priests from the group Opus Dei. Federal workers and tourists attended morning and evening services there. In 1998, a charismatic new director, the Reverend C. John McCloskey, took over. A 44-year-old banker turned priest, he was a regular guest on *Meet the Press*. Hard-charging and unabashedly political, McCloskey liked to say, "A liberal Catholic is oxymoronic." He helped convert a series of prominent conservatives to Catholicism, including the former House Speaker Newt Gingrich, Judge Robert Bork, Kansas senator Sam Brownback, and economist Larry Kudlow. In 2003, McCloskey quietly left his post, and Opus Dei later paid a settlement of nearly a million dollars to a woman who said that he had sexually harassed her.

The center's board of directors remained a nexus of politically connected Catholics. Over time, Barr, Pat Cipollone, a lawyer who had worked as a speechwriter for Barr in the Justice Department, and Leonard Leo, the executive vice president of the Federalist Society, all served on it. In the Trump era, Barr, Cipollone, and Leo would work together to reshape the American judiciary.

. . .

Less than two years after a massive intelligence failure stymied efforts to prevent 9/11, a second historic intelligence failure helped facilitate the US invasion of Iraq. Liberals suspected that the claims of mistakes were a cover-up for a plot by the military-industrial complex to draw the United States into yet another war. Conservatives feared that the intelligence community's hands were tied. Former intelligence officials said that fears of another 9/11 caused them to make a mistake.

In 2003, agency analysts concluded that Saddam Hussein possessed weapons of mass destruction (WMD), providing the Bush administration with a core justification for the invasion of Iraq. Skeptics of the war insisted that the administration, led by Vice President Cheney, had placed political pressure on the CIA to produce the intelligence findings the White House wanted.

In the lead-up to the invasion of Iraq, Joan Dempsey, the former naval intelligence officer from Arkansas who rose to become the CIA's deputy director for community management, attended dozens of meetings where analysts and policymakers debated whether or not Saddam Hussein had nuclear, chemical, and biological weapons. Dempsey said it was clear that some intelligence analysts believed that certain White House officials, such as Cheney and Addington, supported an invasion of Iraq. But she said that she didn't believe that pressure from the White House caused analysts to mistakenly conclude that Iraq had weapons of mass destruction. Instead, the analysts came to that conclusion themselves. "I did not see anything nefarious whatsoever," she said. "They believed it."

Policymakers and intelligence analysts alike feared another 9/11-style attack on the United States, according to Dempsey. "They didn't want to underestimate the threat," she said. "They didn't want to expose US troops by exposing them to chemicals or radiation." Sincere fears of another attack impacted the analysts. "They were largely a group of people who were trying to do their jobs," she said. "It wasn't a conspiracy to doctor intelligence." She added, "we were leaning far forward and we fell."

James Clapper, the Air Force intelligence officer who had feared congressional oversight in the 1970s, was also one of the senior intelligence officials who had failed on Iraq. Two days after the 9/11 attacks, Clapper was named director of the National Imagery and Mapping Agency, the organization that controls the intelligence community's spy satellites. In the lead-up to the Iraq invasion, Clapper's agency identified a group of trucks in Iraq as "mobile production facilities for biological agents." After the US invasion of Iraq, however, American inspectors found out that the trucks were used to pasteurize and transport milk.

The mistake, Clapper said, resulted from the compartmentalization of information. The identity of a key human source—an Iraqi defector known as "Curveball" who lived in Germany—was never revealed to analysts. The defector, a chemical engineer named Rafid Ahmed Alwan al-Janabi, had claimed that Hussein constructed mobile biological weapons laboratories on trucks. It was later revealed that he had fabricated that information in the hopes of remaining in Germany. "I'd never thought to question the CIA's 'spooky source' that had given us all that amazing—too amazing—intelligence," Clapper recalled in his memoir. He said the fault could be found with "administration members who were pushing a narrative of a rogue WMD program in Iraq and on the intelligence officers, including me, who were so eager to help that we found what wasn't really there."

Others in the intelligence community did feel that White House pressure affected analysts' assessments of WMDs in Iraq. Paul Pillar, a retired CIA analyst who was involved in the creation of the CIA's WMD assessment in Iraq, argued that pressure from the White House influenced agency analysts in subtle ways. He believed that the desire to please the CIA's most important consumer of intelligence— the president—led to unconscious bias. "It's much more a matter of a strong awareness of what the policymakers want to see and want to do," Pillar said.

Finally, Richard Blee, the former head of Alec Station, played a role in the establishment of a new covert CIA program against terrorists: armed drone strikes. On June 18, 2004, a Hellfire missile from an American drone killed Nek Muhammad, a young Taliban commander who had been sheltering Al Qaeda members in Pakistan's tribal areas, as well as two other militants and two of their sons. Blee, who was the Islamabad station chief at the time, said such strikes were necessary to safeguard the United States.

Over the next decade, drone strikes would emerge as the primary American weapon against terrorism. Embraced by both Democrats and Republicans, they would kill more than 5,000 suspected extremists and others in Pakistan, Yemen, Somalia, Libya, and other countries. New technology made drone strikes a form of targeted assassinations that appeared precise. But drones would, eventually, be used to kill American citizens without a court proceeding, an unprecedented step in a country where all citizens, particularly those facing a death sentence, expected a trial by jury. And, over time, it would emerge that hundreds of the victims of the drone strikes were civilians, not terrorists.

. . .

In 2004 Bush won reelection, defeating Democratic senator John Kerry, in part due to the apparent success of the American invasions of Afghanistan and Iraq. Flush with victory, the administration launched one of the largest abuses of power in the Justice Department in decades.

On December 7, 2006, seven US attorneys in cities across the United States were fired by Justice Department officials in Washington. At first, each of the US attorneys, who are appointed to four-year terms by the president, were given no reason for their dismissal. Over time, they were given different reasons. David Iglesias, the US attorney in Albuquerque, New Mexico, was told that his district was in need of "greater leadership." Carol Lam, the US attorney in San Diego, was told that she wasn't aggressive enough in investigating immigration and gun cases. John McKay, the US prosecutor, was told he was let go due to policy differences.

All of the prosecutors, though, had one thing in common: they had recently clashed with members of the Bush administration or with Republican members of Congress. Iglesias said he had been pressured by two Republicans, Senator Pete Domenici and Representative Heather Wilson, to file indictments against Democratic politicians before election day. Lam had successfully prosecuted a local Republican congressman, Randy "Duke" Cunningham, for accepting bribes. In 2004, McKay had cut off a conversation with an aide to a local Republican congressman who started asking him detailed questions about an investigation into the disputed election of the state's Democratic governor.

In testimony before Congress over the next several weeks, Attorney General Alberto Gonzales and other senior Justice Department officials denied that the firings were in any way partisan. Members of the Senate Judiciary Committee demanded that the Justice Department turn over all records related to the firings. In March, a series of emails were handed over to Congress showing a wide-ranging effort by White House officials and Gonzales to fire US attorneys who were seen as not sufficiently loyal to Bush. The scheme was a flagrant violation of the post-Watergate practice of not using the Justice Department—or federal prosecutors—as political weapons.

The emails showed that ten months before the firings White House aides had discussed firing 15 to 20 percent of all 93 US attorneys, including those who were not "loyal Bushies." White House Counsel Harriet Miers had raised the idea of firing all 93 attorneys. A White House aide then emailed Miers a chart categorizing the US attorneys into three groups based on whether they had "produced, managed well, and exhibited loyalty to the President and Attorney General." Other emails showed that Gonzales was aware of the planned firings.

In the following months, Gonzales was accused of lying to Congress. Miers was as well. Bush stood by each of them publicly, but both were politically wounded by the scandal. Some defenders of executive power said the firings of the US attorneys were justified under their interpretation of presidential power. But Bush was hesitant to be seen openly defying post-Watergate norms. Democrats, who had taken control of the Senate, threatened intensive investigations of Miers and Gonzales. Miers resigned in January 2007 and Gonzales did so in September 2007. The firings of the US attorneys had shocked many in the legal community. In the end, post-Watergate norms had remained in place. The firings, though, were another sign of the intensifying efforts to politicize the Justice Department. The right attorney general was needed to carry it out.

. . .

In the fall of 2007, Tom O'Connor, the FBI agent who had investigated the *Cole* attack and 9/11, arrived in Baghdad to investigate an incident that illustrated the excesses of the American invasion. Since joining the FBI, O'Connor had made a half-dozen trips abroad, primarily to investigate attacks by Al Qaeda and other militant groups against Americans. This trip was different. He was in Iraq to investigate crimes Americans had reportedly committed against Iraqis. The reversal didn't faze him.

On September 16, 2007, a group of heavily armed American security contractors employed by the Blackwater Security Group claimed they had gotten into a firefight in a traffic circle in Baghdad's Nisour Square. After a bombing in Baghdad, a Blackwater team was bringing a diplomat back into the embassy. Breaking orders to remain in the compound, they drove to Nisour Square to secure it so that the other Blackwater team could drive through it. (The other team took a different route and never passed through the square.) After they arrived in the square, one of the Blackwater guards feared that a white Kia was being driven by a suicide bomber. In fact, the white Kia was being driven by an Iraqi doctor; his mother, also a doctor, was a passenger. The guard shot the driver through the head with a sniper rifle. Other guards fired as well, killing his mother. The guard then fired grenades and hundreds of bullets at other vehicles. All told, seventeen Iraqis were killed and twenty wounded. None of the Blackwater guards were injured.

Investigating the crime appeared impossible. Iraqis feared speaking to American investigators. They also lived in parts of the city where insurgent attacks occurred. O'Connor, who had worked with Iraqi police on counterterrorism investigations on an earlier trip to the country in 2004 and 2005, contacted an Iraqi police officer with whom he had worked. By now an experienced crime scene investigator and team leader, O'Connor and his FBI and Iraqi colleagues came up with a simple plan for how to determine whether the Blackwater guards had murdered innocent people. With the help of the Iraqi officer, O'Connor and his team tracked down all sixteen Iraqi cars and trucks damaged in the shooting. "He helped us find the vehicles," O'Connor recalled. "We would buy the vehicles, as a piece of evidence."

By examining bullet holes in the cars and other forensic evidence, the FBI team concluded that the Blackwater guards had killed all seventeen Iraqis in the square without cause. As a result of O'Connor's work, American federal prosecutors charged five Blackwater guards with fourteen counts of manslaughter and twenty counts of attempted manslaughter in 2008. A year later, a federal judge threw out the case on the grounds that it was too reliant on testimony given in exchange for immunity. O'Connor and his team volunteered to continue to work the case. They were determined to prosecute whoever was responsible for the killing of the Iraqi civilians, regardless of the defendants' nationality.

. . .

The 2008 financial crisis sealed Bush's fate politically. His approval numbers dropped from 90 percent in the weeks after 9/11 to 34 percent when he left office. The war in Iraq had killed roughly 4,500 Americans and 100,000 Iraqis, and cost over $800 billion. No usable weapons of mass destruction were found, and the toppling of Saddam Hussein appeared to have strengthened Iran more than any other country. Bush's legacy in terms of congressional and judicial oversight of America's intelligence agencies was by far the worst of any president since Nixon.

After backing PATRIOT Act legislation that reversed key elements of the Church reforms, Bush, Cheney, and their White House aides confirmed the worst conspiracy theories of the American left and right. An overzealous president had covertly conducted mass surveillance on the American people, operated secret torture facilities abroad, and launched a costly war based on faulty intelligence. Like past presidents, Bush embraced secrecy as a shortcut to achieve his goals. This policy backfired, reducing public trust in government and squandering an opportunity to ease the country's increasingly wide partisan divide. A pattern had taken hold where presidents of the opposing political party were seen as existential threats to the future of the country. As Bush left office, liberals disdained him, dismissing him as a warmonger, torturer, and supporter of the military-industrial complex. As Barack Obama assumed the presidency, conservatives feared that he was weak on terrorism, bent on expanding the "administrative state," curtailing gun and religious rights, and forcing Americans to accept reproductive and gay rights.

EIGHT

Obama, Snowden, and Drones

Barack Obama took office in January 2009, promising to reverse the sweeping use of presidential power that George W. Bush had employed after 9/11. Instead of disputing the roles of the legislative and judicial branches in governing the country, he vowed to respect them. A former professor of constitutional law at the University of Chicago, he pledged to embrace congressional oversight, and strictly adhere to court rulings and the rule of law. Obama initially kept those promises. Over time, though, partisan deadlock in Washington prompted him to rely on executive orders to achieve his policy goals at home. Overseas, he expanded the use of CIA drone strikes to an unprecedented level and used sweeping NSA surveillance as a means to combat terrorism and bring American troops home. Obama's explanations for his actions seemed pragmatic. But skeptics of expanding the powers of the intelligence community, such as Senators Ron Wyden on the left and Rand Paul on the right, warned that they violated the civil rights of Americans and vested dangerous amounts of power in the presidency.

On his second day in office, Obama signed a series of executive orders designed to reverse Bush-era counterterrorism policies. He formally ended the CIA's use of secret detention centers, required interrogators to follow noncoercive methods established in the Army Field Manual, and launched a review process designed to shutter the Guantánamo Bay detention center within a year. However, Obama's executive orders were largely symbolic. Bush had already ended many of his administration's most extreme counterterrorism practices. Beginning in 2003, the CIA had stopped waterboarding prisoners; beginning in 2005, military interrogators were required by law to abide by the Army Field Manual's noncoercive methods; and since 2005 only a handful of prisoners had passed through the CIA's secret prison system. Despite Obama's efforts, Guantánamo would remain open.

Obama broke with Bush in important ways. For example, he expressed a deep skepticism of the country's ability to spread democracy in the Middle East—for Bush, a leading justification for the invasion of Iraq. But Obama legitimized other war-on-terror practices. Over time, he relied more heavily on the CIA, NSA, and FBI to thwart terrorist attacks than on the American military. Those steps were necessary, Obama and his aides argued, to avoid protracted ground wars, to safeguard the country, and to protect the administration from Republican attacks that Democrats were weak on terrorism.

Inside the CIA, operatives initially feared that Obama might put them on trial for using the "enhanced interrogation techniques" authorized by John Yoo and other Bush administration and Justice Department officials. Instead, Obama developed a close relationship with the intelligence community. In an early, reassuring signal to the CIA, Obama appointed John Durham—a Connecticut federal prosecutor—to conduct a probe into whether US laws were broken during Bush-era interrogation sessions. The Bush administration had already asked Durham to investigate the destruction of CIA videotapes depicting torture sessions. The Obama administration simply asked Durham to expand his review to include the techniques employed in those sessions. Durham was known for being politically neutral among government officials. CIA officials were grateful when Durham completed his investigation of the interrogation of 101 detainees and chose to not file criminal charges. But human rights groups said Durham had allowed American intelligence operatives to get away with torture.

Obama's initial choice for CIA director also reassured agency operatives. John Brennan, a little-known retired career CIA analyst, was one of the first former national security officials to endorse Obama for president. Brennan advised the campaign via conference calls and emails, beginning with Obama's breakthrough victory in the Iowa caucuses and continuing through his election as president. When the two men met in person for the first time in Chicago during Obama's transition, they bonded over a shared belief that the Iraq war had been a catastrophic mistake and that there was a way for the United States to combat terrorism without being perceived to be at war with Islam.

Obama's consideration of Brennan seemed to signal that the new president did not intend to enact major changes at the agency. Yet, soon after Brennan's name emerged as Obama's likely CIA nominee, human rights groups questioned whether Brennan was complicit in the agency's Bush-era torture and rendition program. Liberal commentators accused Brennan of "ambivalence and institutional moral cowardice." From 2004 to 2005, Brennan had served as the acting director of the National Counterterrorism Center, an organization created after 9/11 to better coordinate intelligence. But no records could be found of him objecting to the Bush administration's rendition, torture, and mass surveillance programs. At the request of aides to Obama, Brennan withdrew his name from consideration.

Unable to find a CIA director, Obama made a surprise nomination several weeks later: Leon Panetta, a veteran Democratic congressman who had served as Bill Clinton's White House chief of staff. Panetta had chaired the House Appropriations Committee and run the White House Office of Management and Budget. He was known for crunching numbers, corralling members Congress, and other technocratic political skills, not covert operations. His only significant prior work in espionage involved serving as an Army intelligence officer for two years in the 1960s. At the age of 70, Panetta would be the oldest CIA director ever appointed.

Inside the agency, Panetta's appointment sparked dread. A pattern had emerged since the Church reforms: the appointment of partisans as CIA director generally ended in discord. The tenure of Bill Casey, who had served as Reagan's campaign manager before becoming CIA director, ended in disaster for the agency and administration. Career agency workers accused Porter Goss, a congressman and formerly a covert CIA operative in Latin America appointed director by George W. Bush, of placing political allies in senior agency posts and ostracizing staffers perceived as disloyal to the administration. After serving only eighteen months, Goss resigned.

During his two-year tenure, Panetta managed to gain the confidence of both CIA staffers and members of congressional oversight committees. Panetta won the loyalty of CIA staff by ardently defending the agency in White House meetings. He did the same on Capitol Hill, where he had decades-long relationships with some legislators.

Pressure on the CIA and FBI soared after three terrorist attacks occurred in late 2009. On November 5, an Army psychiatrist opened fire on fellow soldiers at Fort Hood, Texas, killing thirteen people, including a pregnant soldier. Before the attack, the FBI had intercepted emails that Major Nidal Hassan had exchanged with the Yemeni-American preacher Anwar al-Maliki, who had joined Al Qaeda, but FBI agents had deemed Hassan not to be a threat. Seven weeks later, Umar Farouk Abdulmutallab, a young Nigerian who had been recruited by Al Qaeda, tried to set off a bomb on a transatlantic flight as it landed in Detroit on Christmas Day. The explosive, sewn into his underwear, failed to fully detonate. Before he could try to ignite the explosive again, a group of passengers wrestled him to the ground, saving the lives of the 290 people on board. Officials later learned that several US intelligence agencies had collected evidence of the plot beforehand but failed to share it with one another.

Five days after the failed "underwear" bombing over Detroit, a Jordanian doctor who had been working as an informant for the CIA arrived at an American military base in eastern Afghanistan to meet his CIA handlers. The doctor stepped out of the car and detonated a thirty-pound suicide vest strapped to his chest. The explosion killed seven CIA officers, including Jennifer Matthews, an intelligence analyst who had worked with Richard Blee at Alec Station in the 1990s. The suicide bombing was the single largest loss of life suffered by the agency in nearly forty years. After the attack, videos appeared online showing the doctor proudly declaring that he had been working as a double agent. In Langley, the attack prompted an intense review of how the agency recruits and interacts with informants. It also deeply damaged morale.

Alarmed, particularly by the Detroit airliner attack, Obama began to employ, with greater frequency, CIA drone strikes and NSA surveillance, two Bush-era counterterrorism tactics. John Brennan, who was appointed White House counterterrorism advisor after withdrawing from consideration as CIA director, played a central role in influencing Obama. Obama was embracing the use of executive power to defend the country, just as his Republican and Democratic predecessors had.

Brennan would prove to be the single most powerful intelligence official during Obama's eight years in office. The son of devout Irish Catholic immigrants, Brennan had grown up in a working-class town in northern New Jersey and attended Catholic elementary and high schools. For college, he chose Fordham University, a Catholic school in the Bronx. He went on to receive a master's degree in government with a concentration in Middle Eastern studies from the University of Texas, and studied for a semester at the American University of Beirut. In 1980, at the age of 24, Brennan joined the agency. During a lie detector test, he disclosed that in 1976 he had voted for Gus Hall, the Communist Party candidate for president, but he was still hired.

Over the next twenty-five years, Brennan worked as the CIA station chief in Saudi Arabia, as daily intelligence briefer for President Bill Clinton, and as a top deputy to CIA Director George Tenet. As the Obama White House counterterrorism advisor, Brennan managed the administration's "kill lists" for drone strikes. During the Obama presidency, the administration carried out 563 airstrikes, primarily by drones in Pakistan, Somalia, and Yemen. US intelligence officials estimated that the attacks killed 2,372 to 2,581 people in 2016, including 64 to 116 civilians. Independent analysts said the death total was much higher, with 3,797 killed, including 324 civilians. In 2015, a US drone strike in Pakistan accidentally killed American aid worker Warren Weinstein and Italian aid worker Giovanni Lo Porto, who were both being held captive by Al Qaeda.

In a series of interviews in 2016, Brennan said that his Jesuit education had given him a tool to wrestle with making such decisions: "just war theory," a centuries-old theological argument that war is justified when waged in self-defense, as a last resort, and minimizes civilian casualties. He declined to comment on specific drone strikes, but defended their use. "I still can look myself in the mirror every day and believe that I have tried to do what is morally right, what is necessary, and what is important to keep this country safe." He also acknowledged being haunted by mistakes. "You question yourself. You beat yourself up. You try to learn from it," Brennan said. "But you also recognize that if you're not prepared to make the tough decisions in the jobs that have been entrusted to you, you shouldn't be in those jobs."

Critics on the left and right criticized the drone strikes as extrajudicial "assassinations." In 2011, Obama authorized a strike that killed Anwar al-Awlaki, the Yemeni-American preacher and US citizen who had joined Al Qaeda in Yemen and had inspired the Fort Hood attack. The killing of al-Awlaki set a new standard for presidential power—an American citizen had been executed by the president with no public court proceeding and no public presentation of evidence. A controversial Justice Department legal memo that authorized the killing was kept secret from the American public. A subsequent strike had killed al-Awlaki's teenage son, one of hundreds of civilians killed in Obama administration drone strikes. Conservatives accused liberals of hypocrisy and argued that a Republican president who carried out such acts would have been decried as a murderer. Liberals said Obama had lost his way. "I have little doubt that Obama chose to rapidly expand the drone war under the sincere belief that it was legal, moral and good policy," James Downie, a *Washington Post* opinion editor, wrote: "But that belief was mistaken; the drone war is an indelible legacy—and shame—of his presidency."

·   ·   ·

In 2010, Obama experienced another intelligence setback. He was forced to fire Director of National Intelligence Dennis Blair, who was faulted for the continuing failure of US intelligence agencies to share intelligence with one another. Privately, Blair had grown deeply frustrated with the DNI's lack of power. Intelligence officials blamed both Bush and Obama for failing to clearly delineate the role of the DNI since its creation in 2004. White House officials in turn blamed the vagueness of the law Congress had enacted. All sides agreed that better coordination was needed by the American intelligence leviathan that had emerged post-9/11, which had grown to include sixteen agencies and one hundred thousand employees, and was sustained by $50 billion a year in spending.

Two weeks before Blair's departure, James Clapper, now a retired Air Force general, had a private fifteen-minute job interview with the president in the Oval Office. Clapper joked with Obama that he was nearly seventy and past his prime. Afterwards, Clapper sent Obama a seven-point letter in which he said he believed the DNI should function as an "avuncular, sage, strong Senate committee chairman" who convened the leaders of the intelligence agencies to discuss the merits of an idea rather than micromanaging the entire community. Lastly, he told Obama that he was a " 'truth to power' guy" and that he would "always insist on giving you privately the facts, to include what we don't know."

Announcing the nomination, Obama said that Clapper "possesses a quality that I value in all my advisors: a willingness to tell leaders what we need to know even if it's not what we want to hear." During his confirmation hearings, Clapper promised closer oversight of drone strikes in Pakistan and tighter monitoring of intelligence spending.

Three months after Clapper became director of national intelligence, the 2010 midterm elections were held. The results were a sign of the growing volatility of American politics. Across the country, the debate focused on the enactment of Obamacare and a massive stimulus package to revive the economy. With unemployment at nine percent, Republicans won a landslide victory, gaining sixty-three seats in the House—the largest win by any party in sixty-two years—and seven seats in the Senate. The Republicans now held a majority in the House, and Democrats were reduced to a narrow, three-seat majority in the Senate. Republicans dominated at the state level as well, winning control of twenty state legislatures and six governorships. A new generation of Republicans emerged, many of them libertarians. South Carolina congressmen Trey Gowdy and Mick Mulvaney, Kansas congressman Mike Pompeo, and Kentucky senator Rand Paul all arrived in Washington eager to curb government growth.

The sound defeat ended the ability of the Obama White House and congressional Democrats to enact legislation independently. It also marked a shift in the tone of American politics. Among conservatives, a narrative of an ever-growing and ever-invasive federal government helped fuel the rise of the Tea Party. Among liberals, Republicans were increasingly seen as obstructionist, bigoted, and backward. Fox News and MSNBC gained larger and larger audiences by becoming increasingly partisan. Cable news anchors made millions casting their political opponents as mendacious, treasonous, and corrupt. Divisiveness was both popular and profitable. Waiting in the wings was a new group of politicians eager to capitalize on the seething disdain members of each party's base felt toward one another.

· · ·

In Obama's third year in office, the CIA achieved the single greatest intelligence triumph in its history, locating the compound where

Osama bin Laden was hiding in Pakistan, and guiding a Special Forces raid that killed the Qaeda leader on May 2, 2011. The raid was a triumph for the agency, the SEALs, Panetta, the Obama administration, and congressional oversight. After the discovery of bin Laden's possible safe house, Panetta had briefed the Gang of Eight: the top party leaders of the Senate and the House and the top Republican and Democrat on the intelligence committees. All of them kept the secret. Oversight had worked as designed, and for once, intelligence had not been leaked for political advantage.

By the end of Panetta's two-year tenure, many intelligence officials and members of Congress viewed him as one of the most effective CIA directors of the post-Church reform era. Panetta maintained a close relationship with Obama and other senior White House officials, delighting agency staffers focused on the CIA's relevance. He also promised to be transparent with the intelligence committees and said he believed it was possible both to respect Congress's oversight powers and keep the country safe. Instead of being angered by committee members' point-scoring during public hearings, he accepted the inherently political nature of Congress. Panetta also began briefing members informally and in private. Using the political skills he had developed during sixteen years in Congress, Panetta charmed Democrats and worked hard not to alienate Republicans. "I made a decision," Panetta said in an interview, "that I would have a series of meetings with them over coffee and donuts."

Obama used the death of bin Laden to overcome what some of his closest aides viewed as attempts to slow-roll the implementation of his policies by unelected officials. Obama never publicly used the term "deep state," but he, like other Democratic presidents, was suspicious of the military. In his first months in office, he had felt that Pentagon officials were trying to box him in during a review of American policy in Afghanistan by proposing a large troop "surge" in the country. Military commanders also hindered Obama's efforts to close the Guantánamo Bay detention center. The Marine general who oversaw

Guantánamo, General John Kelly, slowed the release of medical records that would facilitate the transfer of detainees—despite requests from the detainees and their lawyers that they be made available.

In a nationally televised White House address five weeks after the bin Laden raid, Obama announced that he planned to end the troop surge in Afghanistan and hand over security responsibility to Afghan forces by 2014. Six months after bin Laden's death, Obama, carrying out an agreement negotiated by George W. Bush, withdrew all American troops from Iraq. Most Republicans opposed the Iraq withdrawal, arguing that it was premature, but public opinion polls showed that three-quarters of Americans supported it. For the remainder of his time in office, Obama, choosing the path of many past presidents, would rely primarily on covert action such as drone strikes and Special Operations raids to address complex foreign policy problems.

. . .

When Obama took office, Robert Mueller had two years left in his term as the FBI's director. By the time Obama took office, the bureau had limited the profiling of Muslims and conducting illegal surveillance of mosques that had sparked criticism. Over time, the president and Mueller established a strong working rapport. A month after the killing of bin Laden, Obama asked Congress to extend Mueller's term in office for a further two years, the first time a director's ten-year tenure had been extended beyond the Church reform–mandated length. "In his 10 years at the FBI, Bob Mueller has set the gold standard for leading the bureau," Obama said. While Obama pushed back on the Pentagon, he embraced continuity at the FBI.

As Obama battled Mitt Romney in the 2012 presidential campaign, Mueller was forced to handle a politically sensitive investigation that could affect the outcome of the race. In May of 2012, FBI agents learned that David Petraeus, who had replaced Panetta as CIA director in September 2011, had had an affair with Paula Broadwell, an army intelligence officer who had written a biography of him.

In the summer of 2012, Mueller and Attorney General Eric Holder, who had been appointed by Obama at the beginning of his first term, were informed of the FBI investigation into Broadwell and Petraeus. That spring, Holder had issued a memo urging federal prosecutors to follow an informal Justice Department policy and not announce investigations at a time when they could influence an upcoming election. "Politics must play no role in the decisions of federal investigators or prosecutors regarding any investigations or criminal charges," Holder wrote. "Law enforcement officers and prosecutors may never select the timing of investigative steps or criminal charges for the purpose of affecting any election." The memo reflected a decades-old practice by federal prosecutors and law enforcement officials in which investigations were not announced within sixty days of an election. Mueller consulted with Holder; they decided not to make the Petraeus investigation public, citing the race between Obama and Romney.

On November 6, 2012, Obama won his second term. His administration's success at stabilizing the economy and preventing major terrorist attacks played a central role in his reelection. However, the country remained polarized. Obama's margin of victory was smaller than in 2008. Democrats retained control of the Senate. Republicans retained control of the House. Government remained divided.

That same day, the FBI informed Clapper of the Petraeus affair and its investigation. The following morning, Clapper spoke with Petraeus by phone and advised him to resign. Two days later, Obama accepted Petraeus's resignation. Petraeus publicly apologized for his conduct. After a three-year legal battle, in 2015, he pleaded guilty to a misdemeanor charge of mishandling classified information, admitting that he had lied to FBI agents when, as CIA director, he falsely told them he had not shared classified information with Broadwell. He was sentenced to two years of probation, and fined $100,000. The lenient sentence angered FBI agents, who noted that lying to a federal law enforcement official during a criminal investigation was a felony that carried a sentence of up to five years in prison. Every aspect of the Petraeus investigation would be exhaustively parsed during the 2016 presidential election. The impartiality of the Justice Department and the FBI would be questioned again when it came to Hillary Clinton.

.   .   .

Six months after Obama began his second term, revelations of his administration's secret use of court-approved NSA eavesdropping sparked protests from liberals and conservatives. They angrily asserted that the Democratic president, despite his early pronouncements, was using the same forms of clandestine mass surveillance as the Bush administration. Obama and intelligence officials insisted that the activities were approved by a FISA Court judge and fully lawful, but the political fallout made plain that Americans' deep-seated distrust of the government remained politically potent. Obama, a liberal and constitutional law professor who prided himself on honoring legal norms, now found himself embroiled in a version of the scandals that have consistently plagued presidents—from the FBI's extensive surveillance of political groups in the 1960s to the warrantless wiretapping exposed by Justice Department lawyer James Baker in 2001. The dispute began with a product of the Church reforms—a routine oversight hearing before the Senate Intelligence Committee.

On March 12, 2013, Clapper, who was in his third year serving as the director of national intelligence, testified with other spy chiefs in the committee's annual hearing on national security threats. After opening statements from each of the intelligence chiefs, committee chair Senator Dianne Feinstein opened the session up for questions from committee members. Two hours after the hearing began, Senator Wyden, a liberal Democrat from Oregon and longtime critic of excessive government surveillance, asked Clapper what type of data the government collected from Americans.

"And this is for you, Director Clapper, again on the surveillance front. And I hope we can do this in just a yes-or-no answer, because

I know Senator Feinstein wants to move on. Last summer the NSA director was at a conference and he was asked a question about the NSA surveillance of Americans. He replied, and I quote here, '. . . the story that we have millions or hundreds of millions of dossiers on people is completely false.' The reason I'm asking the question is, having served on the committee now for a dozen years, I don't really know what a dossier is in this context. So what I wanted to see is if you could give me a yes or no answer to the question: Does the NSA collect any type of data at all on millions or hundreds of millions of Americans?"

"No, sir," Clapper replied.

"It does not?" Wyden asked again.

"Not wittingly," Clapper said.

. . .

After the hearing, Wyden's staff asked Clapper if he wanted to correct his answer. Clapper declined.

Later, Clapper said that he had misunderstood Wyden's question: that he thought that Wyden had been asking about surveillance of foreigners under Section 702 of the PATRIOT Act, which authorized the NSA to collect information from non-Americans located outside the United States. The administration had just spent months getting enough votes in Congress to reauthorize Section 702. He did not think Wyden was asking about information collected under a separate statute, Section 215. "I thought immediately of Section 702. I just didn't think he was asking about 215," Clapper said in an interview. "I didn't think about it. Maybe I should have, but I didn't."

Two months later, Edward Snowden, a young NSA contractor, leaked to journalists hundreds of thousands of top-secret documents. Snowden flew to Hong Kong and turned them over to journalists Glenn Greenwald and Ewen MacAskill of the *Guardian* and documentary filmmaker Laura Poitras. Aided by the ease of downloading information in the digital age, Snowden, at the age of 29, had conducted the greatest theft of classified information in American history.

The documents revealed that the NSA had been collecting the telephone metadata of hundreds of millions of Americans for years. The data did not identify Americans by name but listed what numbers they dialed, where they were when they placed their calls, and when each call began and ended. The disclosure led to calls for Clapper to be prosecuted for lying to Congress, and created a diplomatic and political firestorm for the Obama administration. In a series of articles in the *Guardian*, the *Washington Post*, and other news media, the Snowden documents revealed scandal after scandal. American and British intelligence agencies had spied on 122 foreign governments and thirty-five foreign leaders, including such allies as German chancellor Angela Merkel, Brazilian president Dilma Rousseff, and Mexican president Felipe Calderón. The NSA had also spied on foreign leaders, friends and foes alike, at the 2010 G8 and G20 summits in Toronto.

In disclosures that US intelligence officials insisted endangered US national security, the documents revealed that the NSA was hacking into computers, tapping fiber optic cables, and circumventing web encryption programs worldwide. In some cases, the federal government forced American tech companies to secretly create "backdoors" in encryption programs that allowed the NSA to read messages without the public knowing it. Vacuuming up as much information as possible around the world, the NSA collected vast numbers of text messages and emails, and voluminous search engine metadata—all, they said, in the service of protecting the country. On average, the NSA collected information related to two hundred million text messages a day. At times, the agency also collected information from Americans while spying on foreigners. In a final blow to public trust, the stories revealed that the NSA was collecting data from Google and Yahoo data centers without the companies' consent.

Clapper and, initially, Obama himself, argued that the administration had followed all of the legal procedures required by the Church reforms. They pointed out that Wyden and every other member of the House and Senate intelligence committees were aware of the NSA programs. The FISA Court had issued warrants and other legal orders approving eavesdropping on Americans.

The scandal, though, exposed the enormous political dangers created by surveillance in the digital age. Administration officials held that collecting metadata was different from compiling physical, paper dossiers on individual Americans, as the FBI and CIA had done for decades during the Cold War. They asserted that anonymized data was different from recording individual Americans' phone calls and opening their mail.

In a final effort to sway public opinion, the administration also declared Snowden a traitor who had helped the country's enemies by disclosing the NSA's eavesdropping methods. Fearing arrest in Hong Kong, Snowden had fled to Moscow, where he received asylum from Russian president Vladimir Putin. No evidence emerged, though, that Snowden had been working on behalf of the Russian government. Overall, Obama's arguments failed to sway public opinion. Most Americans distrusted the US government more than Snowden. For many on the left as well as the right, Snowden became a folk hero, celebrated as a whistleblower for having duped the country's spymasters and warned the public that they were under surveillance. The revelations fueled the highest levels of American public suspicion of US intelligence agencies since the Church reforms.

A combination of liberal Democrats, led by Ron Wyden, and libertarian Tea Party Republicans, led by Rand Paul, embraced stricter control of surveillance. Wyden argued that the practices, though technically legal, remained more shrouded in secrecy than necessary. As a member of the Senate Intelligence Committee, he understood that surveillance helped protect the country. But he argued that the American people were being told too little about how the Bush and Obama administrations used the surveillance powers Congress granted them after 9/11. "The danger is the emergence of secret law," Wyden said in an interview. "Americans deserve to know more about how the law is being applied."

Clapper said he understood why members of Congress would want to score political points by attacking the spy agencies. Politicians are in office to represent the public, he affirmed. Intelligence officials should recognize that spy agencies will invariably be viewed with suspicion in a democracy. "He's playing to his constituency," Clapper said, referring to Wyden. "There has been and will always be an aura of secrecy and suspicion surrounding intelligence agencies."

Wyden insisted that Clapper had lied to the public. "Regardless of what was going through the director's head when he testified, failing to correct the record was a deliberate decision to lie to the American people about what their government was doing," he said. "And within a few months, of course, the truth came out."

.   .   .

While the debate over surveillance raged, Tom O'Connor, the Massachusetts policeman turned FBI agent, continued his efforts to investigate the Blackwater Security contractors. After a federal judge dismissed the charges against the men in 2009, O'Connor worked with federal prosecutors and FBI agents to build a case against them on new evidence. O'Connor made four trips to Iraq between 2008 and 2010, gathering additional evidence with the help of the Iraqi police. He also made three trips to Afghanistan to investigate attacks on Americans there. Finally, in 2011, a federal appeals court reinstated the charges against four of the Blackwater guards. In 2014, seven years after the shootings, the four men went on trial in a federal court in Washington, DC. O'Connor personally encouraged Iraqi victims and witnesses to come testify at the trial. Although deeply skeptical of the American judicial system, two dozen Iraqi witnesses volunteered to travel to Washington.

Under oath, the Iraqis recounted the confusion and horror they experienced as machine-gun fire from the American convoy riddled Iraqi vehicles. American witnesses from inside the convoy testified that their colleagues had fired recklessly on innocent civilians.

A father wept as he described the death of his nine-year-old son. An Iraqi police officer recounted watching a woman cradle her dead son's head on her shoulder before perishing herself. O'Connor took the stand to testify about FBI ballistics findings.

For 28 days, the jury deliberated. On October 24, 2014, they announced their verdict: the killing of the seventeen Iraqis was not a tragic battlefield accident, but a criminal act. They found one defendant, Nicholas A. Slatten, a sniper who the government said fired the first shots, guilty of murder. They convicted three others—Dustin L. Heard, Evan S. Liberty, and Paul A. Slough—of voluntary manslaughter and using a machine gun to carry out a violent crime. A fifth contractor, Jeremy Ridgeway, had previously pleaded guilty to manslaughter and cooperated with prosecutors.

O'Connor was delighted. He felt that justice had been served.

O'Connor found the work overseas deeply rewarding. In addition to his trips to Kenya, Yemen, Iraq, and Afghanistan, he had investigated crimes in Kosovo, Greece, Indonesia, Pakistan, and Ukraine. He also investigated high-profile crimes in the United States from the Washington-area sniper to the Boston Marathon bombing. His focus inside the United States was on domestic terrorism and stemmed, in part, from one of the last cases he was on as a police officer in Massachusetts. Working with state troopers and a colleague who posed as a gang member, he had helped convict two white supremacist skinheads of assault. The brutality of the group had unnerved him. "When I was a police officer in Massachusetts, I responded to a case where a hippy kid had been attacked," O'Connor said. "They went into the kid's apartment and they beat him with a baseball bat. These two shitheads poured boiling water with noodles on him. I'd never seen that type of scalding before." Over time, he developed expertise in investigating the violent actions of white supremacist groups such as Aryan Nations. O'Connor noticed that the way the groups operated was changing. After 2016, the number of groups declined, but the number of individual adherents grew. More individuals were being radicalized online and acting on their own. He said the threat was always there but it was now growing. The FBI began using a new term for the groups—racially motivated violent extremism.

. . .

A year after the Snowden scandal, the intelligence community committed a second self-inflicted blunder. Following Petraeus's resignation, Obama nominated Brennan to be CIA director, giving the Obama confidant the post he had sought for decades. Soon, however, Brennan created a vast scandal of his own by spying on the Senate Intelligence Committee, which performed oversight of the CIA, and initially lying about it. In March of 2014, Dianne Feinstein delivered an unprecedented speech on the floor of the US Senate in which she angrily accused Brennan's CIA of creating a "constitutional crisis" by secretly hacking into the computers of Senate Intelligence staffers who were investigating the CIA's use of torture.

Hours after Feinstein's speech, Brennan denied her allegations. "Nothing could be further from the truth," Brennan said at an event at the Council on Foreign Relations. "We wouldn't do that. That's just beyond the scope of reason in terms of what we'd do."

Four months later, the CIA inspector general found that in this instance Brennan had either flat-out lied or been grossly ill informed. CIA officers had, in fact, secretly penetrated a computer network used by Senate Intelligence Committee staffers as they worked on the torture report. Agency officers secretly read the emails of Senate investigators and—in an astounding step—asked the Justice Department to prosecute the Senate investigators for stealing CIA documents.

Brennan publicly apologized to Feinstein and asked the CIA inspector general and an accountability review board to investigate. The inspector general found that three of the agency's computer specialists had created false identities and used them to log into a computer network used by the Senate staffers. The CIA specialists were suspicious of how the Senate investigators had gotten access to an internal CIA report, known as the Panetta review, which criticized the torture program. In fact, other CIA officials had given the Senate staffers access to the report. The inspector general added that the three information technology specialists also lied about their actions to investigators.

Some top Democrats said the agency had "unconstitutionally spied on Congress" and demanded Brennan's resignation. The Obama White House, though, again came to Brennan's defense. Press Secretary Josh Earnest said the director had taken "responsible steps" to address the behavior of the CIA employees.

Six months later, the accountability review board found that Brennan himself had encouraged CIA staffers to investigate how the Senate aides received a copy of the Panetta review, making clear "his desire to confront [Senate committee] leadership immediately with information concerning the matter."

.   .   .

The fractious dispute over the CIA's search of the Senate committee's computers came as Feinstein and White House officials were clashing over the release of the committee's 6,000-page report on the use of state-sanctioned torture during the Bush era. Feinstein argued that fully detailing the CIA's abuses—as the Church report had done forty years earlier—would increase public confidence in oversight of US spy agencies. Obama and Brennan argued that releasing the full report would spark attacks on Americans and CIA officers. In the end, Obama again backed Brennan. Only the five-hundred-page executive summary of the torture report was released.

Brennan defended his stance. He said that any interrogation methods used by CIA officials that exceeded the Bush-era guidelines were "reprehensible," but that the vast majority of CIA officers were being unfairly "maligned by individuals who have political agendas." He explained, "When we do things that are within our authorized mandate, things that we are directed to do by our presidents, things that are deemed lawful by our Department of Justice, for us to be dragged through the coals on that, I find that reprehensible as well."

Obama had come to office promising to respect the rule of law; he vowed he would be transparent with the American people and curb the power of the presidency. With time, though, Obama, like so many presidents before him, came to embrace covert action as a means to protect the country from terrorists and to counter rival nations. Three scandals—Snowden's leaks, Clapper's answer to Wyden, and Brennan's battles with Feinstein over torture—undermined Obama's claim of transparency. Liberal Democrats and libertarian Republicans became even more suspicious of the White House and the intelligence community.

In terms of domestic politics, Republicans and Democrats learned during the Obama years that energizing their party's political base produced electoral victories. Voters, it seemed, rewarded the use of executive orders to bypass a deadlocked Congress, the obliteration of bipartisan norms, and the use of blatantly false claims on partisan cable news shows. As Senate majority leader, Mitch McConnell mastered these tactics. Harry Reid and Nancy Pelosi employed them, too, if in more subtle ways.

Eventually, Obama's executive orders and intelligence scandals became fodder for a new Republican narrative. The term "deep state" had not yet been introduced in the American media, but the story line stoked by Fox News was clear. Obamacare, executive orders, and NSA surveillance all flouted individual rights. Federal government overreach reminiscent of the Waco scandal of the Clinton era had returned in even more dangerous forms. To Republicans, Obama and his top aides, from James Clapper to John Brennan to Hillary Clinton, were dangerous authoritarians. In 2016, Donald Trump would take full advantage of those fears.

PART II

PRESIDENTIAL POWER IN THE TRUMP ERA

The accumulation of all powers, legislative, executive, and judiciary, in the same hands, whether of one, a few, or many, and whether hereditary, self-appointed, or elective, may justly be pronounced the very definition of tyranny.

—*James Madison, The Federalist Papers, No. 47*

NINE

The 2016 Campaign

F our years before Donald Trump formally announced his candidacy for president, he debuted the political technique that would carry him to the White House. His ability to weave together hyperbole, fear, and falsehoods into a narrative of aggrievement attracted attention, outrage, and millions of voters. This form of rhetoric, and the way it came to dominate and distort political discourse in the United States, would also erode Americans' faith in their government and one another.

Trump first employed the tactic before a national audience in 2011, when he appeared on *Good Morning America* and *The View* and questioned whether Barack Obama was born in the United States. After Obama released a copy of his long-form birth certificate, Trump offered to donate five million dollars to the charity of Obama's choice if the president would release his college and passport applications. The cunning gambit at once highlighted Trump's wealth, cast aspersions on Obama's academic achievements, and stoked racism and xenophobia.

After Trump chose not to run for president in 2012, he trafficked in new conspiracy theories. While Obama was criticized during the campaign for exaggerating how much Obamacare had reduced health insurance premiums, Trump accused Obama of blocking US military forces from rescuing Ambassador Christopher Stevens and three other Americans, Sean Smith, Glen Doherty, and Tyrone Woods, who died in Benghazi on September 11, 2012.

Once he was reelected, Obama, as well as leading Democrats and the Republican establishment, ridiculed Trump, who remained on the fringe of American politics. What they missed was that Trump, birtherism, and Benghazi were components of a broader shift in the United States. Over the next two years, four different committees of the Republican-controlled House (Oversight, Armed Services, Intelligence, and Foreign Affairs) investigated the attack, but none of them found personal wrongdoing by Obama and Clinton—yet that would not matter in a post-fact era.

Matthew Olsen, the director of the National Counterterrorism Center at the time of the attack, testified at length before each committee. Olsen later said that he had tried to make the center, created after 9/11 as a way to better coordinate information sharing between intelligence agencies, an "honest broker" between Democrats and Republicans. "We were extremely careful about not overstating," Olsen said in an interview. "We knew by then how sensitive it had become."

The findings by the Republican-controlled committees failed to convince conservative commentators that the truth had been found. Conservative cable news and radio shows continued to argue that Clinton and Obama were responsible for the deaths of the four Americans. Benghazi was part of a broader narrative—one that echoed the Clinton years—in which Obama was accused of being an authoritarian ruler who engaged in a massive cover-up in Benghazi, targeted conservative groups with IRS investigations, and concealed his country of birth. The narrative was amplified by a group of multimillionaire conservative commentators, from Bill O'Reilly and Sean Hannity on Fox News, to Rush Limbaugh on radio, to Alex Jones on his online program *InfoWars*. (Jones was by far the most extreme, arguing that the George W. Bush administration had carried out the 9/11 attacks and that the 2012 Sandy Hook Elementary School massacre that killed twenty children was faked. Jones's listeners went so far as to harass the parents of murdered first-graders.)

Trump, at that point a reality television star, promoted the story line on Twitter and in Fox News interviews. He was by no means the leading voice on the right, but he was adept at fueling anger, alarm, and disdain. On May 29, 2013, he tweeted, "House GOP better get its act together. Defund ObamaCare. Out negotiate on debt ceiling. Form commissions on Benghazi & IRS. No excuses!" When US Special Forces soldiers and FBI agents captured a central figure in the Benghazi attack, Ahmed Abu Khattala, Trump belittled the operation. "What took so long to catch only 1 of the Benghazi terrorists? Especially after the killer has been taunting the US in the press f/2 yrs," he tweeted. "The Benghazi terrorist is getting speedier care than our Vets at the VA. Obama has his priorities.'" On August 10, 2015, Trump tweeted, "We must stop the crime and killing machine that is illegal immigration. Rampant problems will only get worse. Take back our country!"

Trump sensed a way to exploit this frustration, alienation, and sense of grievance in rural areas and rust-belt cities that many mainstream politicians, government officials, and journalists were missing. Partisanship and technological change were steadily eroding the authority of post-Watergate institutions and norms. After the congressional investigations of Iran-Contra, Iraq WMDs, and CIA torture broke down along partisan lines, the results of such inquiries seemed to carry less public weight. When Republican congressional inquiries into Benghazi failed to produce evidence of wrongdoing, Twitter, Facebook, and cable news insisted that the conspiracy theories were true.

Most importantly, the nature of politics was changing. The modicum of respect between Democrats and Republicans on the Church Committee, the Iran-Contra Committee, and the 9/11 Commission was evaporating. Instead of creating a basic fact-pattern of events for the American public, congressional investigations sowed confusion. Instead of easing partisan tensions, congressional probes exacerbated political divisions and enabled the spread of conspiracy theories.

Instead of increasing public confidence in government, Congress undermined it.

. . .

At first, it appeared that Clinton wouldn't suffer significant political damage from the Republican congressional investigations into Benghazi. In October 2015, she was questioned about the attack by the House Select Committee on Benghazi chaired by Republican Trey Gowdy for eight hours. Elijah Cummings, the ranking Democrat on the committee, assailed the investigation. "It is time, and it is time now," Cummings said, "for the Republicans to end this taxpayer-funded fishing expedition."

One of the most aggressive questioners was Mike Pompeo, a Republican member of Congress from Kansas with close ties to the Koch brothers, known for his conservatism, combativeness, and ambition. Pompeo accused Clinton of relying on her longtime confidante, Sidney Blumenthal, more than on US intelligence officials for information on Libya. Fact-checkers found that this claim was false, but Pompeo continued to make the allegation. Opinion polls showed that, in the public's view, the hearing initially backfired on Republicans. Clinton had remained calm under questioning, and Republicans had unearthed no new evidence suggesting that Clinton was personally responsible for the deaths. But Pompeo's standing soared among conservatives, who continued to believe that Clinton was involved in a vast cover-up.

Several weeks after Clinton's appearance, Gowdy released a final, 800-page report that rebuked the Pentagon, CIA, and State Department for maintaining facilities in Benghazi they could not protect as other foreign nations withdrew their personnel. The report criticized the State Department Accountability Review Board investigation as token because, in essence, the board allowed Clinton to choose who investigated her actions. It recounted, in more detail than past reviews, the CIA's fluctuating views of whether the attack was a carefully planned strike or a spontaneous response to the posting of an anti-Muslim video. It repeated long-running allegations that the Obama administration had defied oversight by stonewalling congressional demands for documents.

But Gowdy's report found no new evidence that Clinton was personally responsible for the deaths. Instead, it criticized mid-level State Department managers who turned down requests for increased security, and mid-level CIA officials who failed to anticipate an attack. Gowdy was particularly scathing about the Pentagon; there were no US forces in the area that could have arrived in Benghazi in time to save the four Americans. To the delight of Clinton's supporters and to the dismay of her opponents, Gowdy also found no proof of a conspiracy. But in a forty-eight-page addendum, Pompeo insisted that Clinton had engaged in a cover-up and that the State Department had been "seemingly more concerned with politics and Secretary Clinton's legacy than with protecting its people in Benghazi."

Public opinion polls showed a deep partisan divide on Benghazi. Eighty-five percent of Republicans thought that Clinton had acted improperly; thirty percent of Democrats thought that she had. Eighty percent of Democrats thought the Republican-led investigation was aimed at damaging Clinton politically. Sixty-five percent of Republicans said that it raised legitimate concerns. For conservatives, the Benghazi scandal was a Watergate-scale presidential cover-up. For liberals, it was a wholly fabricated Republican smear campaign.

All told, the five different Republican-controlled Benghazi investigations dragged on longer than the inquiries into the attack on Pearl Harbor, the Kennedy assassination, and the 9/11 terrorist attacks. As an example of congressional oversight, it was an abject failure, undermining the concept of objective nonpartisan oversight. It produced little consensus, and no major new findings. Democrats accused Republicans of using their congressional oversight powers purely for political gain. Republicans released their final report without having shared it with committee Democrats.

Adam Schiff, a Democrat on the committee, warned that a new precedent of politicized, partisan oversight had been established. "I hope, what it will do, if there's any positive result that will come out of this, is repudiate the idea of establishing select committees for partisan purposes," Schiff told the *New York Times.* "There's going to be a temptation among Democrats to say, 'They did it to us, maybe we should do a Benghazi to them,' and among Republicans to say, 'We did it before, let's do it to them again.'"

Deputy CIA Director Morell, whom Republicans accused of downplaying the gravity of the attack, said the Benghazi inquiry set a new precedent in terms of post-Church oversight of intelligence agencies. Any pretense of nonpartisan congressional oversight was gone. "I do think Benghazi was a turning point," he said. "I think Benghazi was a use of a foreign policy and intelligence issue solely for political gain. They couldn't care less about the truth." Morell said that Republicans members of Congress privately admitted to him that they had publicly vilified him for political gain. "I can't tell you the number of Republicans who told me, 'Michael, it's just politics,'" he said. The problem, Morell added, was that in the end the Benghazi fishing expedition produced a giant political win. Gowdy's committee confirmed Clinton's use of a private email server. "One of the reasons it was a turning point is that it was successful. It worked spectacularly," Morell said. "By creating a focus on Clinton's use of a private server and the subsequent FBI investigation, it played a major role in her defeat."

.   .   .

On the campaign trail, Trump ignored the findings of all five Republican-controlled committees that Clinton was not personally responsible for the deaths in Benghazi. Instead, he accused her of murder, and Gowdy of letting her get away with it. During Clinton's testimony to Gowdy's committee, he mocked her, tweeting, "Hillary is doing a HORRIBLE job at #BenghaziHearings reading from the script. #pathetic. She is no leader." A week later, Trump's campaign posted a video on Instagram that showed Clinton laughing over footage of the Benghazi consulate in flames. "Hillary has been laughing at our expense for years," the ad said. "Don't let the joke be on us!"

After Gowdy endorsed Senator Marco Rubio for president, Trump savaged Gowdy in four early-morning tweets to supporters. "Rubio finally gets an endorsement—from #Benghazi loser Gowdy," Trump wrote to a supporter. "Face it, Trey Gowdy failed miserably on Benghazi. He allowed it to drag out and in the end, let Hillary get away with murder." Two days later, he called the congressional hearings on Benghazi "a total disaster for Republicans & America!"

By the spring of 2016, Trump had emerged as the presumptive Republican presidential nominee, soundly defeating sixteen rivals and shocking the Republican establishment. In April 2016, Trump again blamed Clinton for the four deaths in Benghazi in his first major foreign policy speech. "Instead of taking charge that night, Hillary Clinton decided to go home and sleep! Incredible. Clinton blames it all on a video, an excuse that was a total lie."

All of the allegations Trump made were misleading or exaggerated. Republican congressional investigators had found that Clinton was awake during the attacks, which killed the four Americans between 4 p.m. and 11:15 p.m. Eastern Standard Time. Two months later, Trump made an even larger series of false claims. He said Clinton's decisions as secretary of state "spread death, destruction, and terrorism everywhere she touched. Among the victims was our late Ambassador Chris Stevens. I mean what she did with him was absolutely horrible. He was left helpless to die as Hillary Clinton soundly slept in her bed."

Trump's vitriol set a destructive precedent. No major-party presidential candidate since Watergate had lied so consistently and boldly in the service of his own political goals. No major-party presidential candidate in modern times had ever before politically weaponized the deaths of four Americans who died serving their country. And no major-party presidential candidate had been rewarded so lavishly for such behavior. The damage, though, went beyond the erosion of political norms. Trump had flatly contradicted the findings of five exhaustive congressional inquiries conducted by his own political party, separate inquiries within the intelligence community, and the investigations by the vast majority of news organizations. Intentionally or not, in an effort to gain a political edge, Trump was undermining public confidence in two institutions that had played significant roles in countering the power of the presidency since the Church reforms and Watergate—Congress and the news media.

Trump's lying continued throughout the general election campaign. He lied two dozen times in his first presidential debate with Clinton, according to fact-checkers, on topics from his business bankruptcies, to the size of the trade deficit, to falsely claiming that Clinton, not Trump, had questioned whether Obama was born in the United States. The *Washington Post* concluded that "There's never been a presidential candidate like Donald Trump—someone so cavalier about the facts and so unwilling to ever admit error, even in the face of overwhelming evidence."

When the *Post* examined the accuracy of a sampling of 92 of Trump's statements, it found that 64 percent were false. By contrast, it found that most politicians, including Clinton, tended to make false or misleading statements 10 to 20 percent of the time— hardly inspiring, but a significant difference in degree. The *Post* found that Trump falsely claimed that he never called women "fat pigs, dogs, slobs, and disgusting animals"; that Barack Obama had spent four million dollars hiding records showing he wasn't born in the United States; that the "real" US employment rate was 42 percent; that the US murder rate was at its highest level in 45 years; that Trump University received an "A" rating from the Better Business Bureau (it received a D− rating); that veterans are "treated worse" than undocumented immigrants; that "scores of recent migrants" in the United States had been charged with terrorism; that the Obama administration "actively" supported terror groups; that Clinton's use of private emails led to an Iranian defector's death; that Clinton would give social security to illegal immigrants. Despite the fact that all of these claims were false, in 2016 tens of millions of voters either believed them or didn't care that they were lies.

.   .   .

During the campaign, the largest question surrounding Trump centered on his relationship with a foreign leader, Russian president Vladimir Putin. Trump's public appeals for Russian help during the 2016 campaign and private contacts between Trump campaign advisors and Russians with ties to Putin embroiled the FBI, the CIA, and the presidency in a bruising political fight that damaged public trust in all three institutions.

As Trump campaigned in the summer of 2016, James Clapper, Obama's director of national intelligence, received unusual reports from American intelligence analysts. A strange pattern was emerging that involved Trump's taunts of Clinton and state-controlled Russian media. After Trump first used the phrase "lying, crooked Hillary" in April, RT (Russia Today), the Russian government–backed television station that broadcasts in the United States and other countries, repeated it, as did internet trolls paid by the Russian government.

Initially, Clapper and other American intelligence officials viewed the activity as the latest version of a decades-old effort by Moscow to undermine the credibility of American elections. The Russians had, for years, carried out operations that they considered payback for CIA meddling in elections in Russia, Iran, Chile, and scores of other countries. For decades RT and Sputnik, a state-controlled news agency, had been spouting propaganda at Americans. Their use of Trump's language in attacking Clinton didn't seem radically different from what the Russians had done before.

During the Cold War, the Soviet Union had repeatedly tried to sway or undermine US presidential elections. In January 1960, the

Soviet ambassador to Washington invited Democrat Adlai Stevenson to his embassy and read him a letter from Premier Nikita Khrushchev offering Stevenson financial support if he would repeat his run for president in 1960. Stevenson declined the offer, documented the conversation, and informed the Eisenhower administration.

In other initiatives, Soviet operatives spread negative information about Richard Nixon and Ronald Reagan, who they viewed as dangerous hawks. In 1976, an unidentified Democratic party activist reportedly attended a three-hour campaign meeting in California with presidential candidate Jimmy Carter while working for the KGB.

For decades, an arm of the KGB known as "Service A" promoted "active measures" campaigns that spread *dezinformatsiya*, or disinformation, designed to exacerbate American political and racial divisions and discredit the United States around the world. In the 1960s, the Soviets funded the publication of books by Western authors that blamed the CIA and FBI for the assassination of John F. Kennedy. They sent letters to the editors of American newspapers alleging that J. Edgar Hoover was a gay transvestite trying to secretly create a "network of like-minded homosexuals." After Martin Luther King Jr. declined to embrace communism, Soviet operatives distributed forged documents depicting King and his aides as "Uncle Toms" who were secretly working with President Johnson to disenfranchise African-Americans. After King was assassinated, the KGB promoted a conspiracy theory that the CIA had killed him.

During the 1970s, "Service A" hatched a plan, never carried out, to set off a bomb in a predominantly African-American neighborhood in New York and blame it on the militant Jewish Defense League. In the 1980s, the KGB helped promote the false theory that adding fluoride to water was a government plot to achieve population and mind control—a belief that still has adherents. Most famously, a KGB program known as "Operation Infektion" promote false stories that the US government was responsible for the creation of the AIDS virus.

In 2005, half of the African-Americans polled believed that the AIDS virus was created by humans in a lab; fifteen percent considered it a type of genocide aimed at the African-American community.

During the first months of the 2016 general election, producers of Russian propaganda appeared to be following the same strategy. They targeted African-Americans and other traditionally disenfranchised groups and urged them not to vote. They amplified the messages—and aided the candidacy—of Donald Trump, who was seen as unlikely to win. And they undermined Clinton. The initial pattern did not surprise Clapper or other senior US intelligence officials. Russian president Vladimir Putin was known to despise Clinton, who he believed had engineered widespread 2011 street protests following legislative elections that demonstrators accused Putin of rigging. Clapper told me that undermining Clinton's reputation inside and outside the United States in 2016 aided Putin at home and abroad. "By definition," Clapper said, "if it hurt Hillary Clinton, it helped him." Over the course of the summer, the Russian activities would intensify.

.　.　.

In the FBI, officials wrestled with how to respond to the Russian interference. Social media allowed Moscow to vastly expand the audience it could reach with propaganda, but it was unclear what impact, if any, the Russians could have on the race. Investigating the Russian interference and the Clinton email case was a political minefield. Whatever decision bureau leaders made, they could appear to be taking sides in the presidential race.

One of the worried FBI officials was James Baker—the Justice Department lawyer who had fought Dick Cheney's warrantless mass surveillance in 2003. In 2014, James Comey asked Baker to serve as the FBI's general counsel. Baker, who had spent several years in the private sector working for Verizon and the hedge fund Bridgewater, happily returned to government service. In 2016, scrutiny of the FBI's is handling of the Hillary Clinton email investigation and Russian election interference would taint the reputation he had carefully built in a quarter century of work at the Justice Department.

From the beginning of the Clinton email investigation, the bureau experienced political pressure regarding the case. Before Comey appeared in a September 2016 congressional hearing, Obama attorney general Loretta Lynch asked Comey to refer to the probe as a "matter," not as a criminal investigation. At the same time, Clinton and her aides obfuscated regarding the emails.

After a series of delays, FBI agents interviewed Clinton's lawyers about exactly how they had determined that half of the 62,320 emails that she sent or received as secretary of state were personal. They interviewed the contactor who deleted the personal emails. They questioned the attorneys who said they couldn't locate any of the thirteen BlackBerrys that Clinton had used with her private server. And they interviewed an assistant who said he had twice destroyed Clinton's old mobile phones by breaking them in half or smashing them with a hammer.

At the same time, Clinton's public explanations for her actions shifted, deepening the decades-old notions among many Americans that the Clinton family was not to be trusted. First, she claimed that she set up her own email for "convenience" because she preferred to carry one smartphone with one email address, rather than two devices. Later, she said that none of the emails on her private server were classified. Then she said that none of the emails on her private server were clearly marked classified.

Finally, days before Hillary Clinton's last interview with FBI agents, Bill Clinton boarded a government jet carrying Attorney General Lynch when their planes were both delayed in Phoenix. After news of the Phoenix meeting broke, Trump declared it an effort by Bill Clinton to pressure the FBI to go easy on Hillary. Democrats privately admitted that the meeting was a public relations debacle. Together, the Clintons had heightened public suspicion rather than eased it.

After consulting with Baker and other close aides, Comey called

Attorney General Lynch on the morning of July 5, 2016, and said he had decided to announce, on his own, the results of the bureau's yearlong investigation of Clinton's use of a private email server. When Lynch asked Comey what he planned to say, Comey declined to tell her. The announcement was an unprecedented step by an FBI director, who usually left prosecution decisions to Justice Department officials. In an impromptu press conference that morning, Comey announced that eight email chains on Clinton's private server were, in fact, top secret, but that the bureau would recommend that Clinton and three of her aides not face criminal charges. One hundred ten emails contained classified information, ranging from "top secret" to "confidential," a lower level of sensitivity. And the FBI had been unable to definitively determine if hostile actors had gained access to Clinton's email system.

In most criminal cases, law enforcement officials disclose no further information. In what Comey later said was an attempt to be evenhanded, he chastised Clinton, saying she had been "extremely careless" in her "handling of very sensitive, highly classified information." As he addressed the press, he added, "Any reasonable person in Secretary Clinton's position should have known that an unclassified system was no place for that conversation."

A review of similar cases, according to Comey, had revealed no examples of an official being criminally prosecuted. "All the cases prosecuted involved some combination of clearly intentional and willful mishandling of classified information; or vast quantities of materials exposed in such a way as to support an inference of intentional misconduct; or indications of disloyalty to the United States; or efforts to obstruct justice," Comey said. "We do not see those things here."

Taking no questions, Comey ended the press conference by asking the American public to trust the FBI as a fair, nonpartisan arbiter: "Only facts matter, and the FBI found them here in an entirely apolitical and professional way."

Comey, in fact, satisfied neither side.

Trump immediately condemned Comey's decision not to prosecute Clinton, tweeting that the process was "rigged" and falsely claimed that "General Petraeus got in trouble for far less. Very very unfair!" Petraeus's actions had, in fact, been worse than Clinton's. He had knowingly given classified information to a journalist with whom he was having an affair and then lied to FBI agents about it.

For the next two weeks, Trump hammered away at the theme of elite corruption. In his acceptance speech at the Republican National Convention in Cleveland, Trump continued his practice of undermining public faith in institutions to score political points. As he had since toying with running for president four years earlier, Trump distorted what had happened, stoking a narrative of outrage and calling Comey's decision proof of corruption at the highest levels of the US government. Following a technique he had honed since toying with running for president four years earlier, Trump exaggerated what had happened in the Clinton case, stoked a narrative of outrage, and called Comey's decision proof of corruption at the highest levels of the US government.

Baker, the FBI general counsel, saw Trump's attacks as perilous to the FBI. The bureau had spent forty years trying to move past the politically biased surveillance, intimidation, and abuse of the Hoover era. It had spent decades trying to be seen by the American public as an apolitical law enforcement organization. Now, Trump was declaring it part of a corrupt cabal.

.   .   .

On July 22, 2016, three days before Hillary Clinton accepted the Democratic Party nomination, WikiLeaks released nearly twenty thousand purloined DNC emails that showed senior DNC officials privately mocking Bernie Sanders during the primaries. The disclosure deeply divided Democrats and marred the convention. Five days later, Trump took a step that no major-party presidential candidate had in American history: he asked a longtime foreign adversary to attack his American political opponent. "Russia, if you're listening, I hope you're able to find the 30,000 emails that are missing," Trump said, referring to the personal emails that Clinton's team had deleted. "I think you will probably be rewarded mightily by our press." Trump then paused and said, "Let's see if that happens. That'll be next."

Trump later claimed he was joking. His announcement, whether he intended to collude with Russia or simply draw press coverage away from Clinton, alarmed American law enforcement and intelligence officials. When Clapper saw clips of Trump's remarks several hours later, he felt chills. In his four decades in the intelligence community, he had never seen an American politician ask for political help from a long-standing American rival.

In late July, Comey, Baker, and other senior FBI officials received a bizarre report from Britain. The Australian ambassador to the UK, Alexander Downer, told FBI agents there that a young Trump campaign aide, George Papadopoulos, had told him that Russian officials had "dirt" on Clinton, including "thousands of emails," and were willing to work together with Trump to defeat her. Three other Trump aides had also been in contact with Russians—Carter Page, Michael Flynn, and Paul Manafort. Alarmed by the Russian release of the hacked DNC emails and the outreach to Trump campaign advisors, Comey, Baker, and a handful of other senior FBI officials launched a counterintelligence investigation of Russian election interference on July 31, 2016. "We had an interest because it was a hostile foreign nation," Baker said in an interview. "The investigation was not about Trump. It was about Russia." The goal, according to Baker, was to understand Russia's intentions.

In August, Clapper held a series of secret meetings with senior national security officials that included Comey, Brennan, Lynch, Secretary of State John Kerry, Defense Secretary Ash Carter, and Department of Homeland Security Secretary Jeh Johnson. The group concluded that the Russian effort to disrupt the election was intensifying. Russian-backed hackers had probed state and local election sites in nearly half the country. Russian state-controlled media and online personas continued to amplify Trump's false claims about Clinton, but there was no clear evidence that Trump was cooperating with Russia.

There was disagreement among administration officials regarding how to respond to Moscow's campaign. Some of them worried that publicizing the Russian interference would enhance its impact. But Clapper and Johnson believed the public should know. Obama believed that a statement from Republican and Democratic congressional leaders warning about the Russian interference would be more credible than one from the administration alone.

Republicans, though, deeply distrusted Obama. They suspected that the administration's talk of Russian meddling was an effort by Obama and his aides to distract the public from the damaging content of the DNC emails. Denis McDonough, Obama's White House chief of staff, said that when he and other administration officials reached out to Republicans during the campaign, GOP officials dismissed the warnings of Russian interference as overblown or a political ploy to aid Clinton. "They are saying there is nothing to worry about," McDonough recalled. "This is recalled. This is partisan."

Obama ordered intelligence officials to conduct briefings for the four top Democrats and Republicans in Congress on the scope of the Russian election interference. Senate Minority Leader Harry Reid, House Speaker Paul Ryan, and House Minority Leader Nancy Pelosi quickly received the briefings, according to McDonough. Senate Majority Leader Mitch McConnell repeatedly said he did not have time to be briefed. When Clapper called McConnell to set up the briefing, he did not respond. McConnell finally received the briefing in early September.

Obama then met with McConnell, Ryan, Reid, and Pelosi in the Oval Office. Ryan had drafted a letter for the four leaders to sign that specifically mentioned the Russian interference. McConnell refused to sign, and told Obama, "You're politicizing intelligence, you stay out of our elections." According to McDonough, Obama implored McConnell to join the effort, saying that he hoped that America's partisan divisions had not devolved to the point where they could not agree on a joint effort to counter foreign influence in a presidential election.

After several tortured weeks of negotiations, the four leaders released a tepid joint letter on September 28. In a victory for McConnell, the letter stated that local officials, not federal ones, were responsible for safeguarding elections. It then warned vaguely of "malefactors" using cyberattacks to "disrupt the administration of our elections," and urged local election officials to "take full advantage" of the public and private sector resources available to help them secure their voting systems. Finally, in another clear win for McConnell, the letter stated that the four leaders opposed "any effort by the federal government to exercise any degree of control over the states' administration of elections." It made no mention of the evidence of the Russian effort to discredit Clinton and, most of all, undermine Americans' faith in their electoral system. At that point, US intelligence officials had not concluded that the Russian effort was designed to aid Trump. They had only determined that it was designed to hurt Clinton and undermine Americans' belief in the fairness of the election. After the election, the intelligence committee received new information that led them to conclude that the Russians also aided Trump.

McDonough said he had two theories regarding McConnell's motives. "One is he has hard-and-fast views on federalism and American elections," McDonough posited, referring to allowing local officials to oversee elections. The other is that "he is the singularly most cynical elected official in the United States of America." Two years later, when the *New York Times* asked McConnell about the criticism of his actions, he bristled. "Well, the Obama administration screwed up the election and then started pointing the finger at everybody else," he said. "They were trying to blame everybody else but themselves," he said again. "Ryan and I did what we thought was appropriate."

· · ·

In late October, twelve days before the election, Baker faced one of the most difficult decisions of his career. FBI agents had discovered thousands of work-related Clinton emails on the computer of Anthony Weiner, the estranged husband of Clinton aide Huma Abedin, while investigating whether Weiner had sent illicit texts to a fifteen-year-old girl. In order for the agents to determine if the laptop's contents could alter the bureau's decision to decline to prosecute Clinton, the FBI needed to obtain a search warrant. The FBI's New York field office appeared to have leaked the news to Trump surrogates. On October 26, former New York mayor Rudy Giuliani went on Fox News and said Trump had "a surprise or two that you're going to hear about in the next two days."

Comey asked Baker if he should inform congressional oversight committees that the bureau was reopening its Clinton investigation. The two men wrestled with the decision for hours. They knew that the 40-year-old oversight system created by the Church Committee was now completely politicized. If they informed members of Congress, Republicans would immediately leak the news in the hopes that it would aid Trump. They were sure that if the situation were reversed, the Democrats would do the same.

At the same time, the traditions established decades before by Edward Levi and William Webster mandated that the Justice Department and FBI demonstrate to Americans that they were politically neutral law enforcement organizations. A commonly understood Justice Department practice discouraged law enforcement officials from making public announcements regarding major criminal investigations 60 days prior to an election.

Baker said he felt like the "fates had thrown him a hundred-mile-an-hour fastball" as he wrestled with the problem in his mind. Baker had been told that between 600,000 and one million new emails had been found on Weiner's laptop. As a result, he believed it was likely that the FBI could find new evidence of wrongdoing by Clinton. As he weighed the decision, his thoughts kept returning to a nightmare scenario. "She wins the election, we go to DOJ, and we recommend that they indict her before she becomes president," Baker said, describing the scenario that haunted him. "That's not a good place for the country. That's not a good place for the FBI."

Baker feared that the credibility of the FBI and the US criminal justice system as a whole would be irreparably damaged if Comey did not inform Congress. "I thought 'what is best for the law enforcement and judicial system?'" he said. "It was better to speak than to not speak." He advised Comey to inform the committee chairs. "I said I thought the director had an obligation to notify Congress," Baker said. "Director Comey agreed with my advice."

On October 28, eleven days before the election, Comey sent confidential letters to the chairs and ranking members of the eight committees that had investigated Clinton's email use. Jason Chaffetz, the Republican chair of the House Oversight Committee, immediately leaked the confidential information. Just before 1 p.m., he tweeted, "FBI Dir just informed me, 'The FBI has learned of the existence of emails that appear to be pertinent to the investigation,' Case reopened." Fox News tweeted at 1:09 p.m., "BREAKING NEWS: @jasoninthehouse; @HillaryClinton email—'Case reopened.'"

Trump hailed the FBI and Justice Department, telling a rally in New Hampshire, "I have great respect for the fact that the FBI and the DOJ are now willing to have the courage to right the horrible mistake that they made."

Clinton's poll numbers immediately slumped. In the final week of the race, her lead in national polls dropped from 5.9 percent to 2.9 percent. In swing states, her lead declined from 4.5 to 1.7 percent. Comey issued a statement two days before the vote that no evidence of wrongdoing had been found. Only a few thousand of the 650,000 emails belonged to Abedin. Many of them were copies of messages that had already been reviewed by the bureau. In hindsight, Comey could have waited until the examination of the emails was completed before publicly reopening the case.

The pollster and pundit Nate Silver argued in a subsequent analysis that Comey's letter to Congress, and the intense media coverage of it, more than any other factor, likely swung the 2016 race to Trump. "The real story is that the Comey letter had a fairly large and measurable impact, probably enough to cost Clinton the election," Silver wrote.

Whatever Comey's intention, he had influenced the outcome of a presidential election in an unprecedented way. Chaffetz had weaponized congressional oversight in an unprecedented way. And Baker's effort to abide by the rule of law would spark an unprecedented assault on the FBI and its credibility.

Multiple factors, of course, led to Trump's win. In an era of spiraling income inequality, he sensed the deep economic frustrations of millions of Americans and promised easy solutions. He deftly played on Americans' historic distrust of Washington and the country's elite. He cynically played on racial and religious fears. Most of all, Trump lied and lied and lied. He lied about Clinton and Benghazi, about his own business achievements, and about the country's complex problems. Russia amplified those lies. In the last twelve days before the election, Trump cited emails stolen by Russia and distributed by WikiLeaks daily. Finally, he benefited from long-term trends in Congress.

Over a forty-year period, deepening partisan divisions had steadily eroded comity in the legislative branch. Since Watergate, congressional leaders had found a way to convey a modicum of bipartisanship regarding investigations involving major national security or constitutional issues. During the Church and Iran-Contra investigations, Senators Frank Church, John Tower, Daniel Inouye, and Warren Rudman found ways to present a façade of cooperation in Congress. That era was over.

TEN

The President-Elect
and the "Deep State"

L ike most observers, Comey and Baker were stunned by Trump's
win. Democrats blamed the FBI for reopening and then closing the investigation into Clinton. Baker was berated by friends
for the bureau's conduct. For the first time in American history, the
FBI had swayed a presidential election. "It's highly personal. Friends
are mad at you. Friends of mine who were Democrats," he said. "People said 'I trusted you guys but you made the wrong decision.'" Baker
stood by their decision to notify Congress. Personally, he attributed
Trump's win to the economic frustrations of average Americans. "If
the system is not generating the blessings of liberty for our people, then
people are not going to be happy about it," Baker explained. "Capital-
ism is not working as it should be."

Career Justice Department officials privately criticized Comey and
Baker's decision to inform Congress of the discovery of the additional
Clinton emails. They said that the decision-making process within
the FBI was too insular. If the FBI leaders had consulted a broader
circle of people, they would likely have been told that software existed
that could determine within days, not weeks, whether the emails
were, in fact, new. Earlier in the probe, investigators had discovered
thousands of copies of Clinton-related emails on other devices. The
discovery of the emails on Weiner's computer fit a past pattern. It was
not unprecedented.

Comey and Baker decided that the best path forward for the bureau was for Comey to try to establish a personal relationship with Trump. They hoped that explaining the myriad post-Watergate rules and norms that governed the actions of the FBI could be a starting point. "I talked with Jim Comey about trying to help the president," Baker said. "The president was not a politician with a lot of experience."

But Comey and Baker were taking an enormous risk. At that point, Trump and the American public did not know that the FBI was still secretly investigating contacts between Russian operatives and Trump campaign officials. Whenever Trump learned of the probe, he would be furious. Democrats would be as well. The FBI had applied inconsistent standards in 2016. It had kept the FBI's Trump-Russia investigation secret and followed the Justice Department practice of making no announcements regarding criminal investigations during the final stage of a campaign. Yet Comey had publicly criticized Clinton in July and disclosed the reopening of the Clinton investigation days before the vote. Baker acknowledged that the FBI's decision-making inadvertently aided Trump and hurt Clinton. But he said that each decision was guided by what he and Comey believed was the best way to uphold the rule of law and maintain the credibility of the FBI. "We acted pursuant to the rule of law," Baker said.

. . .

Clapper and other senior American intelligence officials were surprised by Trump's win as well. When news organizations declared Trump president-elect, Clapper was in Oman meeting with foreign officials. He was surprised by the result, but he blamed himself, in part, for being ensconced in Washington and misunderstanding public sentiment in large parts of the country. "I was disturbed at myself for not understanding the undercurrents in my own country," he said. "I missed it completely."

As the senior representative of the intelligence community, Clapper also tried to build a relationship with the president-elect. The day after the election, intelligence officials gave Trump his first, full President's Daily Brief in Trump Tower and delivered a handwritten congratulatory letter from Clapper. In his note, Clapper promised that the intelligence community would give the president-elect "the best intelligence we can muster." "We will rarely be able to eliminate uncertainty for you and the Vice President," Clapper warned, "but we can at least reduce it, and thus help you manage risk in the face of the many difficult decisions you will undoubtedly face." Clapper then described what he saw as the mission of America's intelligence agencies: "Finally, I hope you will support the basic writ of 'truth to power' in which the Intelligence Community is expected to always 'tell it like it is'—straight, objective, unpoliticized." Clapper had pre-written a similar note to Clinton, in case she had won. As planned, aides shredded the note to Clinton.

After Clapper returned to Washington, he received reports from the FBI and CIA that they were discovering additional evidence of Russian interference. The breadth of what had occurred was greater than what Clapper and other national security officials had been aware of prior to the election. The fact that the Russians interfered was no surprise to Clapper. The difference was how technological change had allowed them to reach far larger numbers of Americans. "The big difference, the big enabler was social media," he said. "Not to mention hacking emails."

Clapper defended the way the Obama administration had handled the election. He said that if Obama had made a televised speech warning Americans of Russian interference in the election, it would have played into Trump's narrative that the election was rigged in Clinton's favor. "Obama, I think, was appropriately concerned about putting his hand on the scale," Clapper said. "If he made a prime-time address about what the Russians were doing it would be considered politicizing it."

Clapper remained surprised at the unwillingness of Republicans, particularly McConnell, to take the Russian meddling more seriously.

"All the previous dealings I had with McConnell, I thought he was a patriot, he cared about the country," Clapper said. "But for whatever reason we were on two different planets when it came to this Russia deal."

Trump adopted the most bellicose position. He dismissed talk of Russian interference as an attempt to undermine the legitimacy of his victory. In a November 28 interview with *Time* magazine, he said, "I don't believe they interfered. That became a laughing point, not a talking point, a laughing point." Asked about the hacking of Democratic Party emails, Trump scoffed, "It could be Russia. And it could be China. And it could be some guy in his home in New Jersey."

At a National Security Council meeting on December 5, Obama asked Clapper and the heads of the CIA, FBI, and NSA to combine their findings into a single report that could be delivered to the new administration and Congress. The deadline was an effort by Obama to ensure that evidence of interference was made public before he left the White House. Clapper, Brennan, Comey, and Admiral Mike Rogers, the director of the National Security Agency, assembled a group of thirty experts from their agencies to prepare a joint report on the Russian interference. Brennan provided them with office space at the CIA.

Four days later, the *Washington Post* broke the story that the CIA had concluded that Russia intervened in the 2016 election to help Trump win the presidency, not simply to undermine the credibility of the vote. "It is the assessment of the intelligence community that Russia's goal here was to favor one candidate over the other, to help Trump get elected," a senior US official, briefed on an intelligence presentation made to US senators, told the *Post*. "That's the consensus view."

Republicans saw the leak of the CIA's finding as an effort by Obama administration intelligence officials to undermine the legitimacy of Trump's victory. Even GOP moderates who were skeptical of Trump questioned the accuracy of the CIA assessment. Privately, they questioned the evidence that Putin himself ordered the operation, and worried that intelligence was being politicized.

As usual, Trump and his closest supporters were more aggressive. Trump's transition team issued a blistering statement that mocked the intelligence community and made an exaggerated claim about the scale of Trump's electoral college victory. "These are the same people that said Saddam Hussein had weapons of mass destruction," the statement read. "The election ended a long time ago in one of the biggest Electoral College victories in history. It's now time to move on and 'Make America Great Again.'" Devin Nunes, the Republican chairman of the House Intelligence Committee and a member of Trump's transition team, dismissed the findings as well. "I'll be the first one to come out and point at Russia if there's clear evidence, but there is no clear evidence—even now," said Nunes. "There's a lot of innuendo, lots of circumstantial evidence, that's it."

.   .   .

Three days later, on December 12, an anonymous columnist who used the pen name "Virgil" published the 4,000-word Breitbart polemic that introduced his concept of the American "deep state" to a broad audience of US conservatives. Peter Dale Scott—the author of the 2007 book *The Road to 9/11*—had defined the "deep state" as the military-industrial complex when he appeared on Alex Jones's far-right conspiratorial program *Infowars*. "Virgil" defined the American "deep state" as something far broader, consisting of the "military-industrial complex," the "establishment" and employees, political supporters, and beneficiaries of ever-growing federal, state, and local government spending. "The term 'Deep State' refers to the complex of bureaucrats, technocrats, and plutocrats that likes things just the way they are and wants to keep them like that—elections be damned," wrote Virgil.

Virgil dismissed the *Post*'s story on the CIA assessment regarding Russian interference as the first of numerous efforts to attack Trump by Democrats, intelligence agencies, and the mainstream media. "Wily in the ways of Washington, the anti-Trumpers are operating behind the scenes, using their well-greased legal and political machinery to block the President-elect, or at least to discredit and de-legitimize him," Virgil wrote. "And as a part of that backroom effort, the MSM is always ready with a supportive, momentum-building headline or two—or two thousand."

Virgil argued that the Obama administration had installed "liberal apparatchiks" across the federal government "even in entities that might be thought of as being on the right, such as the military and other organizations dedicated to national security." The intelligence community had been "highly politicized" under Obama, according to Virgil. All told, "liberal Democrats have controlled the executive branch for 16 of the last 24 years, and so there's been plenty of time to cultivate liberals—even liberal activists—within the ranks and to bring them to the pinnacles of bureaucratic power." (Virgil's choice of time frame was selective. From Reagan to Obama, for example, Republican presidents controlled the federal government for 20 of 36 years.) He concluded by declaring that "a great power struggle is under way: the Deep State vs. Trump." Virgil's polemic was a conspiracy-riddled analysis of American politics. But this narrative of the "deep state" was about to become central to Trump's presidency. Trump himself would soon realize its power and champion it.

. . .

Trump's candidacy and attacks divided military, intelligence, and diplomats in a way that hadn't happened in decades. Post-Watergate, all three groups had generally strived to remain politically neutral. The political activities of some retired intelligence and military officials and diplomats in 2016, though, made the "deep state" narrative more plausible. The hyper-partisanship of the race—stoked by Trump more than any other individual—infected the community of retired national security officials. Fifty former national security officials who had served Republican presidents from Nixon to Bush, including Michael Hayden, a former CIA and NSA director, and John Negroponte, the country's first-ever director of national intelligence, signed a letter that August stating that Trump lacked "the character, values and experience" to be president, and warning that if elected, "he would be the most reckless President in American history."

Michael Morell, the CIA deputy director embroiled in the Benghazi scandal, endorsed Hillary Clinton in an op-ed in the *New York Times*. Michael Flynn, a retired army general and Trump advisor, led chants of "lock her up" at the Republican National Convention. At the Democratic National Convention, another retired general, John Allen, hailed Hillary Clinton in a speech. Two former chairmen of the Joint Chiefs of Staff, Michael Mullen and Martin Dempsey, criticized both Flynn and Allen. "For retired senior officers to take leading and vocal roles as clearly partisan figures is a violation of the ethos and professionalism of apolitical military service," Mullen told the *Post*. "This is not about the right to speak out, it is about the disappointing lack of judgment in doing so for crass partisan purposes. This is made worse by using hyperbolic language all the while leveraging the respected title of 'general.'"

Flynn was one of Trump's most bombastic advisors. The retired military officer contended that Clapper and Brennan were highly politicized spy chiefs. Clapper and Brennan both denied it. In 2014, Clapper and Undersecretary of Defense for Intelligence Michael Vickers had forced Flynn out of his position as the head of the Defense Intelligence Agency (DIA), cutting short a once promising career. Before his ouster, Flynn was widely viewed as one of the most respected military intelligence officers of his generation. Working with General Stanley McChrystal, Flynn had developed a strategy of using night raids by American Special Operations Forces to decimate insurgent groups in Iraq and Afghanistan. Human rights groups said the raids killed large numbers of civilians.

Flynn alienated DIA employees, according to Clapper, when he requested that civilian DIA workers behave like uniformed members of the military. Stories then leaked to the press that Flynn was using intelligence analysts to chase down conspiracy theories, which employees derisively referred to as "Flynn Facts." Flynn also publicly criticized Obama's policy decisions and said the president should refer to terrorists as "Islamic extremists," a step opposed by an administration that believed such terminology alienated Muslims who had joined the United States in battling terrorism.

In a blistering 2016 interview with the *New York Times*, Flynn said that the CIA had become a political arm of the Obama White House. "They've lost sight of who they actually work for," Flynn said, referring to the agency. "They work for the American people. They don't work for the president of the United States." He added, speaking of the agency's leadership: "Frankly, it's become a very political organization." Flynn accused the agency of downplaying the strength of ISIS, Al Qaeda, and the Taliban in order to help Obama achieve his political goals. He also said the CIA had blocked the DIA from examining the documents found in Osama bin Laden's compound because these showed that Al Qaeda remained far stronger than the administration maintained. When Flynn served in Afghanistan in 2009, he issued a paper that was a blistering critique of the work of the nearly 1,000 CIA personnel at work in the country.

"They've really been lying to the American public," he said in the interview, referring to the Obama administration and much of the national security and intelligence establishment. "The Department of Defense and those of us that have allowed this sort of a happy talk— 'We're moving in the right direction, things are working.' It's not. The Taliban are going to come back into power, or ISIS is going to come back into power."

Trump's disdain for the CIA seemed to echo Flynn's views. In the eyes of Flynn and other Trump supporters, a pattern had emerged under Obama, who they viewed as an authoritarian president. Flynn was ousted after publicly questioning Obama's approach to counterterrorism. McChrystal was ousted after he and his aides made disparaging comments about the Obama White House in a *Rolling Stone* interview. Petraeus was ousted after sharing classified information with a retired military officer with whom he was having an affair. Flynn, in particular, was dismayed that the Justice Department and FBI had charged Petraeus, but not Clinton, with mishandling classified information.

Comey argued that Clinton had not intended to mishandle classified information, while Petraeus made a conscious decision to share classified information with his biographer and lied to federal investigators about it. Obama administration officials said that Flynn was removed because of his poor management skills and that his claims were exaggerated and conspiratorial.

After Flynn retired from the military in 2014, he declared the American judicial system "corrupt," called Obama a "liar," and said he was forced out of DIA because of his views on radical Islam. In 2015, Flynn sat next to Vladimir Putin at an RT television anniversary dinner in Moscow. He received a $33,750 speaking fee for attending the event.

. . .

Ten days after winning the election, Trump named Flynn as his national security advisor. In his announcement, the president-elect took a shot at Obama and his intelligence chiefs. "I am pleased that Lieutenant General Michael Flynn will be by my side as we work to defeat radical Islamic terrorism," Trump said, using the term Flynn had urged Obama to adopt. Flynn's appointment was seen as a signal that the new administration would be more aggressive in countering terrorism. In Washington, Flynn's actions before and after Trump took office sparked renewed fears at the FBI of cooperation between the Trump campaign and Russian officials.

On December 29, Obama expelled 35 Russian spies, closed two Russian diplomatic properties, and placed new sanctions on Moscow in retaliation for Russia's election interference. American officials expected Putin to immediately expel a comparable number of Americans from Russia, as had often occurred during the Cold War. "We expected retaliation," Clapper said. Instead, Putin expelled no Americans, invited the children of US diplomats to Christmas parties in the Kremlin, and offered season's greetings to "President Obama and his family" and to "President-elect Donald Trump and the American people." Trump praised Putin's response, tweeting, "Great move on delay (by V. Putin)—I always knew he was very smart."

Putin's muted reaction fueled suspicion in government circles. "The logical question is 'what's going on here?'" Clapper recalled. White House, FBI, and State Department officials began looking for reasons why the Russian leader had displayed such restraint. They eventually focused on a series of phone calls between Flynn and the Russian ambassador to the United States, Sergei Kislyak. Immediately after Obama announced the expulsions and sanctions, Kislyak had called Flynn, who was vacationing with his wife in the Dominican Republic. American intelligence agencies, following standard protocol, monitored all of Kislyak's phone calls and texts. Flynn, as a former intelligence officer, should have known that their conversation would be recorded. Flynn asked Kislyak to refrain from escalating the situation, and the ambassador eventually agreed. Flynn's actions had violated a long-accepted political norm that a president-elect and his aides not act as government representatives until they have assumed office. "There was a general concern about violating the principle of having one president at a time," Clapper said.

In early January, reports circulated that the intelligence community was on the verge of completing its report on the Russian campaign interference. Pushing to control the narrative, Trump tried to discredit the report before its release. On Tuesday, January 3, Trump falsely claimed that his own briefing on the report had been delayed a day, tweeting, "The 'intelligence' briefing on so-called 'Russian hacking' was delayed until Friday, perhaps more time needed to build a case. Very strange!" (According to Clapper, the intelligence officials needed to brief President Obama first.) On Wednesday, January 4, Trump tweeted, "Julian

Assange said 'a 14 year old could have hacked Podesta'—why was DNC so careless? Also said Russians did not give him the info!"

The following day, Clapper, Comey, Brennan, and Rogers arrived in the White House to brief Obama, who had already received a copy of the report. The full report remained classified, but Clapper intentionally made the "key judgments" section identical in both the top secret version and the one released to the public. The report concluded that Putin had personally ordered the Russian interference campaign to "undermine public faith in the US democratic process, denigrate Secretary Clinton, and harm her electability and potential presidency," and that, as Trump emerged as a viable candidate, "Putin and the Russian Government developed a clear preference for President-elect Trump."

The next day, Clapper, Comey, Brennan, and Rogers briefed the Gang of Eight on Capitol Hill on the report. Republican House Speaker Paul Ryan and Republican Senate Intelligence Committee chair Richard Burr asked questions, but McConnell was quiet. "He was very dour. He didn't ask any questions," Clapper recalled. "Ryan asked a couple questions. Richard Burr, he asked a couple questions and evinced that he was interested. Senator McConnell not so much."

They then flew to New York to brief Trump on its findings. Entering Trump Tower through a side residential entrance, the four intelligence chiefs were brought to a fourteenth-floor conference room that the Secret Service had secured. The building bustled with people. "It was chaos," Clapper recalled. "People running around in the halls."

After waiting for ten minutes, Trump arrived, with Vice President–elect Pence, future White House chief of staff Reince Priebus, and several other senior members of his interim national security team. Clapper shook hands with the president-elect and introduced himself. "I know who you are," Trump replied. Trump told him that he had done "a great job" in a recent hearing, adding that "you looked good on TV." Trump also thanked Clapper for the letter he had sent with Trump's first-ever President's Daily Brief. He was friendly toward

Brennan, Comey, and Rogers, introducing them to his aides. Clapper was relieved. "In a setting like that, he is pretty charismatic. He is tall, six-foot three. He was clearly turning on the charm for us," Clapper said. "We had no idea how he was going to behave after that tweet. Was he going to throw us out of the room? Was he going to listen to us? It was actually a fairly professional encounter."

Trump and Pence sat down at the opposite ends of a conference table with eight chairs. Clapper sat to Trump's left, with Brennan beside him. Rogers and Comey took the two seats across from them. Flynn and Priebus took the two remaining seats. Pompeo, Trump's nominee for CIA director, K. T. McFarland, Trump's deputy national security advisor designate, and Tom Bossert, his Homeland Security advisor designate, took seats along the wall.

As planned, the intelligence chiefs made the same presentation they had earlier in the day, but it was more relaxed and conversational, according to Clapper. They explained terms and procedures that they thought Trump and his aides might not know. Trump and Pence both politely asked questions. Trump appeared to take the report seriously. He asked questions about some of the evidence and conclusions, and seemed satisfied with the officials' answers. Pence, in particular, impressed Clapper. "Pence was pretty good," Clapper said. "He seemed like a sane, moderate force."

The meeting lasted ninety minutes, thirty more than planned. Trump and his aides appeared visibly relieved when the officials said the intelligence community's assessment was that the Russians had been unable to change vote totals. Trump's team then asked if the Russian effort had changed the outcome of the election. Clapper said that US intelligence agencies didn't have the authority or the capability to determine what impact, if any, the Russian operation had on the outcome, citing laws barring them from spying inside the United States.

To Clapper's surprise, Priebus began drafting a press statement from the Trump team in front of the intelligence chiefs. Speaking out loud and writing on a pad of paper, Priebus said that US intelligence agencies had concluded that the Russian interference did not change the outcome of the election. Clapper, concerned, pointed out that the intelligence community had not reached a conclusion on whether or not the Russian campaign changed the outcome. "It's a very important nuance," Clapper told me, saying that he corrected Priebus on the point "at least once."

Following a previously agreed-upon plan, Clapper and Rogers left Trump Tower and headed back to Washington. Comey remained in the conference room to privately brief Trump on the "dossier": a thirty-five-page compilation of what Clapper called unverified "pseudo intelligence" compiled by a former British spy and a Washington-based opposition research firm, Fusion GPS. The intelligence community had not been able to confirm the contents of the dossier—which had been funded by the Clinton campaign—but Comey felt that they had a duty to warn the president-elect that it existed. Following a plan he and Clapper had discussed, Comey wanted to explain to Trump how Russian intelligence officials might use compromising information— or the specter of it—as a tool to try and pressure Trump. "Jim felt strongly that he needed to try and educate Trump about the way the Russians would operate. It wasn't whether the dossier was valid or not," Clapper said. "If they don't have leverage, they will try to create leverage. That was a big part of what Jim wanted to convey."

Dozens of reporters and at least two members of Congress already knew of the dossier, which Fusion GPS had been widely sharing for months. In late 2015, the Washington Free Beacon, a conservative news site funded by the billionaire Paul Singer, had hired Fusion GPS to conduct opposition research on Trump and other Republican candidates. In April 2016, Marc Elias, the general counsel for the Clinton campaign and a lawyer for the Democratic National Committee, hired Fusion GPS to continue its opposition research on Trump. In June 2016, Fusion GPS hired Christopher Steele, the former British spy, who began receiving uncorroborated reports from sources inside Russia of collusion between the Trump campaign and Russian officials.

As Fusion GPS received the reports, they shared them with multiple journalists, including me and my colleagues at Reuters. In late November, several weeks after the election, a retired British diplomat gave Senator John McCain a full copy of the dossier. On December 9, McCain gave a copy of the dossier to Comey. Concerned that a news organization would soon publish the dossier, Comey decided it was better to inform Trump about it in a private one-on-one briefing. When Comey summarized the dossier's contents to Trump in New York, Trump said its allegations were absolutely false.

After Comey met alone with Trump, the FBI director departed and Trump's staff issued a statement from the president-elect. "I had a constructive meeting and conversation with the leaders of the Intelligence Community this afternoon," the statement said. "I have tremendous respect for the work and service done by the men and women of this community to our great nation." Trump then added that cyberattacks had "absolutely no effect on the outcome of the election." Looking back, Clapper told me that Priebus's drafting of the press release in front of the intelligence chiefs fit a pattern. "The way they all struck me was no exposure, or outright ignorance, about the way things work in government," Clapper said. "It wasn't malicious, it was born out of ignorance."

.   .   .

During the summer and fall of 2016, while working as an investigative reporter and editor for Reuters, I was one of the dozens of reporters who tried to verify the contents of the dossier. Like many journalists, I met with Glenn Simpson, a co-founder of Fusion GPS. At a July 2016 gathering of national security experts in Aspen, Colorado, I asked John Carlin, then the head of the Justice Department's National Security Division, if he could confirm the Carter Page allegations. Carlin declined to comment on them. In an October 2016 interview in the director's office at CIA headquarters, I asked CIA Director John Brennan if he could confirm any of the contents of the dossier, including that the Russians had a compromising videotape of Trump. Brennan appeared surprised. He then repeatedly said that he would not comment on them in any way. On the record or off the record, Brennan declined to confirm or deny the allegations in the dossier. He also urged me to be very cautious in my reporting. Brennan predicted that I would likely hear numerous rumors and allegations regarding both Trump and Clinton in the final weeks of the campaign. Unless I could thoroughly verify the allegations against either candidate, Brennan urged me to not report them. Unable to corroborate the dossier's claims, Reuters, like the vast majority of news organizations, did not report any of its contents. After Trump's surprise win, we tried to verify its claims again but were unable to do so.

Four days after Comey's January 6 meeting with Trump, CNN published a report on the dossier and BuzzFeed quickly published thirty-five pages of it, saying it made "explosive—but unverified—allegations that the Russian government has been 'cultivating, supporting and assisting' President-elect Donald Trump for years and gained compromising information about him." BuzzFeed maintained that the dossier had been circulating among "elected officials, intelligence agents, and journalists for weeks" and described "unverified, and potentially unverifiable" allegations of contacts between Trump aides and Russian operatives, and "graphic claims of sexual acts documented by the Russians," including that Trump had the prostitutes urinate on one another on the bed in the Moscow hotel where Barack and Michelle Obama had slept.

The following day, Trump tweeted, "Intelligence agencies should never have allowed this fake news to 'leak' into the public. One last shot at me. Are we living in Nazi Germany?" Former government officials complained that Trump was comparing US intelligence officials to Nazis. Jewish groups said that the analogy was false, offensive, and denigrating to Holocaust survivors. Trump declined to back down. At a news conference, he again criticized the intelligence agencies for failing to stop news organizations from publishing the dossier, a power that they, in fact, did not have. "I think it's a disgrace, and I say that—and I say that, and that's something that Nazi Germany would have done and did do."

. . .

Trump's relationship with the FBI and CIA was off to a disastrous start. No president-elect had clashed so openly and bitterly with intelligence officials in the decades since the Church reforms. Intelligence officials felt that the president-elect mocked them publicly and undermined the American people's trust in their work. Privately, they feared that Trump was working with Putin. Trump, in turn, saw the intelligence community as a political arm of the Obama administration that was unabashedly working to undermine the legitimacy of his election. In his public statements, Trump echoed the views of Flynn and Nunes that the agencies pretended to be neutral but were, in fact, Obama's minions. The calamitous start fueled concerns about national security. If the new president and his intelligence chiefs could not agree on basic facts, agreeing on policies could prove chaotic. As Trump prepared to take office, his presidency represented the gravest threat to the standing of the intelligence community of any presidency since Nixon.

Michael Morell, the former deputy CIA director who had backed Hillary Clinton, said in an interview that he believed that the intelligence community made mistakes in their initial interactions with Trump, both when he was a candidate and as president-elect. Morell now regretted endorsing Clinton's candidacy. His *New York Times* op-ed piece—"I Ran the C.I.A. Now I'm Endorsing Hillary Clinton."—reinforced Trump's view of the CIA as a highly political organization, not a neutral arbiter of intelligence. An intermediary told Morell that his endorsement of Clinton infuriated Trump. "It's important to look at this from Trump's perspective," Morell said. "I think during the campaign Trump perceived that the intelligence community was a political animal. He's a political animal and therefore he saw everyone else as one too, and this tendency on his part was reinforced by the comments of former senior IC officers."

Morell said that he was not excusing Trump's smears of the CIA and FBI and his false claims. As a candidate and as president-elect, Trump had insulted and disparaged intelligence leaders to a greater extent than any modern president. But Morell contended that it was important to recognize that he and other former intelligence officials made a mistake by violating Church-era norms and engaging in partisan attacks on Trump. Taking the bait and responding in kind to Trump's insults inadvertently aided Trump, weakened public trust in the FBI and CIA, and abetted the growth of hyper-partisanship. "He saw Michael Hayden take out a scalpel and just slice and dice him and his foreign policy and worldview," Morell said. "He saw me, a former deputy director and acting director, endorse his opponent and say he was an unwitting agent of Russia." Morell believed that Clapper and Comey's decision to brief Trump on the Russian election interference findings and the dossier was well intentioned, but that those actions also reinforced Trump's view of the intelligence community as a threat. "He sees former intelligence and law enforcement officials criticizing him," Morell said. "I'm sure it has added to his view of the 'deep state.'"

ELEVEN

The Transfer of Power

On January 20, 2017, Trump took the oath of office and delivered one of the most ominous inaugural addresses in American history. He began the speech with a declaration and a warning. "Today we are not merely transferring power from one administration to another, or from one party to another," Trump said. "But we are transferring power from Washington, DC, and giving it back to you, the American People."

As he had throughout his campaign, Trump laid out an enthralling narrative to the Americans who had voted for him. Its themes were grievance, corruption, and inequity. Its heroes were average Americans. Its villains were the members of the Washington elite. "For too long, a small group in our nation's Capital has reaped the rewards of government while the people have borne the cost. Washington flourished—but the people did not share in its wealth. Politicians prospered—but the jobs left, and the factories closed," Trump said. "The establishment protected itself, but not the citizens of our country. Their victories have not been your victories; their triumphs have not been your triumphs; and while they celebrated in our nation's Capital, there was little to celebrate for struggling families all across our land."

The harsh rhetoric of the address, written by Steve Bannon and Stephen Miller, surprised analysts but fit the themes of Trump's campaign: embattled Americans being cheated out of their just rewards. Trump did not use the term "deep state," but his message was clear: he would expose the Washington cabal defying the will of the American people. "That all changes—starting right here, and right now, because this moment is your moment: it belongs to you," he said. "January 20th, 2017, will be remembered as the day the people became the rulers of this nation again."

Reactions were deeply divided across cable news and social media. On Fox News, the new president was praised for boldly declaring, "this American carnage stops right here and stops right now." On MSNBC and CNN, these same words were cited as Trump stoking grievance and fear and exaggerating the country's ills for political gain. Twitter and other social media served largely as echo chambers, reinforcing each side of the political divide.

The next morning, Trump visited the CIA headquarters in Langley, Virginia. Observers expected him to make a speech reassuring the intelligence community that he fully supported it. Trump's nominee for CIA director, Mike Pompeo, the Kansas Republican who had attacked Clinton during the Benghazi hearings, was sailing through the confirmation process.

Instead, standing in front of a wall of stars representing the 117 agents who had died serving their country, Trump delivered a rambling, fifteen-minute, stream-of-consciousness speech unlike any address ever given to the CIA by an American president. After thanking agency employees for their work, Trump claimed that the vast majority of members of the military and intelligence communities had voted for him in the 2016 election. "We were unbelievably successful in the election with getting the vote of the military," Trump said. "And probably almost everybody in this room voted for me, but I will not ask you to raise your hands if you did." (Preelection polls showed that members of the military had supported Trump over Clinton by a two-to-one margin. No such poll existed for the CIA.)

Trump then blamed the news media, not himself, for any tensions he had with the intelligence community, ignoring the fact that, ten days earlier, he had falsely accused US intelligence officials of leaking the Steele dossier and compared them to Nazis. "I have a running war with the media," Trump said, sparking laughter from some in the audience. "They are among the most dishonest human beings on earth. Right? And they sort of made it sound like I have this feud with the intelligence community."

Trump lauded his own intelligence, joked that the United States should seize Iraq's oil, and hinted that he might again allow the CIA to torture detainees. He exaggerated the size of the crowd at his inauguration. (Trump claimed that his inauguration drew 1.5 million people, almost three times the most common estimate of between 300,000 and 600,000 people.) He falsely claimed that he had set an "all-time record" for *Time* magazine cover stories. (*Time* later said the record for cover stories was held by Richard Nixon, who had fifty-five.)

Some of the four hundred CIA employees who voluntarily attended the speech on a Saturday afternoon applauded Trump's remarks; his promise to stop being "restrained" in the fight against ISIS was welcomed by members of the agency's clandestine service. In an echo of the Carter administration, the Directorate of Operations felt hamstrung by what they saw as a micromanaging and risk-avoidant Obama White House. Former agency officials said John Brennan, Obama's outgoing director, was very controlling, and engaged in "a lot of 'mother may I.'" Trump promised to end that.

And yet for older CIA and military veterans, Trump's boast that he had received the overwhelming majority of votes cast by American soldiers and intelligence officers was shocking. To have a sitting president suggest the American military and intelligence community was more loyal to him than to another political leader was unprecedented. For decades, intelligence and military leaders had strived to build organizational cultures that centered on apolitical service to a duly-elected president, regardless of party. The long-running tradition dates back to James Madison and other Founding Fathers, who feared the armed forces taking sides in a political dispute or carrying out a coup. (At one point near the end of the Revolutionary War, Continental soldiers who had not been paid threatened to revolt.) Some American military officers embrace the apolitical role so fervently that they decline to vote in elections. Privately, many disdain politics and politicians. They embrace loyalty to their fellow service members far more than fealty to a political party.

In the CIA, intelligence officers have a long tradition of distrusting politicians. A cynical lot, spies often joke that they are a president's best friends when the commander-in-chief needs a foreign threat addressed quietly. When things go wrong, though, the historical pattern is clear. From the Bay of Pigs to Iraq WMDs, politicians scapegoat the agency. The Church reforms and the restrictions that they imposed—in some ways—protected the CIA. They laid out clear guidelines for how intelligence gathering could be carried out without CIA officials fearing being abruptly fired, publicly humiliated in congressional hearings, or, potentially, prosecuted for breaking the law. Joan Dempsey, the Arkansas native who rose to be the number-three official at the CIA, said in an interview that officers came to grudgingly appreciate the system because it protected both the agency and officers. "There is great potential for corruption," she said, referring to the spy agency's vast powers. "But a lot of the safeguards that have been put in place are not that easy to undermine."

Again, the reaction to Trump's visit to the CIA cut along ideological lines. Commentators on Fox News praised the speech. Pundits on MSNBC and CNN mocked it. Twitter filled with pro-Trump boosterism and anti-Trump barbs. Such diametrically opposed reactions were nothing new in 2017. What was unusual was a tweet that appeared that afternoon. Two days after leaving office, former CIA director John Brennan had a spokesman post a blistering statement about Trump's speech. "Former CIA Dir Brennan is deeply saddened and angered at Trump's despicable display of self-aggrandizement in front of CIA's Memorial Wall of Agency heroes," the statement read. "Brennan says that Trump should be ashamed of himself." He was not alone. Michael Hayden, the former NSA and CIA director, told NBC News, "I was heartened that the President gave a speech at CIA. It would have been even better if more of it had been about CIA."

Less than a week into Trump's presidency, former senior intelligence officials were voluntarily breaching a norm of their own. Since the founding of the CIA, former agency directors had largely refrained from publicly attacking politicians, particularly presidents. "It creates a perception in the public that the intelligence community is political," Morell, the former deputy director, said. "You're already a secret organization operating in a democracy," he added. "You lose the American people. Or at least half of them."

TWELVE

Loyalty

A week after his inauguration, Trump called Comey on January 27 and invited him to dinner that evening in the White House. The dinner was the first in a series of meetings where Trump, according to Comey, pressured him to limit FBI investigations of Flynn and other Trump loyalists.

Comey arrived at the White House assuming he was attending a group dinner with Trump. In order to avoid the perception that the president was using the FBI for political purposes, FBI directors had avoided dining alone with a president since the days of J. Edgar Hoover doing so with Nixon. Comey was surprised and concerned to see that he would be dining alone with Trump. During the dinner, according to Comey, Trump repeatedly asked him if he wanted to stay on as director of the FBI. Comey believed that Trump was trying to create a patronage relationship by forcing Comey to ask to keep his job. Later in the dinner, Trump told Comey, "I need loyalty, I expect loyalty." Comey changed the subject, but Trump brought it up again as the dinner came to a conclusion, saying for a second time, "I need loyalty." Comey replied, "You will always get honesty from me."

"That's what I want, honest loyalty," Trump said.

Comey assured him, "You will get that from me." Soon after, the dinner ended.

Comey left the White House convinced that Trump did not understand that the bureau had spent forty years trying to distance itself from the abuses unearthed by the Church Committee and the perception that the FBI was a tool for the president to attack his political enemies. That night, the FBI director wrote a memo memorializing his conversation with Trump, something he had not done after sessions with other presidents or senior FBI officials.

Three days before Comey had dinner with Trump, Flynn's behavior had again alarmed FBI officials. In a January 24 interview, Flynn lied to FBI agents, saying that he did not ask Kislyak to refrain from escalating the situation after the Obama administration expelled Russian spies and imposed sanctions on Moscow. Flynn also falsely stated that he did not remember a follow-up conversation where Kislyak said that Russia would limit its response as Flynn had requested. Flynn had lied to Spicer, the White House spokesman, Vice President Mike Pence, and other officials, about the content of the calls as well.

On January 26, Deputy Attorney General Sally Yates and Mary McCord, a senior Justice Department official, visited the White House and took the unusual step of informing White House Counsel Don McGahn that Flynn had lied to Pence and Spicer. Yates warned that Flynn's continued false statements made him vulnerable to blackmail by Russian officials, who could threaten to reveal that Flynn had misled the vice president. It was an extraordinary moment. The White House national security advisor—the senior-most official charged with protecting the country—was vulnerable to Russian blackmail. The Justice Department was performing exactly as it should have. Yates and McCord were sharing damaging information with the president, not shielding him from it. McGahn reviewed Flynn's behavior and concluded that no laws had been broken. Priebus and other staffers, though, believed Flynn could no longer be trusted. Trump agreed. On February 13, Flynn resigned as Trump's national security advisor, fueling further calls for an investigation into Trump's possible ties with Russia. Trump's White House was descending into chaos just weeks after he took office. The president was acting in ways that could allow him to be investigated for obstruction of justice.

Later that day, Comey arrived at the Oval Office for a scheduled counterterrorism briefing with the president. At the end of the meeting, Trump said that he wanted to speak to Comey alone in the Oval Office. According to Comey, Trump argued that Flynn had done nothing wrong in speaking with the Russians, but had to be let go because he had misled Pence. Trump said, "He is a good guy and has been through a lot." Trump then became more aggressive, according to Comey, saying, "I hope you can see your way clear to letting this go, to letting Flynn go. He is a good guy. I hope you can let this go." Comey agreed that Flynn "is a good guy," but made no commitment to stop investigating Flynn.

After the meeting, Comey immediately wrote a memorandum describing what Trump had said, and gave copies to Baker and his other senior staff. Comey was again shocked by Trump's behavior. The president was asking the director of the FBI to drop a criminal investigation of a close aide. Worse, the aide had lied to FBI agents about his contacts with Russia, a foreign power that had intervened in the election to help Trump. The behavior smacked of a cover-up.

.   .   .

Over the next several weeks, press reports continued to uncover multiple contacts between Trump aides and Russian officials. Attorney General Sessions had not fully disclosed his own contacts with Russian ambassador Kislyak during his Senate confirmation hearings. As Democratic criticism of Sessions grew and press coverage intensified, Sessions announced on March 2 that he was recusing himself from any FBI investigation of contacts between the Trump campaign and Russian officials. He claimed that he was abiding by the advice of career Justice Department ethics officials. He said that he had made the decision on his own and informed the White House counsel that morning. "They don't know the rules, the ethics rules, most people don't," Sessions said, referring to White House officials. "But when you evaluate the rules I feel like I am—I should not get involved investigating a campaign I had a role in."

Two days later, in an early morning tweet barrage, Trump shifted the political debate and news coverage by making another blatantly false claim that heightened public fears of a "deep state." At 6:35 am, Trump accused the Obama administration of wiretapping his phones. "Terrible! Just found out that Obama had my 'wires tapped' in Trump Tower just before the victory. Nothing found. This is McCarthyism!" A half hour later, the president again accused his predecessor of wiretapping his phones, an act that would be unprecedented in US history. "I'd bet a good lawyer could make a great case out of the fact that President Obama was tapping my phones in October, just prior to Election!" Trump tweeted. And, then, in his final tweet of the morning, he said, "How low has President Obama gone to tapp my phones during the very sacred election process. This is Nixon/Watergate. Bad (or sick) guy!"

Trump was exaggerating. The FBI had obtained a FISA Court warrant to wiretap former Trump advisor Carter Page, who had met with Russian officials in July 2016. Major FBI errors occurred in the Page investigation, but Obama played no role and Trump Tower was never wiretapped.

Two weeks later, on March 20, Comey disclosed during testimony to the House Intelligence Committee that since late July the FBI had been investigating whether "coordination" had occurred between the Trump campaign and Russian officials. When asked if the president was personally under investigation, Comey said he could not comment on an ongoing investigation. During the hearing, Comey stood by the US intelligence community assessment that Putin had intervened in the election to aid Trump. When asked, Comey said it was "impossible to say" how long the investigation might take.

When asked about Trump's claim that Obama had wiretapped Trump Tower, Comey gave a legalistic answer. He correctly stated that Trump Tower was not being wiretapped but did not reveal that the FBI was currently wiretapping former Trump advisor Page. "I have no information that supports those tweets," Comey said. The director of the National Security Agency, Admiral Mike Rogers, testified that he had no evidence of the NSA wiretapping either. He also denied a rumor that British intelligence had surveilled Trump Tower.

Comey's testimony infuriated Trump. The FBI director had given an enormous boost to Democratic claims that Trump may have conspired with Putin to win the election. No such allegation—conspiring with a foreign adversary—had ever been made against an American president. And now, by refuting Trump's claim that Obama had wiretapped Trump Tower, Comey was publicly calling the president a liar. Over the next several weeks, Trump would pressure the leaders of the FBI, the Justice Department, and the intelligence community to help curtail the investigation. They resisted him.

On March 21, the president, furious that Comey had publicly revealed the FBI investigation, repeatedly called White House Counsel McGahn and asked him to intervene with the Justice Department. The president was "getting hotter and hotter, get rid?" McGahn's chief of staff wrote in his notes. In a phone conversation, McGahn told Dana Boente, the acting head of the Justice Department's National Security Division, that the president was under a cloud that made it hard for him to govern. Boente responded that there was no good way to shorten the FBI investigation, and trying to do so could erode public confidence in the independence of the investigation. Trump asked to speak to Boente directly, and McGahn told the president that Boente did not want to speak with him.

The next day, March 22, Trump asked Dan Coats, a former Indiana senator who had succeeded Clapper as the director of national intelligence, and Mike Pompeo, who had succeeded Brennan as CIA director, to speak alone with him in the Oval Office after his morning intelligence briefing. In an extraordinary request to aid him politically, Trump asked the country's top two intelligence officials if they would say publicly that no link existed between Trump and Russia. Coats responded that his office had nothing to do with criminal investigations and it was not his role to make public statements regarding the Russia investigation. Pompeo later told investigators that he had no recollection of Trump asking him to stay behind after the briefing. He simply recalled Trump regularly urging officials to get the word out that the president had not done anything wrong related to Russia.

Three days later, the president called Coats and complained again about the Russia investigations, saying, according to Coats, "I can't do anything with Russia, there's things I'd like to do with Russia, with trade, with ISIS, they're all over me with this." Coats told the president that the investigations were going to continue and the best thing to do was to let them run their course. (Coats later testified in a congressional hearing that he had "never felt pressure to intervene or interfere" with an ongoing investigation.)

The next day, Sunday, March 26, Trump called NSA Director Rogers and said that he was frustrated with the Russia investigation and that it made relations with Moscow difficult. He asked Rogers if he could do anything to refute the news stories linking him with Russia, which he said were false. Rogers's top aide, Deputy NSA Director Richard Ledgett, who was present for the call, later told investigators the conversation was the most unusual thing he had experienced in forty years of government service. Typically, a president would never ask an intelligence official to do such a thing. Rogers did not perceive the president's request to be an order, and the president did not overtly ask Rogers to push back on the Russia investigation itself. But it was unprecedented for a president to pressure his top three intelligence officials to push the FBI to curtail an investigation of his own conduct. Not even Nixon had dared make such a request.

At least twice in March, Trump began President's Daily Briefs by saying that there was no collusion with Russia and that he hoped a press statement to that effect could be issued. Pompeo recalled Trump venting to him about the investigation on multiple occasions, and complaining that there was no evidence against him and that nobody would publicly defend him. Rogers remembered a private conversation with the president in which Trump complained about the investigation and said he had done nothing wrong; Trump told Rogers, "The Russia thing has got to go away." Coats recalled that Trump brought up the Russia investigation so many times that, finally, he told the president it was his job to provide intelligence, not to get involved in investigations.

The specter of another Watergate-scale scandal was hanging over Trump, his White House aides, and the country's top Justice Department and intelligence officials. For the first time since Nixon occupied the Oval Office, a president was pressuring law enforcement and intelligence officials to clear him of potential criminal wrongdoing. Trump was tempting fate and risking impeachment. Ordering an end to the investigation amounted to obstruction of justice, an impeachable offense. Trump was also benefiting from the post-Watergate norms that his Republican and Democratic predecessors had respected and strengthened. Trump's White House advisors, as well as top Justice Department and intelligence officials, were leery of engaging in criminal conduct themselves and being prosecuted and publicly humiliated as Nixon's aides had been. So far, they listened to Trump, but declined to act on his requests.

Trump was also calculated in his behavior. He had not explicitly ordered any one of his aides to stop Comey's investigation. He was, he could argue, merely expressing frustration, portraying himself as a victim, and making it clear to his aides what he would like them to do about Mueller.

.   .   .

On March 30, Trump crossed a new line. In a phone call, he asked Comey what could be done to "lift the cloud" of the Russia investigation. Comey, according to notes he took at the time, explained "that we were running it down as quickly as possible and that there would be great benefit, if we didn't find anything, to our Good Housekeeping seal of approval, but we had to do our work." Comey also told Trump that he told congressional leaders that the FBI was not investigating the president personally. Trump said several times, "We need to get that fact out." Trump then hedged, saying that if there was "some satellite" that did something, "it would be good to find that out." (Comey assumed that Trump meant an associate or campaign worker.) But Trump insisted that he himself had not done anything wrong, and he hoped Comey "would find a way to get out that we weren't investigating him."

Two weeks later, on April 11, 2017, Trump called Comey again. The president said he was following up to see if Comey had done what Trump "asked him to do last time." Comey said that he had passed the request to Boente at the Justice Department, but not heard back, and he told Trump that the traditional channel for such a request would be to have the White House counsel contact the leadership of the Justice Department. Trump said he would take that step, and added, "Because I have been very loyal to you, very loyal, we had that thing, you know."

On May 3, Comey testified before the Senate Judiciary Committee and said he had no regrets about how he handled the Clinton email investigation. He added, though, that it made him "mildly nauseous" to think he might have affected the outcome of the election. The comment angered Trump, who thought that it again undermined the legitimacy of his election victory. Five days later, on May 8, Trump met alone with Sessions and the new deputy attorney general, Rod Rosenstein, to discuss Comey. Rosenstein expressed concerns about how Comey had handled the Clinton email investigation and other decisions in the 2016 campaign. Trump tweeted that night, "The Russia-Trump collusion story is a total hoax, when will this taxpayer funded charade end?"

.   .   .

On May 9, 2017, White House spokesman Sean Spicer announced that Trump, acting on the "clear recommendations" of Sessions and Rosenstein, had fired Comey. Spicer released a letter from Sessions to Trump and a memo from Rosenstein as justification for the firing. Democrats immediately called for the appointment of a special counsel and accused Trump of trying to obstruct the FBI's Trump-Russia investigation. When Rosenstein learned that the White House had cited his memo as a justification for Comey's firing, he reportedly threatened to resign. Trump had ordered Rosenstein to write the memo, and then, without warning, used it to justify firing Comey.

The White House, struggling to control the narrative, changed its explanation for the firing and said the dismissal had been Trump's personal decision. White House Deputy Press Secretary Sarah Huckabee Sanders said that Comey had committed "atrocities" while overseeing the Clinton email investigation, compromised public trust, and undermined morale in the bureau. "He wasn't doing a good job," Trump told reporters. "Very simple. He wasn't doing a good job."

Trump had misjudged the reaction to Comey's removal. Critics compared it to Richard Nixon's "Saturday Night Massacre," when his firing of Independent Counsel Archibald Cox resulted in the resignations of Attorney General Elliot Richardson and Deputy Attorney General William Ruckelshaus. Comey's deputy, Andrew McCabe, now the acting director of the FBI, was so alarmed by Trump's behavior that he formally opened a counterintelligence inquiry into whether the president himself had been working on behalf of Russia. He also expanded the investigation to include whether Trump had obstructed justice. McCabe then met alone with Rosenstein on May 12 and urged him to appoint an independent counsel.

Three days later, former FBI director Robert Mueller met with Trump at the request of White House aides to describe to him how the FBI functioned as an independent institution. The following day, Rosenstein appointed Mueller as special counsel.

Sessions was with the president conducting interviews for a new FBI director when he received a call from Rosenstein. Sessions stepped out of the Oval Office to speak with Rosenstein, who told him about Mueller's appointment. Sessions then returned to inform Trump of the news. The president slumped in his chair and said, "Oh my God.

This is terrible. This is the end of my presidency. I'm fucked." He lambasted Sessions for his decision to recuse himself from the investigation, asking, "How could you let this happen, Jeff?" The president then told Sessions to resign as attorney general. Sessions agreed to submit his resignation and left the Oval Office. Hope Hicks, the White House Director of Strategic Communications, saw the president shortly after Sessions departed and described the president as being extremely upset. Hicks said that she had only seen the president like that one other time: when the *Access Hollywood* tape in which Trump bragged about groping women came out.

.   .   .

Democratic politicians who had been calling for the appointment of a special counsel were delighted. Acting FBI director McCabe, who considered the appointment of a special counsel the most important thing he could support as director, was pleased as well. In hindsight, firing Comey was the largest single mistake of Trump's first year in office. Trump's own actions had increased suspicions of a cover-up. Instead of ending the investigation, the firing had simply shifted it from the FBI to a special counsel. Mueller had the full authority to subpoena documents, convene a grand jury, and prosecute crimes.

Officials in the Justice Department and FBI, from Comey to Yates to Rosenstein, had all declined to carry out actions that they believed violated post-Church reform norms, or, in some cases, the Constitution. In the first five months of Trump's presidency, the Justice Department and the FBI and senior intelligence officials proved to be the most formidable resistance that the president encountered in the federal government. A struggle for power that would define Trump's presidency had begun.

THIRTEEN

Obstructing the Mueller Investigation

T he appointment of Robert Mueller as special counsel immediately put Trump's every act, word, and tweet under the intense scrutiny of an investigative team that was, to him, the living embodiment of the "deep state." More than at any point in his career as a real estate developer and reality television star, Trump now faced political and legal jeopardy. Democrats yearned to impeach Trump. Legions of reporters chased what appeared to be the biggest political story of the twenty-first century—an American colluding with Russia to win the presidency. And while the powers of special counsels had been weakened since Congress and Jimmy Carter formally created the position in 1978, Mueller's writ remained formidable. Prosecutors and FBI agents working for Mueller could subpoena Trump's tax returns, campaign documents, and financial records. They could subpoena his campaign staff, business associates, and White House aides. Any witness who made false statements could be prosecuted for lying to FBI agents. The probe could also, at Mueller's discretion, expand its focus to new matters and continue on indefinitely, as Lawrence Walsh's investigation of Iran-Contra and Ken Starr's investigation of Whitewater did.

Yet Trump's primary tactic in response to Mueller's appointment was to lie. Just as during his 2016 campaign and his business career, Trump invented conspiracy theories, painted himself as a victim, spun false narratives for the press and social media, and stalled. He lied about Comey. He lied about Mueller. He lied about his closest White House aides. And he called the journalists who accurately reported his actions liars as well. In the most dangerous step for himself and the country, Trump privately and publicly tried to interfere with Mueller's investigation and badgered his aides to commit improper and illegal acts. By his own actions, Trump created the gravest constitutional crisis since Watergate.

The day after Mueller's appointment, on May 18, 2017, Sessions met with Trump in the Oval Office and handed him a resignation letter, as Trump had requested. The letter stated simply, "Pursuant to our conversation of yesterday, and at your request, I hereby offer my resignation." Trump placed the resignation letter in his pocket and then asked Sessions several times if he wanted to remain attorney general. Sessions told Trump that he wanted to stay in the position but he served at the pleasure of the president. Eventually, Trump said that he wanted Sessions to stay. At the end of the meeting, Trump baited his attorney general: he shook Sessions's hand but kept the resignation letter in his pocket.

When White House Chief of Staff Reince Priebus and Chief Strategist Steve Bannon learned that Trump was holding onto the resignation letter, they worried that it could be used by the president to influence the Department of Justice and, therefore, become evidence of obstruction of justice. Priebus told Sessions that the letter could function as a kind of "shock collar," an instrument of threat and restraint on the attorney general, and that Trump had "DOJ by the throat." Trump was toying with a member of his cabinet and playing his aides against one another; he was, at the same time, creating evidence of potential obstruction of justice that Mueller could use against him.

After only five months in office, Trump was trying to eviscerate the post-Watergate norms created by Edward Levi, the University of Chicago president who served as a model post-Watergate attorney general during the Ford administration. His actions appeared erratic, but he pursued a clear strategy. Trump believed that he was locked in a struggle for his political survival—that Mueller and his investigators, a cabal of Democrats and "deep state" members, were trying to force him from power.

. . .

In public, Trump's initial response to Mueller's appointment was, by Trump standards, calm. On the day of the announcement, the White House issued a statement from the president, saying, "A thorough investigation will confirm what we already know—there was no collusion between my campaign and any foreign entity. I look forward to this matter concluding quickly. In the meantime, I will never stop fighting for the people and the issues that matter most to the future of our country."

Republican supporters of the president applauded Mueller's appointment as well. "Robert Mueller is superb choice to be special counsel," former House Speaker Newt Gingrich tweeted. "His reputation is impeccable for honesty and integrity. Media should now calm down."

For a brief political moment, it seemed as if Mueller's credentials and credibility might ease the hyper-partisanship that Trump had helped exacerbate since 2016. Supporters of the decorated war veteran and career law enforcement official said Mueller was just the type of nonpartisan public official Republicans and Democrats could trust to produce an objective, fact-based history of the chaotic events of 2016. Despite the unpredictable nature of the Trump presidency, there was some initial hope that the Mueller investigation would restore public confidence in government and spark needed reforms, as the Watergate, Church, and 9/11 investigations had.

. . .

Instead, Trump publicly attacked Mueller and tried to discredit his investigation. On June 16, 2017, Trump, invoked the term "deep state" with his 60 million followers for the first time. The president retweeted a post by Fox News host Sean Hannity urging viewers to watch a segment on his show that night on ties between the "deep state" and the news media. Use of the term had now spread from former UC Berkeley professor Peter Dale Scott, to online conspiracy theorist Alex Jones, to Breitbart's "Virgil," to Newt Gingrich, the former House Speaker, to Fox News pundit Sean Hannity, to the president of the United States.

Meanwhile, Trump tried to find ways to fire Mueller. As a first step, he attempted to force out Sessions and replace him with an attorney general who would protect him. On July 22, 2017, while flying on Marine One helicopter to Norfolk, Virginia, Trump instructed Priebus to get Sessions to resign immediately, saying that the country had lost confidence in Sessions and the negative publicity was intolerable. Trump told Priebus to say that he needed a letter of resignation on the president's desk "immediately" and that Sessions had "no choice" but "must immediately resign," according to notes Priebus took at the time. Priebus warned Trump that if they fired Sessions, they would never get a new attorney general confirmed and that the Department of Justice and Congress would turn on the president. Trump responded that he could make a recess appointment to replace Sessions. (Trump was exaggerating his powers as president and flouting the Constitution. He could temporarily appoint an attorney general while the Senate was in recess, but his nominee would have to be confirmed by the Senate after it returned.)

Priebus called White House Counsel Don McGahn and asked for advice, explaining that he did not want to pull the trigger on something that was "all wrong." Although Trump claimed he wanted Sessions to resign because of his negative press coverage and poor performance in congressional testimony, Priebus believed Trump's decision was being driven by his anger at Sessions's recusal from the

Russia investigation. McGahn told Priebus to ignore Trump's order, adding that they should both consult their personal lawyers, with whom they had attorney-client privilege. McGahn and Priebus discussed the possibility that they would both have to resign eventually rather than carry out the president's command to fire Sessions. The moment was extraordinary. Trump's efforts to obstruct the Mueller investigation were so blatant that both his White House counsel and his White House chief of staff were considering resigning. Again, no president since Nixon had asked his aides to engage in such blatant acts of obstruction.

That afternoon, Trump followed up with Priebus, asking, "Did you get it? Are you working on it?" Priebus recalled. At that point, Priebus believed that his job depended on whether he followed Trump's order to remove Sessions, although the president had been careful to not explicitly say so. Knowing that he did not intend to carry out Trump's order, Priebus tried to placate the president and said he would get Sessions to resign. But he had every intention of trying to derail the effort. Later that day, Priebus called Trump and explained that it would be a calamity if Sessions resigned because Priebus expected Rosenstein and Associate Attorney General Rachel Brand to resign as well. Priebus again warned the president that he would be unable to get anyone else confirmed as attorney general by the Senate. Trump agreed to hold off on demanding Sessions's resignation until after the Sunday talk shows the next day. Aides in the Trump White House frequently hoped that the president's attention and anger would shift to other issues over time. Priebus's strategy worked. By the end of that weekend, Trump relented and agreed not to demand Sessions's resignation.

Over the next several days, Trump publicly called on Sessions to investigate Clinton. "Attorney General Jeff Sessions has taken a VERY weak position on Hillary Clinton crimes (where are Emails & DNC server) & Intel leakers!" he tweeted on July 25. The following day, he tweeted, "Why didn't A.G. Sessions replace acting FBI director Andrew McCabe, a Comey friend who was in charge of Clinton investigation." In response to the attacks from Trump, Sessions prepared another resignation letter. For the rest of the year, he carried it with him in his pocket every time he went to the White House.

In the late spring of 2017, according to Sessions, Trump called the attorney general at home and asked him if he would "unrecuse" himself so that Sessions could direct the Justice Department to investigate and prosecute Hillary Clinton. Sessions said the "gist" of the conversation was that the president wanted him to unrecuse himself from "all of it," including the special counsel's Russia investigation. Sessions said he listened but did not respond. Sessions did not reverse his recusal and did not order an investigation of Clinton. He also refused to resign, infuriating Trump. Trump believed that the attorney general's job was to protect him, not enforce the law.

· · ·

In fact, Trump's staff was saving him from impeachment. Trump's attorney general, White House counsel, chief of staff, deputy chief of staff, staff secretary, and former campaign manager had all refused to carry out the president's orders to end or limit the Mueller investigation. More than any other factor, the refusal of his aides to obstruct or end Mueller's investigation had saved Trump's presidency. But the damage Trump was doing to the rule of law—and public faith in it—was unparalleled. He relentlessly politicized the work of the FBI and Justice Department, reversing decades of efforts to convince Americans that both institutions applied the law equitably.

FOURTEEN

The Collapse of
Congressional Oversight

O n July 12, 2017, Christopher Wray walked into a wood-
paneled hearing room on Capitol Hill with his wife and
two children. Dozens of photographers encircled Wray,
recording hundreds of images of the multimillionaire corporate lawyer and former Justice Department prosecutor. For the next several
hours, Wray's Senate confirmation hearing to succeed James Comey
as director of the FBI would be broadcast live on national television.
Dressed in a navy-blue suit and purple tie, Wray looked uncomfort-
able and nervous. He had good reason to be. Democrats, Republicans, and former colleagues all had doubts about his ability to lead the
bureau through its most tumultuous period since the death of J. Edgar
Hoover. If confirmed, Wray would, at best, preserve the notional air of
independence the bureau had gained after decades of effort by Webster, Freeh, Mueller, and Comey. Or he would be badgered by Trump
into returning the bureau to its Hoover-era practice of pleasing the
president by collecting dirt on his political rivals. The president could
also ignore Wray and achieve his goals by other means.

Former Justice Department colleagues saw Wray as well intentioned but weak. A wealthy introvert, Wray had little experience running large organizations. Former prosecutors wondered if he could
relate to FBI agents, many of whom hailed from working-class families. Conservatives feared that Wray would undermine Trump. Liber-

als questioned why Wray, as a young lawyer in the Justice Department, never spoke out against the Bush administration post-9/11 use of torture. Friends worried, most of all, about Wray's ability to hold his own in the most partisan Washington in decades. All sides wondered if he had the guts to stand up to Trump if asked to do something improper.

Wray, who was 50, appeared youthful compared to members of the Senate, an archaic institution that seemed increasingly out of touch with the country. While younger Americans disrupted tech, entertainment, and other industries, the average age of a US senator had steadily risen since the 1980s and was now 62. (The average age of Americans of all professions is 42.) Charles Grassley, the Judiciary Committee chair, was 83 and had served in the Senate for 36 years. Dianne Feinstein, the committee's ranking Democrat, was 84 and the country's oldest sitting senator. Wray could have been either senator's son.

In his opening statement, Wray vowed to prevent the bureau from being politicized. "I will never allow the FBI's work to be driven by anything other than the facts, the law, and the impartial pursuit of justice. Period," he said. "My loyalty is to the Constitution and the rule of law." As members of the committee began to ask questions, it quickly became clear that Republicans and Democrats were describing two different realities. Senator John Cornyn, a conservative Republican from Texas, used his time for questions to defend Trump's firing of Comey. Senator Orrin Hatch, Republican of Utah, asked Wray about the rise in violent crime—a statistic Trump had exaggerated during the 2016 campaign. Senator Lindsey Graham asked Wray about press reports of an effort by the Ukraine government to hurt Trump's candidacy and influence the 2016 election. Wray promised to look into it. Asked by Graham if he believed that Mueller was engaged in a witch hunt, Wray replied, "I do not consider Director Mueller to be on a witch hunt."

Democrats used their questions to coax Wray into criticizing Trump. Responding to questions from Feinstein, Wray promised to inform the committee of any efforts to interfere with Mueller's work, and called the special counsel a "consummate straight shooter." Asked by Senator Patrick Leahy if he believed that Russia had tried to aid Trump in the 2016 election, Wray replied, "I have no reason whatsoever to doubt the assessment of the intelligence community." Asked what he would do if Trump asked him to do something illegal, Wray responded, "First, I would try to talk him out of it, and if that failed I would resign." After the hearing, Wray's performance was widely praised. Some called him more impressive than the members of Congress.

Feinstein and other Democrats announced they would support Wray's nomination. Three weeks later, Wray was confirmed by the Senate in a 92–5 vote. The new FBI director, it appeared, would report to the committee any effort by Trump to obstruct Mueller's investigation. But the president had learned a lesson from his interactions with Comey. He would hide wrongdoing from Wray and find others who would help him achieve his goals.

. . .

Trump's behavior during his first six months in office frustrated Will Hurd, a Republican congressman from West Texas. A 39-year-old former undercover CIA operative, Hurd had run for Congress because he was infuriated by the cartoonish understanding members of Congress had of intelligence work. Two weeks before Donald Trump took office, Hurd had joined the House Intelligence Committee as its newest Republican member. A political centrist with a sterling résumé, Hurd was social media–savvy and a rising star in the GOP. As a former member of the agency's Directorate of Operations, he knew firsthand how oversight could succeed or fail. After spending nine and a half years at the agency, he had quit and run for Congress, and, perhaps naively, hoped to improve oversight. "I thought I could help the intelligence community in a different way," Hurd said. "So I ran."

Hurd represented how the CIA had changed. The agency was no longer dominated by Ivy League–educated WASPs. Since the end of the Cold War and particularly after 9/11, its ranks had grown more diverse. Hurd's father, Bob, is African-American, born and raised in Texas. Hurd's mother, Mary Alice, is white and grew up in Indiana. The two met at a business meeting in Los Angeles, when he was a textiles salesman and she was a fabric buyer for a department store. After they were married, they settled in San Antonio. For more than a year, they struggled to buy a home. When Mary Alice viewed a house alone, realtors told her it was available. When her African-American husband joined her, realtors announced it was no longer on the market. They settled in a working-class neighborhood, where Will, the youngest of three children, attended public school and studied computer science. A childhood lisp resulted in kids nicknaming him "Hurd the Nerd." He dreamed of attending Stanford, but after a high school guidance counselor urged him to visit Texas A&M, he fell in love with the school's campus life and commitment to public service. Six feet, four inches tall and a computer science major, he mounted a long-shot bid for class president in his senior year and won.

That fall, Hurd received a late-night call from a panicked friend and was told there had been a terrible accident. A Texas A&M tradition—the construction of a massive bonfire before its annual football game against the University of Texas—ended in calamity when the pyre collapsed and killed twelve students. Hurd arrived at the scene and found students frantically trying to remove logs, as trapped friends screamed for help. Firefighters, fearing another collapse, urged students not to touch the pile. Hurd tried to calm the groups as he struggled to remain composed himself. Over the next several weeks, he consoled hundreds of students and parents, gave interviews on national television, and sat beside former president George H. W. Bush at a wrenching memorial service. Twenty years after the incident, he said it haunted him more than anything he had seen at the CIA. "When I think of chaos and carnage," he said. "I think of going out onto that field."

While an undergraduate, he took a course, "Cold War Rhetoric and Intelligence," taught by former CIA operative James Olson. "He told these stories and I was like, wow," Hurd said. "I thought it would be cool to serve my country in all these exotic, crazy places." Shocking his family, Hurd applied to work at the CIA. Hurd spoke no foreign languages fluently, and had limited experience abroad. Yet he wanted to serve as a clandestine officer overseas. Armed with recommendations from Olson and Robert Gates, the former agency director and the interim dean of Texas A&M's Bush School of Government and Public Service, the agency accepted him in 2000.

Hurd moved to Washington and started receiving training as an undercover operative. He was first told to expect a posting in Latin America. Then, in the summer of 2001, colleagues told him they were concerned something big was going to happen but they didn't know what. Hours after the September 11, 2001, attacks, Hurd volunteered for any service the agency needed. At 4 am on September 12, he received a phone call and was told to immediately report to the basement of CIA headquarters. There, he joined the first-ever CIA Counterterrorism Center Special Operations Division. Many of the veteran CIA officers were anguished and frustrated at the agency's failure to stop the attacks. The fury of one official, in particular, struck him: Richard Blee, the director of the Counterterrorism Center.

Hurd learned to speak Urdu, the official language of Pakistan, grew a beard, and worked undercover in South Asia. He was serving as an undercover operative in Kabul when a visit from members of the House Intelligence Committee changed the course of his career once again. As was customary, he and other CIA officers briefed the delegation on the situation in the country. At one point, a member of the committee asked Hurd if the agency could cut short its briefing so that the members could go shopping in the bazaar. The question infuriated Hurd. "It wasn't even a real bazaar," Hurd recalled. "It was inside the embassy." Later, a different member of the delegation asked Hurd what the difference was between a Sunni and Shia Muslim. Exasperated, Hurd replied mockingly, "I don't know, Congressman, what is the difference?" The retort offended the congressman and frustrated Hurd's boss, the CIA station chief, who simply wanted to get the briefing over with.

Hurd made a snap decision. "I pushed my chair back and I walked outside," he recalled. He telephoned a college friend who had been urging Hurd to run for Congress from San Antonio, his hometown. On the spot, Hurd accepted. Hurd resigned from the CIA after nearly ten years of service, shocking his colleagues and friends, and bought a house in San Antonio. "Everybody told me that I was crazy to leave the CIA."

In his first major political mistake, Hurd underestimated the challenge of winning his home district, the twenty-third. The largest in Texas, it spanned 58,000 square miles of remote desert, including 820 miles of the US-Mexico border. It was the heavily Republican state's only swing district, evenly divided between Republicans and Democrats. Each two-year election cycle, both national parties spent millions of dollars trying to gain or hold control of the seat. A year after he left the CIA, his gambit into politics ended in failure. Hurd narrowly lost the 2010 Republican nomination for the twenty-third district by 700 votes.

After spending four years working in a consulting firm run by other former covert CIA officers, Hurd won the seat in 2014, defeating the incumbent Democrat by 2,500 votes. In his first term in Congress, Hurd authored more bills that passed and were signed into law than any other member of Congress. He did so by introducing modest, nonpartisan measures that would benefit constituents, such as overtime pay for border patrol members. On a personal level, he was surprised by the warmth members of Congress displayed in private, even after they had battled bitterly in public to score political points. Hurd was also struck by the willingness of veteran House members to ask new members for advice on certain issues.

During the 2016 presidential campaign, Hurd distanced himself from Trump. He criticized the Republican nominee's "nasty rhetoric" toward Latinos and Muslims. He declared Trump's $8 billion wall along the US-Mexico border "the most expensive, least-effective way to do border security." A month before the election, Hurd went a step further and said he would not vote for Trump. "I never endorsed Donald Trump, and I cannot in good conscience support or vote for a man who degrades women, insults minorities, and has no clear path to keep our country safe," Hurd said. "He should step aside for a true conservative to defeat Hillary Clinton." Hurd was narrowly reelected by three thousand votes. Trump lost to Clinton in Hurd's district but easily won the statewide vote in Texas, taking all thirty-six of the state's electoral votes.

After Trump nominated Congressman Mike Pompeo to be CIA director, House Speaker Paul Ryan gave Pompeo's seat on the House Intelligence Committee to Hurd. "Ultimately, Paul wanted people who actually understand how the intelligence community works," Hurd said. While hearings could devolve into partisan posturing, Hurd believed in them. "I think coming forward and having to answer the American people is a hallmark of our democracy," he said. At Hurd's first-ever intelligence hearing, several former agency colleagues served as witnesses. Some of the questions from members of the committee were good, Hurd recalled. Others showed that members did not understand how the CIA was structured. When the CIA officials said that they didn't know the answers to one question, Hurd knew it was because certain information was compartmentalized inside the agency. The committee member, though, reacted suspiciously. "The lack of a response was viewed as cagey," Hurd said, "when, in fact, they didn't know."

At first, the committee functioned as designed and resisted pressure from Trump to split along party lines. After Trump falsely claimed in March that Trump Tower had been wiretapped by the Obama administration, the committee's chair, Republican Devin Nunes and its ranking member, Democrat Adam Schiff, held a joint news conference and refuted the conspiracy theory. "We don't have any evidence that took place," Nunes said.

Two weeks later, Nunes was summoned to the White House on a Tuesday night to view highly classified documents. (Journalists dubbed his trip the "midnight run.") The next day, without sharing the documents with other committee members, Nunes held an impromptu press conference and suggested that the Obama administration had improperly surveilled the Trump transition team. "What I've read seems to me to be some level of surveillance activity—perhaps legal, but I don't know that it's right," Nunes said. "I don't know that the American people would be comfortable with what I've read."

Relations between Democrats and Republicans had been strained in the past, but no committee chair had dared take such a step. Nunes made a damaging allegation without releasing any concrete details, which made it impossible to disprove. He hinted at a "deep state" conspiracy against Trump that played on Americans' long-running fears of government surveillance. Over time, it emerged that Nunes was referring to the fact that senior Obama administration officials, primarily National Security Advisor Susan Rice, had asked for the identities of the Trump campaign aides who had been trying to set up communications with Russian officials. Democrats said Rice was simply doing her job. Nunes said she was part of a vast attempt by Obama administration officials to surveil Trump aides. Nunes's allegation set a new precedent for the use of intelligence as a political weapon. Democrats dismissed it as an effort to distort information, spread a conspiracy theory, and distract Americans from the unprecedented FBI probe of Trump's campaign that Comey had announced.

Furious, Schiff attacked Nunes at a press conference of his own hours later. "The chairman will either need to decide if he's leading an investigation into conduct which includes allegations of potential coordination between the Trump campaign and the Russians, or he is going to act as a surrogate of the White House," he told reporters. "Because he cannot do both." Several days later, Schiff went farther. In an interview on *Meet the Press*, the ranking Democrat said that new evidence had emerged in the Russia investigation. "There is more than circumstantial evidence now," Schiff said. "I will say that there is evidence that is not circumstantial, and is very much worthy of investigation." Republicans accused Schiff of lying and insisted there was no clear evidence of Trump colluding with Russia. Democrats accused Nunes of revealing classified information for political gain. The House committee was paralyzed.

．　．　．

Trump's firing of Comey in May 2017 briefly revived bipartisanship on the Hill. Schiff and every Democrat in the House and Senate hailed the appointment of Robert Mueller as special counsel. Republican House Speaker Paul Ryan and Senate Majority Leader Mitch McConnell, Nunes, and most Republicans praised it as well. "This is the right decision at the right time, and the right man was chosen for the job," said Nunes.

Hurd and many moderate Republicans believed that Trump had committed a catastrophic political mistake by firing Comey. The Russia investigation could now continue for years. "I wouldn't have done it that way," Hurd said, referring to Trump's removal of Comey. "But he's defending himself the way he knows how to defend himself."

Privately, Hurd was exasperated with Trump, Nunes, and Schiff. He felt that Schiff's statement about new evidence of "beyond a reasonable doubt" exaggerated the facts. "The Democrats were acting as if they had access to something that nobody else had access to," he said. Hurd, like many Republicans, did not believe that Trump had coordinated with the Russians. One current White House official said he agreed with Senator Lindsey Graham, saying, "I don't think [Trump] colluded with the Russians because he doesn't collude with his own staff."

Hurd felt a special counsel investigation was needed to restore American faith in Trump's election and the FBI. He questioned the decision of a handful of senior officials to surveil former Trump campaign aide Carter Page. But he thought Trump's and Nunes's suggestions of an Obama administration–wide conspiracy were overblown and undermined public trust in the FBI and CIA. "You can criticize the leadership," Hurd said. "But appreciate the work of the organization."

In the Senate, the Republican and Democratic members of the Intelligence Committee overwhelmingly endorsed Mueller's appointment, but the committee was deadlocked in a different way. Unlike the leaders of the House Intelligence Committee, Chairman Richard Burr, a Republican from North Carolina, and Vice Chairman Mark Warner, a Democrat from Virginia, had a strong working relationship and rarely feuded in public. The committee was conducting its own investigation of Russian interference, which was widely viewed as more credible than the House investigation. Privately, though, the Senate committee was also divided. Republicans believed that Democrats were inflating the importance of the Trump-Russia investigation to undermine the legitimacy of Trump's presidency. Democrats believed that Trump was a threat to American democracy. The committee agreed to issue a series of reports on Russian interference but left for last the most contentious issue—possible Trump campaign coordination with Russia.

Seven months after taking office, Trump had paralyzed the House and Senate intelligence committees. The president's embrace of conspiracy theories, firing of Comey, and public attacks on the FBI and CIA created tremendous pressure on the panels. With time, Nunes succumbed to it and began trafficking in conspiracies himself. Schiff, like many Democrats, feared that Trump would impede the Mueller investigation and that the president was, potentially, a Russian asset. Hurd decided to bide his time and see what Mueller found. Overall, the largest source of the dysfunction was clear: Trump himself. The president had single-handedly exacerbated Washington's partisan differences and caused the collapse of an oversight system that had worked effectively for forty years.

FIFTEEN

The Disinformation Presidency

Throughout American history, presidents have typically dominated the country's political discourse. Teddy Roosevelt's description of the presidency as a "bully pulpit" remains true. The White House is an unmatched platform for pushing a political agenda and swaying the views of American voters. Presidents have also always manipulated facts, but in the post-Watergate era they generally lost public support after being caught telling outright lies. Bill Clinton's declaration that "I did not have relations with that woman, Miss Lewinsky," hurt him politically. George W. Bush's infamous "mission accomplished" speech following the invasion of Iraq did the same.

In his campaign and the first year of his presidency, Trump showed a brazen willingness to lie. Aides tried to restrain Trump, but he continued to use his Twitter feed and, to a lesser extent, his public comments, to make false and exaggerated claims. Trump also took pride in dismissing the advice of experts.

At the same time, Trump, like all American presidents, was barraged with information. Foreign intelligence services mounted disinformation campaigns designed to influence his thinking. Democrats and other domestic political rivals tried to damage him politically. Aides jostled to advance their personal ambitions and agendas, including some who fed the president false claims clearly designed to play to his long-held beliefs and biases.

Under Trump, though, the amount of false information emanating from and circulating inside the White House was remarkable, current and former administration officials said. Disinformation, false information that is deliberately spread and designed to deceive, mixed with misinformation, false information spread unintentionally. The primary source of the dynamic was Trump himself. The president welcomed the chaos and infighting and, it seemed, had no misgivings regarding the use of misleading facts. He also sometimes ignored information that aides presented to him. "He's very engaging but he didn't seem to read anything we gave him," said a former White House aide who asked not to be named. "What you see is what you get. There's no hidden genius there."

Some current and former officials blamed some of Trump's initial advisors for exacerbating the dynamic. One former senior official singled out Steve Bannon for criticism. "He was not there to serve the president," the official said. "He was there to manipulate decisions." (Bannon declined an interview request.) The former senior official said that Bannon fed Trump rhetoric that reinforced the president's biases and ended up in Trump's speeches and tweets. Bannon constructed narratives that played on fear—such as illegal immigrants "invading" the country or longtime allies "cheating" the United States—that appealed to Trump's prejudices. Bannon and his allies "would deliberately feed misinformation to the president," he said, and called Bannon "a master manipulator of Trump, in particular." The former official said that Bannon also fed Trump "deep state" conspiracy theories to get the president to distrust the advice of career government officials who opposed Bannon's policy goals.

Current and former administration officials said that Trump did consistently express some clear policy goals in private—from confronting Chinese trade practices to ending prolonged American wars in the Middle East. "When he is briefed well and served well, he will make good decisions," the former senior official continued. "He will also change his positions." A current official who asked not to be named said that while Trump's public rhetoric toward Iran and North

Korea was bombastic, the president himself adamantly opposed engaging the United States in an armed conflict. "I have never worried about a reckless decision involving matters of war and peace," he said. "This is not a warmonger president." A second current official said that the failure of the Clinton, George W. Bush, and Obama administrations—and the Washington elite as a whole—to address economic inequality, the loss of high-paying manufacturing jobs, and the opiate crisis, created an opening for Trump's rise. "They saw us kowtow to China for thirty years—and it proved to be economically disastrous. And they've seen two wars that sacrificed 6,500 Americans but made no sense," this official said. "They just feel abandoned and betrayed by Washington. That there are a lot of people benefiting more than them."

Many aides continued to try and manipulate the president after Bannon left the White House in August 2017. Many cabinet members, several former aides said, played to Trump's ego by flattering the president or telling him that if he took certain policy actions he would look strong. "I think he is easy to manipulate because of his deep insecurities," one of the former officials said. Trump's family members and other senior aides tried to ensure that the president was given reliable information and honest advice, but he sometimes ignored it. "Like any leader, he came to the office with certain weaknesses and vulnerabilities," said one of the former senior officials. "He is in an environment that exacerbates them."

.   .   .

For members of the Washington national security establishment, the President's Daily Brief should have provided Trump with relatively reliable information. The Church reforms, the 9/11 attacks, and the Iraq WMD scandal had led to repeated efforts to make the briefings as politically neutral as possible. Skeptics on the left and right scoffed at the notion that the intelligence agencies would not have political motives of their own. At the very least, the agencies would want to continue to convince the presidents, as well as members of Congress, to increase their budgets. Clapper and other current and former officials contend that intelligence officers have learned from the scandals of the past that "speaking truth to power" is best for national security, presidents, and the agencies themselves.

The way Trump received the briefing differed from his immediate predecessors. Bush had received a written copy of the PDB each morning in a leather-bound briefing book, read it, and then went over each item in face-to-face meetings with CIA Director George Tenet and a handful of aides. He often asked his intelligence briefers rapid-fire questions, according to Michael Morell, who was one of them. Obama received an electronic version of the PDB on his iPad, read it alone, and shared it with thirty of his top aides. He asked fewer questions during in-person daily briefings. After he took office, Trump received his briefing as he sat behind the "Resolute" desk in the Oval Office. At his request, as many as fourteen of his senior aides attended, including CIA Director Mike Pompeo, Director of National Intelligence Dan Coates, National Security Advisor H. R. McMaster, and, at times, his son-in-law, Jared Kushner. Trump asked for the presentation to be primarily oral and visual. Written briefings on specific topics were kept to one page. Pompeo told the *Washington Post* in 2017 that the new president enjoyed poring over visuals—charts, maps, videos, photos, and "killer graphics." Trump interrupted briefers with questions and asides. Trump preferred a free-flowing conversation over one-way lectures. "It's a very oral, interactive discussion, as opposed to sitting there and reading from a text or a script," Pompeo said.

Staffers on the National Security Council initially generated multipage memos for Trump, as they had for Bush and Obama, that outlined detailed policies and strategies. He also received a thick briefing book each night. Over time, it became clear that Trump, unlike Bush and Obama, rarely read these. An order came down from senior officials to reduce the NSC memos to a single page. Eventually, aides came to the conclusion that the best way to raise an issue in writing was to prepare a long, narrow card, made of heavy paper stock, with "The White House" written across the top. One former aide said the information that needed to be relayed to Trump had to be reduced to "two or three points, with the syntactical complexity of 'See Jane run.'"

During meetings, McMaster tended to address Trump in a formal manner that the president viewed as lecturing. Aides encouraged McMaster to joke with the president. He tried to do so, saying, "Mr. President, just seventeen quick points on that!" Trump reacted with disdain. Former aides said that McMaster believed his job was to present the president with honest advice and clear options. Privately, they came to see McMaster's approach as naive. "This was his first job in Washington," a former aide said. "He didn't know how to play the game."

Supporters of Pompeo praised the strong personal relationship he developed with the president, which they said protected the agency from Trump's attacks. "Pompeo can be the president's best friend because he's a back-slapper who speaks his language," said a former aide. As had been true since the agency's founding, CIA staffers believed it was critical to establish and maintain access to the president—the intelligence community's most important customer. At the same time, Pompeo's willingness to take risks and delegate authority made him popular in the agency's Directorate of Operations, which carried out covert operations. Pompeo also lifted Obama-era limits on the CIA's role in American drone strikes. Both moves were seen as a reversal of the micromanagement and risk aversion of the Obama White House that operatives had complained about for much of the previous eight years.

Critics of Pompeo emerged in the agency and administration as well. They accused him of self-aggrandizement, referred to him as pompous, and said he remained in Trump's good graces by telling him what he wanted to hear. "He will make compromises in the short term to keep his constituencies happy, including the president," the former official said. "He will hold back his views." In more alarming behavior, in some national security meetings Pompeo voiced his own policy views rather than the more neutral findings of the intelligence committee. He made statements regarding misconduct by Iran that did not match carefully vetted intelligence-community assessments. At times, Pompeo even pitched covert CIA operations to Trump without being asked to prepare them.

All of those steps were a radical break in the protocol that had taken hold in the four decades since the Church reforms. Intelligence officials clearly had biases. Like many other government officials, they were loyal to their organization and favored its success and growth. But a consensus had formed that briefings should be as fact-based and politically neutral as possible. From the Bay of Pigs to Vietnam to faulty Iraq WMD intelligence, bias in the presentation of intelligence had helped cause some of the largest foreign policy debacles in US history. From Clapper to Blee to Hurd, three generations of American intelligence officials had generally embraced the approach of needing to present facts that might anger a president or a policymaker. Now, Pompeo, aides feared, was telling the president what he wanted to hear.

Former aides reported on another habit of Trump's that impacted the information he received. Throughout his career, Trump tended to be skeptical of the recommendations of his own staff at times, and often turned to outsiders for feedback and advice. This habit continued in the White House. Trump cultivated a coterie of informal advisors. At the time, information that Trump received from them surprised White House staffers. The problem emerged during a July 19, 2017, National Security Council meeting regarding Afghanistan. In the two-hour session, Trump indicated that he had been deeply influenced by a meeting he had recently had with a group of Americans who had fought in Afghanistan. According to officials, Trump said the veterans told him NATO forces had not been helpful, and that China was making money off of mining in Afghanistan while American troops were fighting the Taliban. One official reported that Trump expressed frustration at the slow pace of an effort to help American businesses obtain rights to those mines instead. Finally, he repeatedly criticized his military advisors and called for the firing of General John Nicholson, the four-star general then in command in Afghanistan. Trump suggested that the veterans who fought in the war were better able to advise him on Afghanistan. He then compared the administration's Afghanistan policy review with the renovation of a famed New York restaurant in the 1980s. Trump said that the restaurant, Manhattan's elite 21 Club, had shut its doors for a year and hired an expensive consultant for a renovation. After a year, Trump said, the consultant's only suggestion was that the restaurant needed a larger kitchen. (The restaurant had, in fact, closed for only two months, and the renovation was extensive and widely praised.)

At roughly the same time, some aides were telling Trump that he should adopt a proposal from Erik Prince, the brother of Education Secretary Betsy DeVos, to use private contractors rather than American soldiers to secure Afghanistan. A former national security official who asked not to be named said that Trump presented the option at the meeting in an appealing but unrealistic way. "An American company will do this cheaper and better without young Americans in uniform dying," he said, paraphrasing the argument made by backers of the plan. In fact, deploying Prince's army was completely unrealistic. Thanks in part to an investigation by FBI agent Tommy O'Connor, guards from Prince's former private-security company, Blackwater, had been convicted of killing more than a dozen civilians in a 2007 shooting in Baghdad. Deploying a large number of Blackwater-like security contractors, which had gone disastrously in Iraq, would likely fuel a surge in anti-American sentiment among Afghans, and aid the Taliban insurgency.

.　.　.

In January 2018, Trump's appetite for conspiracy theories sparked chaos in Congress and the White House. On January 10, 2018, the White House issued a statement supporting the renewal of Section

702 of the FISA Amendments Act, a post-9/11 program that allows US intelligence agencies to collect the communications of foreigners overseas without a warrant—including when they are speaking with Americans. The next morning, on *Fox & Friends*, Andrew Napolitano, the network's top judicial analyst, personally appealed to Trump to change his position on the bill. "Mr. President, this is not the way to go," Napolitano said. "Spying is valid to find the foreign agents among us. But it's got to be based on suspicion and not an area code."

Napolitano then invoked the debunked conspiracy theory that British intelligence agencies had spied on Trump Tower during the 2016 campaign. Napolitano had first floated the theory in early 2017; it was repeated by Sean Spicer, then the White House press secretary. Stunned British intelligence officials, in a rare public rebuke, had dismissed the claim as "nonsense" and "utterly ridiculous." The Republican-controlled Senate Intelligence Committee also investigated the claim and found it to be false.

Forty-five minutes after Napolitano asked Trump to oppose the renewal of Section 702, the president tweeted, "This is the act that may have been used, with the help of the discredited and phony Dossier, to so badly surveil and abuse the Trump Campaign by the previous administration and others?" Fearing that the legislation would fail to pass without Trump's support, White House Chief of Staff John Kelly, National Security Advisor H. R. McMaster, Director of National Intelligence Dan Coats, and CIA Director Mike Pompeo convened an Oval Office meeting; Speaker of the House Paul Ryan joined by phone. Together they convinced Trump to reverse his reversal. "Today's vote is about foreign surveillance of foreign bad guys on foreign land," he tweeted. "We need it! Get smart!"

Several former aides told me they came to the conclusion that Trump's character flaws prevented him from delivering on his agenda. A former senior national security official told me he lost faith in Trump after observing his decision-making. Presidents George W. Bush and Barack Obama both did a better job of weighing information. "That's why the president gets the big bucks," he said. "To discern where the preponderance of the evidence lies, to discern where the more persuasive argument lies." The former senior official who was critical of Bannon said that he supported Trump's goal of aiding the middle class, confronting China, and reforming immigration. Bold changes were needed but, over time, he saw that Trump could not deliver them. "What kills me with Trump is, we needed a disruptive leader," the official said. "But his fundamental flaws got in the way."

Other aides recognized Trump's personal flaws but remained committed to helping him achieve his policy goals. The second current official said he realized that Trump alienated some Americans. "The constant narcissism and the showmanship, it often gets carried away," he said. "I can understand why so many people can't stand the guy." He acknowledged Trump could be abrasive. "He's definitely selfish. He's a damaged person, for whatever reason in his childhood. But I don't think he's evil." The official argued that the people who voted for him—and the democratic mandate they gave Trump—should be respected. He predicted that Trump's legacy would be different than what his critics now see. "I think in the deep distant future, people will look and see that he did not get us involved in another war," he said. "And he injected friction into China's ambitions to be a global empire."

SIXTEEN

The Loudest Voice

A s Trump's aides worked to help Americans who had voted for him, the president continued to look for ways to thwart the Mueller investigation and launch criminal investigations of his political enemies. His primary focus remained on Attorney General Jeff Sessions. On October 16, 2017, Trump met with Sessions and said that the Justice Department was not investigating the individuals that he wanted scrutinized. Rob Porter, the White House staff secretary, attended as well. Trump mentioned Clinton's emails and said, "Don't have to tell us, just take look," according to notes taken by Porter. As he had in the past, Sessions stood firm and offered no assurances that the Justice Department would investigate Clinton.

Two days later, on October 18, 2017, Trump used Twitter to publicly pressure Sessions to investigate Comey and Clinton. He tweeted, "Wow, FBI confirms report that James Comey drafted a letter exonerating Crooked Hillary Clinton long before investigation was complete. Many people not interviewed, including Clinton herself." (Nearly all of Trump's claims in the tweet were false or exaggerated. Clinton had been interviewed before Comey announced the bureau's findings.) The following day, Trump tweeted, "Uranium deal to Russia, with Clinton help and Obama Administration knowledge, is the biggest story that Fake Media doesn't want to follow!"

Trump was referring to a debunked, three-year-old conspiracy theory circulated during the 2016 campaign by Peter Schweizer, a Breitbart News editor. Schweizer claimed in his 2015 book *Clinton Cash* that while Clinton was secretary of state, the US government had authorized the sale of a Canadian company that controlled twenty percent of the US uranium supplies to a Russian-controlled firm. The owner of the Canadian company subsequently made $145 million in donations to the Clinton Foundation. Fact-checkers at the *Washington Post* and other organizations had found Schweizer's allegation to be false. Clinton played no personal role in the sale of the company, which was approved by a nine-agency US government review board. The State Department official who served on the board said that Clinton never contacted them regarding the issue.

Four days after Trump's tweet, Fox News host Tucker Carlson raised the allegation again. "Why did Hillary's office and the Obama administration sign off on giving the Russians a fifth of our uranium?" Carlson asked. Three days after that, Nunes, the chair of the House Intelligence Committee, said in an interview with Fox, "How is it that our government could approve a sale of twenty percent of our uranium at the same time that there was an open FBI investigation?" (Carlson's and Nunes's claims, like Trump's, were exaggerated or false.)

On October 29, Trump sent out a series of tweets again pressuring Sessions, "Never seen such Republican ANGER & UNITY as I have concerning the lack of investigation on Clinton made Fake Dossier (now $12,000,000?), . . . the Uranium to Russia deal, the 33,000 plus deleted Emails, the Comey fix and so much more." Trump then ended the tweet chain with "DO SOMETHING!" The president was calling for the criminal prosecution of his political opponent—after multiple prosecutors, including his own attorney general, had declined to press charges. No modern American president had so clearly and publicly enlisted the Justice Department to take such overtly political actions.

On November 22, 2017, Trump's pressure paid off. Sessions sent a letter to John Huber, a former federal prosecutor in Utah, instructing him to determine if a criminal investigation into the uranium deal was merited. Eleven months after taking office, despite the appointment of a special counsel, Trump had pressured the attorney general into launching an inquiry into discredited Clinton claims. (Two years later, in January 2020, the *Washington Post* reported that Huber found no wrongdoing and had filed no charges in the case.) To the president, the opening of an investigation appeared to be more important than what was actually found. Clinton had been tarred as corrupt. Trump's strategy was working.

.   .   .

On December 2, Trump received an extraordinary boost that reinforced two of the central narratives of his presidency: conspiracy and grievance. The *New York Times* and *Washington Post* reported that the senior FBI agent who helped lead the Hillary Clinton email and Trump-Russia investigations had sent derogatory text messages about Trump during the 2016 campaign. Mueller immediately removed the agent, Peter Strzok, from his team of investigators. Strzok, the bureau's top counterintelligence investigator and an army veteran, had exchanged the texts with Lisa Page, an FBI lawyer with whom he was having an affair. For Trump, the texts immediately called into question the fairness of the Clinton email probe, the FBI, and the Mueller investigation. On the day the story broke, Trump tweeted that the FBI's reputation was now in "Tatters—worst in History!" The next day, he said the tweets confirmed why Clinton had not gone to jail: "Now it all starts to make sense!" Within hours, his message had been retweeted 24,000 times.

Unquestionably, the texts between Page and Strzok were politically biased, pejorative, and sneering. "Just went to a Southern Virginia Walmart," Strzok wrote. "I could SMELL the Trump support." Page called Trump an "enormous douche" and asked Strzok, "Trump's not ever going to become president, right?" Strzok replied, "No. No, he won't. We'll stop it." (Strzok later told congressional investigators that he was saying "the American people" would stop Trump.) In another exchange, Strzok said of Trump, "Omg he's an idiot." Page replied, "He's awful." Page said, "She just has to win now. I'm not going to lie, I got a flash of nervousness yesterday about trump." Strzok called Trump "a f***ing idiot" and said "F Trump." The message that got by far the most interest was an August 2016 text in which Strzok mentioned an "insurance policy." "There's no way he gets elected—but I'm afraid we can't take that risk," he wrote. "It's like an insurance policy in the unlikely event you die before you're 40."

Trump, Nunes, and conservatives said that "insurance policy" referred to the Trump-Russia investigation. They also said the FBI had not filed charges against Clinton due to political bias. Comey, James Baker, and lawyers for the two agents said that they did not allow political bias to impact the investigation. Christopher Wray, the new FBI director, denied there was political bias in the agency. Tom O'Connor released a statement as the president of the FBI Agents Association, defending the bureau's integrity. "FBI agents are dedicated to their mission," O'Connor said, adding that they demonstrated "unwavering integrity and professionalism." He asserted that "suggesting otherwise is simply false."

Trump and his allies scoffed at the claim. Over the course of December, the House Intelligence Committee held a series of raucous hearings in which Strzok tried to defend himself. Democrats declared Strzok a victim, ignoring the clear bias he showed in the texts. Republicans and Strzok berated one another and traded insults. Republican Louie Gohmert of Texas taunted Strzok about his extramarital affair. "I can't help but wonder, when I see you looking there with a little smirk," the congressman asked, "how many times did you look so innocent into your wife's eyes and lie to her about Lisa Page?" Members of the panel and Strzok then started shouting. Later, Strzok accused South Carolina Republican Trey Gowdy of twisting his words, saying, "I don't appreciate what was originally said being changed." Gowdy thundered back, "I don't give a damn what you appreciate, Agent Strzok. I don't appreciate an FBI agent with an unprecedented level of animus working on two major investigations in 2016." Strzok insisted that his superiors and colleagues followed strict procedures designed to prevent political bias from impacting a case. "The suggestion that I, in some dark chamber somewhere in the FBI, would somehow cast aside all of these procedures, all of these safeguards, and somehow be able to do this is astounding to me." Any semblance of the bipartisan fact-finding that had emerged during Abscam, Iran-Contra, and the Iraq WMD congressional investigations was gone.

The texts further hardened partisan divisions. For Trump supporters, they confirmed that Trump was, in fact, the victim of a "deep state" conspiracy. Fox News legal commentator Greg Jarrett told host Sean Hannity that Mueller "has been using the FBI as a political weapon," and that the FBI had become America's secret police. "Secret surveillance, wiretapping, intimidation, harassment, and threats. It's like the old KGB that comes for you in the dark of the night banging through your door." Hannity then commented, "This is not hyperbole you are using here." A year after Trump had compared American intelligence agencies to the Nazis, conservative news outlets were doing it on a nightly basis.

To opponents of Trump, the allegations of a coup were overblown and nonsensical. If senior FBI officials or Strzok had wanted to block Trump from winning the presidency, they could have leaked the Trump-Russia investigation to the press. The existence of the probe, though, remained secret until the end of the 2016 campaign. In what many Democrats considered a pro-Trump FBI double standard, Comey publicly discussed the FBI's investigation of Clinton's email use without disclosing that Trump was under investigation for potential contacts with Russia. If the FBI hurt a candidate in 2016, they argued, it was Clinton.

Trump, though, continued to attack Comey and his aides. Hours before Andrew McCabe, Comey's former deputy, was to retire with his pension, he was fired in March 2018 for not being fully truthful with FBI investigators about his media contacts. In a tweet, Trump hailed his dismissal as "a great day for democracy" and again talked about "lies and corruption" at the "highest levels of the FBI." Former CIA director John Brennan replied to Trump, "When the full extent of your venality, moral turpitude, and political corruption becomes known, you will take your rightful place as a disgraced demagogue in the dustbin of history." The dispute continued that evening, with Fox News host Tucker Carlson citing Brennan's tweet as proof of the existence of the "deep state." "No wonder people are afraid of the deep state," Carlson told viewers. "This is what it looks like when it bares its fangs. Thwart us, and we'll destroy you. In case you are looking for a real threat to American democracy, and there are some, there you go." Brennan and Trump's bitter public sparring continued, and Trump, at one point, announced that he was revoking Brennan's security clearance.

For a sitting president and a former CIA director to express such open disdain for one another was another first in American history. In the first fourteen months of the Trump presidency, forty years of consensus between presidents and intelligence chiefs on the importance of keeping politics out of the intelligence world were erased in a few keystrokes.

Clapper, after decades of avoiding the press, began speaking out against Trump as well. He was more measured than Brennan but became a CNN contributor and regularly criticized Trump on the network. Clapper said he felt he had a duty to speak because he genuinely feared for the future of American democracy.

Some current and former intelligence officials believed that Brennan's tweets and Clapper's interviews played into Trump's "deep state" narrative. A former senior intelligence official told me that Clapper and Brennan were undermining public trust in the CIA and FBI. "John Brennan's tweets are exhibit A for Trump supporters that there is a deep state," the official said. "I don't think John's tweets are changing anyone's minds. I think they are putting more pressure on the intelligence community."

Over the remainder of 2018, Trump forced out his secretary of state, defense secretary, national security advisor, and attorney general. He assailed Mueller and his team of investigators as "thugs" and as "angry Democrats" who were "totally discredited." He disputed the CIA assessment that Saudi Arabia's crown prince was involved in the murder of journalist Jamal Khashoggi. He met with Russian president Vladimir Putin in Helsinki and said he believed Putin's denial of Russian interference in the 2016 election more than the assessment of US intelligence officials. He pressured the FBI to conduct a cursory review of sexual abuse allegations against Supreme Court nominee Brett Kavanaugh and then claimed that Kavanaugh had been "proven innocent." He publicly offered his former campaign manager Paul Manafort a pardon when it appeared that Manafort, then facing tax evasion charges, might become a cooperating witness. Most of all, Trump maintained extraordinary message discipline, falsely claiming, over and over, that he had brought unprecedented economic growth to the country, was the victim of an FBI witch hunt, and would fare well in the midterm elections.

In fact, in the 2018 midterm elections, Republicans were trounced, losing forty-one House seats. Led by a record number of female and minority candidates, Democrats took control of the House and vowed to launch congressional investigations of Trump and his administration. Adam Schiff, now the chair of the House Intelligence Committee, vowed to restore the "normal order" of the past to the committee's work. As they had with Nixon, Democrats vowed to use the power of Congress to restrain a wayward president.

Trump, in turn, was determined to counterpunch. He continued to use the politics of grievance and conspiracy to fire up his political base. He continued to fear an attempt to remove him from power and reverse his 2016 election win. On the day after the midterms, he began a search for a new attorney general. Trump craved a forceful, Roy Cohn–style advocate who would zealously defend him from what continued to be the largest threats to his presidency—Congress and the Mueller investigation.

Democrats and Republicans braced for the most intensive political and legal clashes between the executive and legislative branches since the 1970s. Both sides believed that nothing less than the future of American democracy was at stake.

SEVENTEEN

Trump, Barr, and the Gutting of Congressional Power

B ill Barr was late to join the Trump revolution. In the 2000s, the former Bush administration attorney general had grown rich. GTE had merged with Bell Atlantic and the two companies formed Verizon, the country's largest telephone company. From 2001 to 2007, Barr was paid an average of $1.7 million a year in salary and bonuses, in addition to stock options, the use of a company jet, and a spending allowance. When Barr took an early retirement in 2008, he received twenty-eight million dollars in deferred income and separation payments—a large enough sum that a watchdog group cited the payouts as an example of poor corporate governance. Barr had amassed a fortune that Forbes recently estimated at forty million dollars, and he made millions more serving on corporate boards, including those of Time Warner and Dominion Energy. He also joined Kirkland & Ellis, a Washington firm known for its leading conservative lawyers. Barr designed his own home, a sprawling house in McLean, Virginia, a few miles from CIA headquarters.

In July 2012, Barr learned that his youngest daughter, Meg, had a recurrence of non-Hodgkin's lymphoma. Meg, who was then 27 years old, faced a roughly twenty percent chance of survival. He stopped working and focused on his daughter's care. The family had Meg treated at the Dana-Farber Cancer Institute in Boston, and Barr and his wife moved to be near her. After Meg underwent chemotherapy and a stem-cell transplant, Barr rented a house in the town of Scituate, outside Boston, so that Meg could be isolated from other patients and avoid infection. They read books, walked on the beach together, and talked about what Meg would do if she survived. "Those three months were the best and worst of times," Meg told Fox News in 2019. "The hardest part of my illness was accepting the randomness of it, the fact that you can't control the outcome. Both my father and I tend to be control freaks." Meg survived. But, Barr told Fox, "Meg's illness changed our family. It changed me." Friends of Barr's said that he approached both his professional life and his personal life with a renewed zeal. Chuck Cooper, the conservative lawyer who worked with Barr in the Reagan administration, said, "I think he has an intense appreciation for life and our tenuous hold on it. And that to squander any of it is unforgivable."

Before Meg's illness, Barr's primary form of political activity had been making campaign donations to Republican political candidates. In the 1990s and early 2000s, he donated more than half a million dollars to Republican candidates, mostly such mainstream figures as George W. Bush, John McCain, and Mitt Romney. (Barr even supported Jeff Flake, the Arizona senator whose occasional criticisms of Trump ended up turning constituents against him.) In 2016, Barr gave twenty-seven hundred dollars to Trump's campaign—and about twenty times that amount to support Jeb Bush.

After Trump won, though, Barr demonstrated a convert's enthusiasm, writing op-eds for the *Washington Post* in which he endorsed Trump's controversial positions. In February 2017, after Sally Yates, the acting attorney general, refused to carry out a ban on travelers from predominantly Muslim countries, Barr accused her of "obstruction," and assailed news coverage of the situation. "The left, aided by an onslaught of tendentious media reporting, has engaged in a campaign of histrionics unjustified by the measured steps taken," he wrote. In July 2017, Barr criticized Robert Mueller for hiring prosecutors who had donated to Democratic politicians—but did not disclose his own donations to Republicans.

In November 2017, the *New York Times* contacted ten former attorneys general for comment after Trump's demand that a special counsel be appointed to investigate Clinton's role in the uranium sale. Barr was the only member of the group to reply. "There is nothing inherently wrong about a president calling for an investigation," he said. Barr added that he saw more basis for an investigation in the uranium deal than in any supposed collusion between Trump and Russia.

In June 2018, Barr sent an unsolicited, nineteen-page legal memo to Rod Rosenstein, the deputy attorney general, who was overseeing the Mueller investigation. He spent much of the letter elaborating an argument that a president's Article II powers rendered him essentially incapable of obstructing justice. He acknowledged that such blatant acts as destroying evidence and encouraging perjury were impermissible. But, he wrote, "Mueller's core premise—that the President acts 'corruptly' if he attempts to influence a proceeding in which his own conduct is being scrutinized—is untenable." Benjamin Wittes and Mikhaila Fogel, of the blog Lawfare, described the memo as "bizarre." Barr, without firsthand knowledge of the facts in the case, had devised a legal theory of obstruction, attributed it to Mueller, and then declared it "fatally misconceived."

After the midterm elections, Trump forced out Sessions and nominated Barr as attorney general, calling him "my first choice since Day One." Barr had strong advocates. Pat Cipollone, his former speechwriter, had become White House counsel. Laura Ingraham, the Fox News host, lobbied on his behalf as well.

On January 15, 2019, Barr arrived on the Hill for confirmation hearings, accompanied by his wife and daughters. Many Democrats in Congress, particularly those who hadn't studied Barr's record, hoped that he would be an institutionalist who would curb Trump's legal excesses. They also faced a stark political reality: they did not have the votes to block his nomination. Ignoring the advice of some aides, Democrats did not dwell on Barr's statements regarding criminal justice, or on whether his religious beliefs might affect his views.

Most of the hearings focused on how Barr would handle the release of the Mueller report. In his opening statement, he repeated a reassuring pledge that he had made at his confirmation hearings as Bush's nominee: "The Attorney General must ensure that the administration of justice—the enforcement of the law—is above and away from politics." He testified that he believed that Mueller, a longtime associate whom he described as a "good friend," should be allowed to complete his investigation. But he also signaled skepticism about the idea that Trump had colluded with Russia, and repeatedly expressed support for the president's policies. Four weeks later, he was confirmed, in a largely party-line vote, as Trump's second attorney general.

.   .   .

Tom O'Connor and other FBI agents started leaving bags of canned food in a break room in the bureau's Washington field office. They were concerned about colleagues who had been working without pay for the last three weeks. The federal government had shut down on December 22, after Democrats in Congress declined to approve a request from President Trump for $5.7 billion to fund a border wall between Mexico and the United States. The impromptu food pantries in Washington, New York, Dallas, and Newark FBI field offices allowed staff to discreetly leave food for colleagues in need. No one monitored who entered and left the room. No one tracked what disappeared. Employees could take what they needed without feeling ashamed.

O'Connor, the former Massachusetts police officer who was now the head of the FBI Agents Association, found himself in another awkward political position. As the shutdown dragged on, he was getting calls from dozens of journalists asking if it was curtailing FBI operations. O'Connor did not want to blame either side in the dispute. That would have been a betrayal of the nonpartisan ethos that he believed in. At the same time, he was trying to find ways to pressure politicians from both parties to solve the issue. "It's discouraging that this is the way people who put their lives at risk are being treated by the federal government," O'Connor told me at the time. "To be treated this way is wrong."

O'Connor said that the majority of the bureau's thirteen thousand agents were working without pay, and morale was plummeting. Agents continued to work cases, but the shutdown was "slowing F.B.I. investigations, and it will only get worse as it drags on." In some field offices, employees were going to their supervisors in tears and asking for help. Others feared that they would be unable to make a mortgage or credit card payment; as a result, they might fail the bureau's routine financial-background checks, which could cause them to lose their security clearance and, with it, their job. With five thousand of the bureau's approximately thirty-five thousand employees on furlough, all vacations had been cancelled, requests to work second jobs were rising, and retirements were being delayed.

Agents' salaries vary based on where they live and their years of experience. At the outset of their careers, agents in the New York area earn roughly $65,000 a year. By the time they retire, they earn, at most, about $100,000 a year. The highest-ranking FBI executives are paid $190,000 annually. O'Connor said the long-term fear was that, given that the private sector pays more than the bureau, the FBI and other federal law-enforcement organizations would both lose experienced agents and be unable to recruit new ones.

In the weeks before the shutdown, Trump had continued to accuse the FBI of conducting illegal searches, smearing him, and secretly protecting Democrats. On December 16, Trump falsely accused the FBI of breaking into the office of his former attorney, Michael Cohen. The president tweeted, "Remember, Michael Cohen only became a 'Rat' after the FBI did something which was absolutely unthinkable & unheard of until the Witch Hunt was illegally started. They BROKE INTO AN ATTORNEY'S OFFICE!

Why didn't they break into the DNC to get the Server, or Crooked's office?" (A federal judge had, in fact, issued the FBI a search warrant.)

Two days later, the president falsely claimed that the bureau had intentionally deleted thousands of texts between Strzok and Page. He tweeted, "Biggest outrage yet in the long, winding and highly conflicted Mueller Witch Hunt is the fact that 19,000 demanded Text messages between Peter Strzok and his FBI lover, Lisa Page, were purposely & illegally deleted. Would have explained whole Hoax, which is now under protest!" (In fact, the Justice Department's inspector general found that the bureau's automated system for collecting messages from staffers' mobile phones had failed.)

O'Connor declined to comment on Trump's attacks, saying only that agents strongly believe that the FBI must remain fully independent. "The F.B.I. is an apolitical organization," he told me. Christopher Wray, the bureau's new director, had made no public comments since the shutdown began. Since taking office, he had adopted a strategy of ignoring the attacks and avoiding public fights with Trump. The result, though, was that Trump had, in effect, silenced the FBI director.

Trump's attacks divided opinion among retired agents, just as they divided opinion across the country. Some former agents supported Comey and saw Trump as undermining the rule of law. Others criticized Comey and said that his call for Americans to vote for Democrats in the 2018 midterm elections made the bureau appear politically biased. Kevin Brock, a former assistant director of intelligence, felt that the text messages between Strzok and Page raised legitimate questions about the neutrality of the Trump-Russia investigation. Brock told me that the texts had shocked and angered many agents, who felt that they were gross violations of the bureau's culture. "In my twenty-four years, I recall having one political discussion, one time, that lasted about five minutes. It's just not a conversation that happens," he said. "Agents had just never heard anything like those texts." O'Connor, while more cryptic, was also upset about the texts.

He cited a Hoover-era FBI dictum that he had learned while attending basic training in Quantico: Don't embarrass the bureau.

.   .   .

In an Oval Office ceremony on February 14, 2019, Chief Justice John Roberts administered the oath of office to William Barr, as President Trump and Barr's wife, Christine, looked on. For Barr, it was a personal triumph. He became only the second American to serve as attorney general twice. (John Crittenden served twice in the 1800s.) The Justice Department that Barr took over was plagued by dissension and low morale. Trump's public attacks on Sessions and Mueller had unnerved staffers. And though career employees supported Sessions's decision to recuse himself from the Mueller investigation, some staffers said that he was distant and seemed over his head in meetings. "When he got confused or distracted, which seemed pretty often, he would tell some story about a bank robbery in Mobile," a former department official said. "He was a nice enough man, but I don't think he had any idea what we did for a living."

Current and former Justice Department officials told me that the main problem was not Sessions but Trump, whose administration required them to defend contorted legal positions. Under Sessions, the department defended the travel ban, a prohibition on transgender people joining the military, a policy of separating immigrant children from their parents, and a dismissal of claims that the president had violated the emoluments clause. Several career officials declined to put their names on legal memos. "Morale has been low since Trump came in," Matthew Collette, a former senior official who worked for thirty years at the Justice Department, said in an interview. "The incredibly controversial and difficult cases started and kept coming."

When past presidents resisted sending materials to Congress by claiming "executive privilege," Justice Department lawyers tried to help resolve the disputes. Under Trump, that practice stopped, according to Senator Sheldon Whitehouse. As Brett Kavanaugh was going through confirmation hearings for the Supreme Court, Congress requested documents describing his work in the George W. Bush administration. The White House refused access to more than a hundred thousand pages of them. Blank sheets of paper arrived on Capitol Hill stamped "Constitutional privilege," a category that members of Congress said they had never heard of before.

Rather than avoiding the partisanship of the Trump era, Barr placed the Justice Department at the center of it. One of the most divisive fights was over immigration. In March 2018, the administration announced that it intended to add a citizenship question to the forthcoming national census—a measure that liberals said was designed to disadvantage Hispanics. The effort fueled bitter division in the department. Collette said that lawyers were comfortable with implementing a new administration's policy priorities, but not with "twisting legal views to fit the personal views or needs of the President."

After taking office, Barr intensified Trump's crackdown on immigrants. He directed judges to deny some migrants the opportunity to post bail, and restricted migrants' ability to claim asylum based on connections to family members who face threats of violence. The Justice Department tried to reverse a court decision that helped protect people from fast-track deportations. It also sued "sanctuary cities," in California and other states, which offered to protect migrants fleeing the crackdown.

In June 2019, the Supreme Court ruled against the administration in its bid to add a citizenship question to the census. In a 5–4 decision, Chief Justice John Roberts concluded that the "sole stated reason" for the change "seems to have been contrived."

Trump responded to the defeat by issuing an executive order giving the president the ability to collect the citizenship data by other means. Legal experts widely dismissed the order as a pointless fig leaf, but in a Rose Garden ceremony, Barr declared it a triumph. Standing a few feet from Trump, he said, "Congratulations again, Mr. President, on taking this effective action."

Most importantly, Barr protected Trump from the fallout of the Mueller investigation. When the special counsel released his findings, Barr released a sanitized four-page summary before the full report was made public, which the president immediately used to declare himself cleared. Barr's summary was carefully crafted. He quoted part of a sentence saying that no conclusive proof of collusion had been found, but left out the rest, which suggested that Russia and the Trump campaign had worked at arm's length toward similar goals. He mentioned that the report identified potential incidents of obstruction of justice, but did not enumerate or describe them. (There were ten, including Trump's firing of the FBI director James Comey, who had declined to promise him loyalty.)

Three days later, Mueller wrote Barr a letter, complaining that the summary "did not fully capture the context, nature, and substance" of his report and had created "public confusion about critical aspects of the results of our investigation." Mueller had prepared an introduction and executive summaries, and he urged Barr to release them. Barr declined, and took another three weeks to redact the full report, allowing Trump's claim of "total exoneration" to dominate the news.

When Barr finally released the Mueller report, he held a press conference before journalists had access to it, which prevented them from asking detailed questions about its contents. Barr repeated four times that no collusion had been found and argued that "the President was frustrated and angered by a sincere belief that the investigation was undermining his Presidency, propelled by his political opponents, and fueled by illegal leaks." Four days later, congressional Democrats subpoenaed Don McGahn, the White House counsel, who had witnessed some of Trump's potential acts of obstruction; the Justice Department issued a legal opinion that he was not required to testify.

At the behest of the president, Barr launched an investigation of the FBI's Trump-Russia probe and the intelligence community's assessment that Russia tried to aid Trump in the election. Rather than seek a nonpartisan commission, Barr appointed a federal prosecutor, reinforcing the president's claims of a "coup." A government official who asked not to be named told me that while Barr does not believe that the "deep state" is plotting to force Trump from power, he is convinced that there was something nefarious in the FBI's conduct of its investigation. Last April, Barr spoke about the matter before a Senate subcommittee. "Spying on a political campaign is a big deal," he said. "I think spying did occur. The question is whether it was adequately predicated."

At the time, the Justice Department's inspector general, Michael Horowitz, was already investigating the FBI's handling of the Trump-Russia probe. But Barr, at Trump's bequest, began his own investigation. Trump gave Barr a far-reaching power: to unilaterally declassify top-secret documents in order to review the work of the country's intelligence agencies.

To conduct the probe, Barr appointed John Durham, the US attorney in Connecticut, who, during the Obama administration, had investigated the CIA's use of torture against suspected terrorists. Barr and Durham made trips to the UK and Italy, where they asked officials for evidence of misconduct by the FBI and the CIA. Ron Wyden, a Democratic senator from Oregon who has served on the Intelligence Committee since 2001, said in an interview that Barr was ignoring Justice Department norms: "He is flying around the world trying to get evidence that would confirm these bizarre conspiracy theories and exonerate Russia." Intelligence officials worried that the trips would make longtime allies hesitant to share information with the United States, for fear of being drawn into a partisan fight.

David Laufman, a former senior counterintelligence official at the Justice Department who helped investigate Russian interference, said that the probe has also sent a clear message to US officials: challenge Trump at your peril. "We're into Crazy Town," Laufman said in an interview. The investigation, he said, was "evocative of regimes in history that conduct purges for perceived disloyalty."

. . .

Months after being sworn in, Barr had emerged as the most feared, criticized, and effective member of Trump's cabinet. Like no attorney general since the Watergate era, he acted as the president's political sword and shield. Both men believed that any constraint on presidential power weakened the United States. Both men combined the pro-business instincts of traditional Republicans with a focus on culture clash and grievance. And both men shared a sense of being surrounded by a hostile liberal insurgency. Barr, a devout Catholic, was one of many religious conservatives who have embraced the president. Under Trump, conservative Catholics have achieved a degree of influence rivaling that of evangelicals in the George W. Bush administration. Along with Barr and Cipollone, there are the acting chief of staff, Mick Mulvaney; the White House counselor, Kellyanne Conway; the National Economic Council director, Larry Kudlow; and the former chief strategist, Steve Bannon. Leonard Leo, of the Federalist Society, has guided Trump in his selection of judges.

An administration official acknowledged that religious leaders "are acutely aware of Trump's shortcomings" but also recognize his value to their cause. "Name a political leader who has done more for conservatives," the official said. Trump has reshaped the country's legal system, appointing two Supreme Court justices and a hundred and sixty-two other judges, most of whom can be counted on to rule with conservative principles in mind. Barr's Justice Department has supported efforts to restrict access to abortion, and has aided attempts to secure taxpayer funding for Christian schools. Barr has also helped Trump restore the use of the federal death penalty, which presidents of both parties have frozen for sixteen years.

Barr likes to describe Trump as the heir to Ronald Reagan. But in some ways his administration, with its fixation on enemies and its willingness to bend laws for political gain, is more reminiscent of Richard Nixon's. Reaganites believed that any government intervention in private enterprise was a step on what the libertarian economist

Milton Friedman called "the road to serfdom." Under Barr, the Justice Department has been accused of using its influence to punish the president's opponents. In September 2019, Honda, Ford, Volkswagen, and BMW agreed with California to observe emissions standards tougher than those endorsed by the White House. After the administration derided the move as a "P.R. stunt," the Justice Department opened an antitrust investigation of the automakers.

The administration has also been accused of favoritism in awarding government contracts. At the request of Democrats, the Pentagon inspector general launched an investigation in December 2019 of reports that Trump personally pushed for the awarding of a $400 million contract for border wall construction to a North Dakota company run by a Republican donor who made multiple appearances on *Fox News* contending that his firm would do a better job than the companies previously chosen by the government. Since taking office, Trump has repeatedly attacked Jeff Bezos, who owns Amazon and the *Washington Post*, and falsely accused him of ordering the *Post* to produce negative coverage of the president. In December, Amazon filed a lawsuit alleging that Trump's attacks had caused the Pentagon to unfairly award a $10 billion contract to Microsoft.

Barr's work on the president's behalf extends to keeping his tax returns secret. In 2019, Trump's personal lawyers argued that his financial records should not be given to New York City prosecutors, who were investigating whether he had made an illegal payment to the adult-film actress Stephanie Clifford. The Justice Department filed an amicus brief, arguing that turning over the records would "impose substantial burdens on the President's time, attention, and discharge of his constitutional duties." Stephen Gillers, a legal ethics professor at New York University Law School, argued that Barr was failing to challenge Trump when he should. "We don't have an Attorney General now," he said. "We have an additional lawyer for the President."

. . .

On June 11, 2019, Tom O'Connor arrived on Capitol Hill to attend a hearing by the House Judiciary Subcommittee on the Constitution, Civil Rights, and Civil Liberties. It did not relate to Trump-Russia, the Mueller report, or Barr. Instead, it focused on fifteen members of the FBI who had died of cancer in recent years. Different types of cancer had killed them, and their ages and backgrounds varied, but all of them had been first responders to the World Trade Center or the Pentagon on 9/11. They were among the 2,355 first responders, volunteers, and others who had died from 9/11-related health problems in the years after the attacks, according to the World Trade Center Health Program, which is administered by the Centers for Disease Control and Prevention. The hearing threw into relief the growing exasperation of rank-and-file law enforcement officials with American political leaders from both parties. Their alienation from politics and disgust with elected officials had steadily grown.

Years after the attacks, cancers, respiratory problems, and other illnesses thought to stem from toxins released by the attacks were claiming new victims. Several of the agents who died had worked alongside O'Connor at the Pentagon. He knew that he, too, might one day be diagnosed with a 9/11-related illness, but expressed pride at his service that day. "It was an honor," he said. "There was no place I would rather be."

O'Connor took a seat in the middle of the third row. Dozens of other current and former law enforcement officials were present to demand that Congress fully fund the September 11th Victim Compensation Fund, which covered medical expenses and death benefits. As the population aged, the number of 9/11-related cases had nearly doubled from 56,000 in 2011 to 95,000 in 2019, with roughly 500 to 900 new cases being identified each month. To continue to compensate expected victims adequately, Congress needed to appropriate an additional $11 billion.

For the next several hours, dozens of reporters in the room focused on two men in the front row. One was Luis Alvarez, a New York City

Senator Frank Church of Idaho (left), the chairman of the Church Committee, and Senator John Tower of Texas (right), vice chairman, display a poison dart gun created by the Central Intelligence Agency for assassinations in 1975. (AP PHOTO / HENRY GRIFFIN)

US Attorney General Edward Levi, who ended the FBI's illegal domestic spying on Americans and brought nonpartisanship to the Justice Department after the corruption of Watergate, testifies before the Senate Intelligence Committee in 1976. (KEYSTONE PRESS / ALAMY STOCK PHOTO)

Mel Weinberg, a New York con man turned FBI informant who played a central role in Abscam, a public corruption scandal that sent six members of Congress to jail for accepting bribes, arrives at federal court in Brooklyn in 1980 to testify. Abscam was the basis for the 2013 film *American Hustle*. (AP PHOTO / DAVID PICKOFF)

William Webster, the only American who has served as director of both the CIA and FBI, at a memorial event for FBI agents in 2011. Told that some Americans believed that he is a member of the "deep state," Webster responded, "What is the deep state?" (AP PHOTO / ALAN DIAZ)

Attorney General Ed Meese testifies to the congressional committee investigating the Iran-Contra affair in 1987. (AP PHOTO / JOHN DURICKA)

Reagan administration CIA director William Casey in 1981. (AP PHOTO)

Lieutenant Colonel Oliver North testifies before the joint House-Senate committee investigating the Iran-Contra affair in 1987. (AP PHOTO / LANA HARRIS)

Senators Warren Rudman (R-New Hampshire) and Daniel Inouye (D-Hawaii), co-chairs of the Iran-Contra Committee, releasing its final report in 1987. (TERRY ASHE / CONTRIBUTOR / THE LIFE IMAGE COLLECTION VIA GETTY IMAGES)

The compound of the Branch Davidian religious community burns on April 19, 1993, after FBI agents attempted to end a fifty-two-day standoff near Waco, Texas. Seventy-five people, including twenty children, perished in the fire. (AP PHOTO / RON HEFLIN)

Janet Reno, a prosecutor from Miami who served as US attorney general for the entire eight years of the Clinton administration, testifies before the 9/11 Commission in 2004. (AP PHOTO / DENNIS COOK)

Secretary of State Colin Powell gives a speech at the United Nations describing
evidence of weapons of mass destruction in Iraq on February 5, 2003.
(AFP / STRINGER VIA GETTY IMAGES)

Former CIA staffer and contractor Edward Snowden in Moscow in 2017.
Snowden carried out the largest leak of classified material in US history.
(BAIKAL / ALAMY STOCK PHOTO)

Senate Intelligence Committee ranking member Dianne Feinstein (D-California) and Chairman Richard Burr (R-North Carolina) confer before a hearing on Capitol Hill in 2016. (CHIP SOMODEVILLA / STAFF VIA GETTY IMAGES)

CIA director nominee John Brennan testifies during his Senate confirmation hearing in 2013. (ZUMA PRESS, INC. / ALAMY STOCK PHOTO)

Director of National Intelligence James Clapper testifies before the Senate Armed Services Committee in 2017. (AP PHOTO / EVAN VUCCI)

FBI Director Christopher Wray, CIA Director Gina Haspel, and Director of National Intelligence Dan Coats wait to testify before the Senate Intelligence Committee in 2019. (AP PHOTO / JOSE LUIS MAGANA)

Attorney General William Barr testifying to a House committee on Capitol Hill in 2019. (SHUTTERSTOCK)

Former FBI general counsel James Baker in 2020. (KRISTEN NYMAN)

Republican Congressman Will Hurd of Texas, a former undercover CIA officer, speaks during the House Intelligence Committee impeachment hearings in 2019. (SHUTTERSTOCK)

Former US ambassador to Ukraine Marie Yovanovitch testifies during impeachment hearings held by the House Intelligence Committee in November 2019. (MEDIAPUNCH INC. / ALAMY STOCK PHOTO)

Former White House national security aide Fiona Hill testifies during impeachment hearings held by the House Intelligence Committee in November 2019. (AP PHOTO / JOSE LUIS MAGANA)

Joan Dempsey, a Navy cryptologist who rose to become one of the highest-ranking intelligence offices of her generation, in 1985. (COURTESY OF JOAN DEMPSEY)

Tom O'Connor, a retired FBI agent who investigated Al Qaeda members, Blackwater security guards, and Aryan Nations white supremacists over the course of his twenty-year career, in 2019. O'Connor summed up his job as to "investigate evil in whatever form it takes." (COURTESY OF THE FBIAA)

Police detective and 9/11 first responder stricken with colorectal cancer three years earlier that doctors linked to the attack. The other was the comedian Jon Stewart, who had spent years demanding that 9/11 first responders be properly compensated. When Alvarez spoke, the room grew hushed. Emaciated from his illness, he spoke softly but clearly: "Less than twenty-four hours from now, I will be starting my sixty-ninth round of chemotherapy. Yeah, you heard that correct. I should not be here with you, but you made me come." Alvarez expressed the pride he took in responding to the attacks, to "help people first and then to help their families bury someone or something." He said there was no place he would rather have been than Ground Zero. "We were part of showing the world that we would not back down in the face of terrorism and that we could all work together, no races, no colors, no politics." He concluded by urging Congress to act. "I will not stand by and watch as my friends with cancer from 9/11 like me are valued less than anyone else because of when they get sick. You made me come here the day before my sixty-ninth round of chemo. I'm going to make sure that you never forget to take care of the 9/11 responders."

O'Connor and the other first responders stood up behind Alvarez and gave him a standing ovation. Some members of the committee did as well. Stewart spoke next. Infuriated by the small number of House members who showed up for the subcommittee hearing, he lambasted Congress as a whole. "As I sit here today, I can't help but think what an incredible metaphor this room is for the entire process that getting health care and benefits for 9/11 first responders has come to," Stewart said. "Behind me, a filled room of 9/11 first responders, and in front of me, a nearly empty Congress. Sick and dying, they brought themselves down to speak to no one. Shameful. It is an embarrassment to the country and it is a stain on this institution. You should be ashamed of yourselves and those who aren't here, but you won't be because accountability is something that appears to not happen in this chamber."

Videos of Stewart and Alvarez went viral. Contempt for lawmakers filled social media. The following day Alvarez was too disoriented to receive his scheduled round of chemotherapy. Medical tests showed that his liver was failing. Within a week, his family admitted him to hospice. Three weeks after his testimony, Alvarez died. He was 53.

In the week after the hearing, the House passed a bill fully funding the program, 402–12, and the Senate passed it, 97–2. A month after Alvarez's death, Trump signed the bill into law in a Rose Garden ceremony with first responders. Reading from a prepared statement, Trump praised them for their heroism. At one point, he appeared to veer off script. "I was down there also, but I'm not considering myself a first responder," Trump said. "But I was down there. I spent a lot of time down there with you." The statement was false, the latest in a series of unproven claims Trump made about his personal response to 9/11, from seeing Muslims celebrating the attacks to watching through a "solid gold" telescope in his office as victims jumped from the buildings—which were four miles away. From the empty seats at the congressional hearing to Trump's lies in the Rose Garden, America's political class had failed its civil servants and itself. The social compact—which created a system for law enforcement officials and politicians to work together—was fraying.

. . .

On July 24, after weeks of speculation, Robert Mueller testified before the House Judiciary and Intelligence committees regarding his final report. For weeks, Mueller had signaled that his testimony would not go beyond what was in his report, but Democrats were still eager to have him testify. In his first exchange with Democratic House Judiciary chairman Jerry Nadler, Mueller appeared to make news. The former special counsel directly contradicted one of Trump's primary claims regarding the Mueller investigation. Speaking in lawyerly terms, Mueller said that his report had not exonerated the president on allegations of obstruction of justice.

"The president was not exculpated for the acts that he allegedly committed," he said, referring to obstruction of justice. Mueller agreed that the report was not the "total exoneration" that Trump claimed.

After that exchange, Mueller's testimony devolved into a five-hour battle of conflicting narratives. Democrats insisted that Trump was guilty of obstruction of justice and rampant lies. Republicans insisted that Trump was the victim of a vast conspiracy involving a cabal of FBI agents. At times, Mueller appeared sober and in command. At other times, the special counsel, who was 74, seemed "Dazed and Confused"—as the Drudge Report put it. He declined to answer many questions, in a seemingly sincere effort to remain neutral and nonpartisan. Overall, he failed to answer questions with the clarity that would have helped Americans struggling with what to make of the affair.

Questions from Democrats followed a predictable script. They tried to coax the former special counsel, over and over, into recounting the most damaging findings of his report. On some points, Mueller helped. On others, he did not. Mueller said that Russia had systematically intervened in the election to aid Donald Trump, but he declined to comment on whether Trump should be impeached, repeatedly saying, "I'm not going to talk about that issue."

Questions from Republicans conveyed a polar-opposite narrative: that Trump was the victim. They argued that a group of politically biased FBI officials had launched a spurious investigation of Trump's supposed ties with Russia. Representative John Ratcliffe, a Republican from Texas, accused Mueller of smearing Trump by saying his report did not "exonerate" Trump of obstruction of justice. Ratcliffe urged voters to ignore the "Democrats and socialists on the other side of the aisle" who cited that part of Mueller's report. Fact-checkers found Ratcliffe's claim of an FBI conspiracy to be false, but he ended his appearance on a note of indignation. "I agree with the chairman this morning when he said Donald Trump is not above the law. He's not," Ratcliffe said, his voice rising. "But he damn sure shouldn't be below the law."

Representative Will Hurd, the former CIA officer and moderate Republican from Texas, took a different tack. Hurd asked Mueller if he believed it would be good for the US government to have a strategy to respond to disinformation from foreign governments. "That sounds like a worthwhile endeavor," Mueller replied. "In fact, one of the other areas we have to look at is that many more countries are developing capability to replicate what the Russian government has done." Hurd then asked Mueller if he believed Russia would continue to try to meddle in US elections. "It wasn't a single attempt," Mueller said. "They are doing it as we sit here. And they expect to do it during the next campaign."

In the end, the hearings were most remarkable for what they revealed about the state of American politics. Distrust was the defining dynamic. Each political party accused the other of committing, in effect, acts of treason.

.   .   .

Four days after the hearing, it was clear why Ratcliffe, the Republican from Texas, had been so aggressive in questioning Mueller. Trump nominated Ratcliffe to be the most powerful intelligence official in the country, replacing Dan Coats, who was stepping down as the director of national intelligence. Administration sources told the *Times* that Trump enjoyed watching Ratcliffe aggressively question Mueller, though they also denied that this was the reason the Texas congressman got the job. Senate Minority Leader Chuck Schumer, of course, disagreed, issuing a statement that said, "It's clear that Representative Ratcliffe was selected because he exhibited blind loyalty to President Trump with his demagogic questioning of former Special Counsel Robert Mueller."

Ratcliffe was playing his part in Trump's war against the "deep state." Coats, a leader of the Republican establishment, had stood up and repeatedly contradicted Trump regarding the threat posed by Russia, and also publicly questioned Trump's worldview. He had challenged Trump's optimistic assessments of North Korea's willingness to give up its nuclear weapons and the extent to which ISIS had been eradicated. Ratcliffe, a Trump loyalist who echoed the president's narratives, was his natural replacement.

Most important, Ratcliffe was a full-throated backer of Trump's practice of trafficking in conspiracy theories for political gain. Ratcliffe repeatedly claimed that Hillary Clinton, not Donald Trump, colluded with Russia, and that a cabal of CIA and FBI officials, working with foreign intelligence services, carried out a global conspiracy to entrap Trump aides.

James Clapper said that the appointment of Ratcliffe to replace Coats sent an unmistakable message to thousands of members of the intelligence community: "Obviously, the President wants someone in this position whose first priority is loyalty to Donald Trump." Clapper also expressed concern about the effect that appointing Ratcliffe could have on intelligence officials whose job it was to present apolitical information to policymakers. "I worry about the people in the intelligence community, and the impact of being directed to write intelligence analyses that comport with the president's worldview, and not their best judgment as to the facts," he said. "Over time, this could be very dangerous to the country. 'Truth to power' is a crucial, bedrock tenet of US intelligence, and Dan Coats upheld that."

Senator Angus King, a Maine Independent who caucuses with the Democrats and serves on the Senate Intelligence Committee, warned of the dangers of politicizing intelligence. "We have gotten in trouble in this country in the past when we have cherry-picked intelligence for political purposes or to suit the needs of the president," he said. "That is the worst thing that can happen."

Republicans believed that intelligence agencies were plotting against the president; Democrats, in turn, were convinced the president was silencing intelligence chiefs who disagreed with him.

Days after Ratcliffe's nomination was announced, press reports emerged that he had exaggerated his qualifications. Ratcliffe's office had claimed in biographical documents that he had prosecuted major terrorist cases as a federal prosecutor in Texas. It also claimed that Ratcliffe single-handedly had "over three hundred illegal immigrants" arrested in a single day. Both claims were, at best, exaggerations. Trump and his aides had been impressed with Ratcliffe's questioning of Mueller and his interviews on Fox News, but they had not thoroughly vetted his background. Senator Burr of North Carolina, the chairman of the Senate Intelligence Committee, and other Republican senators pressured Trump to pick another nominee. Five days after announcing Ratcliffe's nomination, Trump withdrew his name from consideration and promptly took to Twitter to blame the press. "Rather than going through months of slander and libel, I explained to John how miserable it would be for him and his family to deal with these people," he wrote. "John has therefore decided to stay in Congress where he has done such an outstanding job representing the people of Texas, and our Country."

EIGHTEEN

Checks and Balances

On September 26, 2019, the American people had an opportunity to judge the "deep state" for themselves. A meticulous nine-page whistleblower complaint was released by the House Intelligence Committee. In the document, an unnamed CIA official described an effort by President Trump to use the powers of his office to pressure Ukraine's newly elected president, Volodymyr Zelensky, into launching a criminal investigation of Trump's political rival, Joe Biden. The whistleblower wrote, "The White House officials who told me this information were deeply disturbed by what had transpired in the phone call."

Normally, a phone call of this nature would have been described in a memorandum shared with Cabinet members. Instead, according to the whistleblower, it was transferred into a separate system reserved for documents involving sensitive national security information, where far fewer officials would see it. The whistleblower described this act as evidence that White House officials understood the "gravity" of what had occurred on the call. The pressure on the Ukrainian leadership to do Trump's bidding was intense. Russia, which had already sent military forces to annex Crimea, was carrying out military operations in eastern Ukraine. At the same time, Trump was asking for a "favor" while withholding nearly $400 million in military aid. Zelensky, whose previous career had been as a comic actor, was now caught in a very real, high-stakes geopolitical struggle with the most powerful leader in the world.

And yet, Trump's plan had been derailed by the whistleblower. The emergence of the complaint showed that—despite Trump's pressure—the system created in the 1970s to prevent waste, fraud, and abuse by presidents, intelligence agencies, and individual federal workers alike still functioned. The Church reforms remained intact. The civil service rules dating back to the 1935 Hatch Act and the reforms enacted by Jimmy Carter still stood.

Joan Dempsey, the former Navy cryptologist who became a top CIA official, praised the system, particularly the Hatch Act, which bars federal civil servants from engaging in political activity at work. "The Hatch Act is singularly important to an apolitical civil service," Dempsey said. "We do not let politics come into the workplace because it is illegal to do so. We bend over backwards to remain apolitical because it is required by law." She praised the whistleblower for following procedure and not leaking the information to the press. "It was an extraordinary statement, very well written. I would expect that from an intelligence officer," she said. "The whistleblower went through channels. They didn't go to the press. They didn't go to the Hill."

As the whistleblower was supposed to do under the law, he or she had filed the complaint with the inspector general of the Intelligence Community, one of the independent watchdogs created in 1978 by Congress and Carter to counter waste, fraud, and abuse. Inspector General Michael Atkinson then deemed the whistleblower's complaint "credible and urgent" and, again following the law, forwarded it to the acting director of national intelligence, Joseph Maguire. Maguire, a former Navy SEAL, agreed with the inspector general that the complaint was credible.

When Maguire attempted to take the next step in the process by law—sharing the complaint with the House and Senate intelligence committees—he was blocked by the White House and the

Justice Department. Again, Barr's Justice Department was aiding Trump politically. Barr claimed he had played no role in the decisions, but the department issued two legal opinions that protected the president. First, the Office of Legal Counsel ruled that the complaint was not an "urgent concern" and therefore did not need to be handed over to congressional oversight committees. Then the department's Criminal Division dismissed the whistleblower's allegation that the president had broken a federal law forbidding candidates to solicit support from foreigners. The department reasoned that a publicly announced Ukrainian investigation into Biden's conduct cannot be a campaign contribution, because there is no way to precisely enumerate its value.

With the release of the complaint to Congress blocked, word of the whistleblower complaint was leaked to the *Washington Post* and the *Wall Street Journal*. In the first of a series of stories, the *Post* reported that the complaint related to a phone call between Trump and a foreign leader. Then it reported that the call related to Ukraine. In a final story, several days later, the newspaper reported that the complaint related to President Trump's effort to pressure Ukraine to dig up dirt on the Democratic candidate Joe Biden.

Trump tried to discredit the claim and blame it on a conspiracy. He dismissed the whistleblower as a "political hack," questioned whether the person was "on our country's side," and declined to hand the complaint over to the House Intelligence Committee. After the dispute dragged on for several days, the Constitution's checks and balances set in. Congress invoked its most powerful political and legal weapon against a president: House Speaker Nancy Pelosi announced the opening of a formal impeachment inquiry of Trump over his refusal to hand over the complaint. Faced with potential impeachment, Trump released a summary of his call with Ukraine's president and forwarded the whistleblower complaint. The Constitution's checks and balances were at work.

Instead of ending the controversy, the release of the documents intensified calls for impeachment. The summary of the call corroborated the whistleblower's claim. And in testimony before the House Intelligence Committee, Maguire hailed the whistleblower. "As public servants, we have a solemn duty to report waste and abuse," Maguire said. "I think the whistleblower did the right thing. I think he followed the law every step of the way."

Dempsey said she did not know if the whistleblower's complaint would be fully corroborated. But the whistleblower deserved praise and protection, given Trump's record of attacking critics, which ranged from public vilification to threatening to remove security clearances to eliminating pensions. "It is a benefit to the country to have a skilled, apolitical civil service that functions on behalf of the country, not a particular person or political party," she said. Dempsey argued that the career civil servants who have come forward deserve support instead of being declared part of a conspiracy. "I have seen bad behaviors, I have seen failures, but ultimately it is an extraordinary professional civil service," she said. "This whole thing of a 'deep state' is to discredit the civil servants who are trying to help the country."

Richard Blee, the former undercover CIA officer, said he was impressed by the quality of the whistleblower's complaint and dismissed claims that a "deep state" existed. "In my career, there was no nefarious 'deep state,'" he said. "I never viewed the bureaucracy negatively. The bureaucracy kept the state running."

The battered oversight system still stood. From the whistleblower, to the Intelligence Community inspector general, to the *Washington Post*, to the House Intelligence Committee, to the House of Representatives, each part of the system had functioned as designed. It was unclear if the allegations would be proven. It was doubtful that the revelations would significantly shift the political balance in the country. But an effort by backers of the power of the executive branch to withhold information from the legislative branch and the public had failed.

.   .   .

The reaction to the whistleblower complaint filled James Baker with optimism. In 2017, Baker had been ousted from his position as the FBI's general counsel, after President Trump fired Comey. Trump had welcomed the news of Baker's removal in a tweet: "Wow, 'FBI lawyer James Baker reassigned.'" In subsequent tweets and retweets, the president accused Baker of lying to Congress and being part of an "Unconstitutional Hoax" and an "attempted coup."

Baker considered Trump's claims about him to be completely false, but he said nothing publicly at the time. "I believed that, once I was out of the FBI, I could resume a normal life and avoid the spotlight," he said. "But that was inaccurate, because the damage had already been done by the president's tweets and stories about me on Fox News and other outlets."

Once considered one of the government's most trusted national-security officials, Baker found that Trump's attacks impacted his ability to find a job. "Certain corporations and law firms thought that I was too controversial and didn't want to hire me," Baker said. "It surprised me and was dispiriting." Over time, Baker decided to push back. "At a certain point, I became unafraid of Donald Trump," he said. "I felt, OK, I can speak out. And also, I have an obligation to speak out." In May of 2019, Baker had begun publicly criticizing what he called Trump's "false narrative that there was a coup, and a conspiracy, and treason."

Two weeks after the release of the whistleblower complaint, Marie Yovanovitch, a career foreign-service officer and the former US ambassador to Ukraine, also decided to push back against Trump. In nine hours of closed-door testimony to impeachment investigators, Yovanovitch responded to months of attacks from Trump and his allies. She said that Trump had pressured State Department officials to remove her from her ambassadorship based on made-up allegations. "Although I understand that I served at the pleasure of the president," she said, "I was nevertheless incredulous that the US government chose to remove an ambassador based, as best as I can tell, on unfounded and false claims by people with clearly questionable motives."

When Yovanovitch testified in a public hearing a month later, Trump mocked her on Twitter and Barr gave a fiery speech at the annual meeting of the Federalist Society where he defended the power of the president. As the audience cheered, Barr accused liberals of violating norms, not Trump. "In waging a scorched-earth, no-holds-barred war of resistance against this Administration, it is the left that is engaged in the systematic shredding of norms and undermining the rule of law," he said. Barr portrayed the president as a victim of "encroachment" by the other branches of government. "There is a knee-jerk tendency to see the legislative and judicial branches as the good guys, protecting the people from a rapacious would-be autocrat," Barr said. "This prejudice is wrongheaded and atavistic."

Baker remained hopeful and believed that Trump's failure to discredit the whistleblower had weakened his power to silence current and former officials. "He tried to smash the whistleblower, and it didn't work," Baker said. "One of the things that Donald Trump has trafficked in is fear. And, once people are no longer afraid of him, I think more people will come forward."

The likelihood that Yovanovitch, Baker, or other government officials could significantly undermine Trump's messaging appeared low. Baker, though, believed that it was worth trying to counter Trump's narrative. As part of his personal effort, he published an essay, in May 2019, on the Lawfare website: "Why I Do Not Hate Donald Trump." In it, he argued that deriding the president and his supporters was the wrong tactic. Instead, Baker suggested responding with grace and facts. He conceded that this approach may strike many as naive. "All I know is that I have a small grain of sand that I can contribute to the effort, and I want to put it on the right side of the scale," Baker told me. "If many people do that, then it can make a difference." He commended Yovanovitch, saying, "She's taking a risk and putting her grain of sand on the scale. It sounds like she is pursuing the truth with the goal of helping protect the American people and upholding the Constitution."

Over time, though, some Republicans had come to view government workers with distrust and, in some cases, disdain. A Reagan-era veneration of the private sector prompted some conservatives to question why anyone would want to work in government. They viewed government workers as inept and morally bankrupt. A former White House official told me that Trump's personal distrust of career government workers had grown since he took office. Fearing that government officials would not obey his orders, the president increasingly announced new policies on Twitter, without any vetting from aides or experts. A Democratic senator said that based on his private conversations a growing number of Republicans believe a "deep state" exists. "Half of the Republicans in the Senate are true 'deep staters,'" he said. "They believe they are all under assault by an establishment made up of journalists and government officials." He paraphrased Republican sentiment as, "Yeah, maybe Trump didn't do everything right. Now, they're out to destroy us. We are the only ones who are here to defend conservative values."

.   .   .

On October 11, two months after the whistleblower complaint was filed, Barr appeared at Notre Dame Law School to make a case for ideological warfare. Before an assembly of students and faculty, Barr claimed that the "organized destruction" of religion was under way in the United States. "Secularists, and their allies among the 'progressives,' have marshalled all the force of mass communications, popular culture, the entertainment industry, and academia in an unremitting assault on religion and traditional values," he said. Barr blamed the spread of "secularism and moral relativism" for a rise in "virtually every measure of social pathology"—from the "wreckage of the family" to "record levels of depression and mental illness, dispirited young people, soaring suicide rates, increasing numbers of angry and alienated young males, an increase in sense-less violence, and a deadly drug epidemic."

The speech was less a staid legal lecture than a catalogue of griev-ances accumulated since the Reagan era, when Barr first enlisted in the culture wars. It also included a series of contentious claims. He argued, for example, that the founders of the United States saw religion as essential to democracy. "In the Framers' view, free gov-ernment was only suitable and sustainable for a religious people—a people who recognized that there was a transcendent moral order," he said. Barr ended his address by urging his listeners to resist the "constant seductions of our contemporary society" and launch a "moral renaissance."

Donald Trump does not share Barr's long-standing concern about the role of religion in civic life. What the two men have in common is a willingness to traffic in fear and aggrievement. A few days after Barr's speech, Trump told an audience at the conservative Values Voter Summit, "Extreme left-wing radicals, both inside and outside gov-ernment, are determined to shred our Constitution and eradicate the beliefs we all cherish. They are trying to hound you from the work-place, expel you from the public square, and weaken the American family, and indoctrinate our children." As the impeachment investi-gation intensified, Barr's and Trump's political interests converged. Barr was committed to defending the presidency from congressional efforts to weaken it as an institution. Trump was committed to his own political survival, and using any means to achieve it.

. . .

Two weeks later, on October 31, Pelosi held the first impeachment-related vote in the House. With evidence mounting and Trump mocking the inquiry and congressional oversight, Pelosi was under pressure from her own political base to move ahead with impeach-ment. The measure asked House members to formally authorize a pub-lic impeachment inquiry led by the House Intelligence Committee.

Forty-three years after it was created as part of the Church reforms, the Intelligence Committee would play a leading role for the first time in the potential impeachment of a president. The vote would be the first indication of whether the whistleblower complaint and the revelations in the closed-door testimony of Yovanovitch and other career diplomats had swayed public opinion. It would also signal whether Trump's defense of his actions was resonating with Republicans.

In a bitter debate on a packed House floor, Pelosi insisted that the future of American democracy was at risk. With a picture of the American flag at her side, Pelosi read from the preamble of the Constitution and declared, "What is at stake in all of this is nothing less than our democracy." She attacked Trump's expansion of executive branch powers. "That is in defiance of the separation of powers. That is not what our Constitution says." House Minority Leader Kevin McCarthy argued that the Democrats, not Trump, were being undemocratic. "Democrats are trying to impeach the president because they are scared they cannot defeat him at the ballot box," Mr. McCarthy said. "Why do you not trust the people?"

As Pelosi read the final vote tally on the House floor, Republicans members of Congress shouted "objection" and tried to drown out Democrats as they proceeded with subsequent votes. Given the House's Democratic majority, the measure easily passed by a vote of 232–196 that broke down nearly entirely along partisan lines. Two Democrats voted against the resolution—Collin Peterson of Minnesota, whose district backed Trump by 31 points, and Jeff Van Drew of New Jersey, whose district backed Trump by nearly five points. Justin Amash, a Republican turned independent who had concluded that the Mueller report showed that Trump had committed impeachable offenses, voted in favor of the measure.

The real focus, though, was on whether any moderate Republicans would break with Trump and support the launching of an impeachment investigation. One of the most closely watched votes was that of Will Hurd, the moderate Republican and former CIA officer who had declined to back Trump in 2016. Hurd had publicly criticized Trump's conduct in office and was not running for reelection. Hurd had said the whistleblower's complaint should be taken seriously and that texts from American diplomats that appeared to corroborate the complaint were "damning." Hurd also called for Trump to recognize Congress as a "coequal" branch of government and stop blocking White House officials from testifying before the Intelligence Committee. When Trump publicly called for China to investigate the Biden family, Hurd had condemned it. "I think it's terrible," Hurd said. "It's something that I wouldn't have done."

Hurd, though, said Schiff was conducting the investigation in a duplicitous manner. He questioned why the oversight hearings were carried out behind closed doors when none of the information was classified. He complained that Democrats were selectively leaking information. To Hurd, no clear, firsthand evidence had emerged proving that Trump personally ordered security assistance be withheld from Ukraine until its government investigated the Bidens. So far, he felt the Democrats were hyping their findings. "They are saying that they have a smoking gun," he said, "and they don't have one."

With no clear definition of an impeachable offense delineated in the Constitution, Hurd, like other members of the Congress, had come up with his own definition for what act would merit impeachment. "For me, it's a violation of law," he said. "Is there a crime? Is there a violation?" Hurd, added, though, that the evidence of a crime had to be clear. He said that the actions that Trump was accused of carrying out regarding Ukraine could merit impeachment, but he didn't feel that Democrats had proven their case. "If a president used the office for personal gain to get information on an opponent, that's a problem," he said. "But we don't have proof of that." Hurd voted against the Democratic measure.

Schiff and his Democratic colleagues had an opportunity to carry out the most significant congressional hearings of Trump's presidency.

They had an opportunity to sway public opinion and, potentially, the votes of a handful of moderate Republicans like Hurd. Most intriguingly, their star witnesses were not former aides to the president, as in Watergate; they were career diplomats and military officials. Americans would be able to see and hear members of the "deep state."

NINETEEN

Impeachment

O n November 13, 2019, the House Intelligence Committee held its first public hearing of its impeachment inquiry. In his opening statement, Democratic committee chairman Adam Schiff said, "If the president can simply refuse all oversight, particularly in the context of an impeachment proceeding, the balance of power between our two branches of government will be irrevocably altered." Schiff added, "That is not what the Founders intended. And the prospects for further corruption and abuse of power in this administration or any other will be exponentially increased."

The Trump presidency, Schiff contended, threatened to reset the traditional balance of power between coequal branches of government. He said Trump's refusal to provide any documents—or allow any administration officials to testify—before an impeachment inquiry was unprecedented. Congress was exerting its ultimate check on a president—impeachment—and Trump was mocking the legislative branch and stonewalling its investigation. If Trump was not held accountable for his actions, Schiff argued, it would permanently embolden future presidents and enfeeble Congress.

Schiff hoped to lay out a simple narrative. Democrats claimed that Trump had withheld nearly $400 million in US security aid to Ukraine and an official White House visit in order to get Ukrainian president Zelensky to announce an investigation of the Bidens. When members of Congress asked administration officials to testify before Congress about what occurred, Trump blocked them from doing so. In constitutional terms, the Democrats believed that Trump both committed a high crime and was now obstructing Congress from investigating it.

Schiff was also tacitly arguing that the Ukraine call reflected how Trump had conducted himself as president: he had inflated his powers, used his position for personal political gain, and incessantly lied about his conduct and that of his rivals. The tenor of the proceedings did not in any way resemble the work of the Church, Iran-Contra, and 9/11 commissions, or the Nixon impeachment. Under Trump, the distrust and disdain between Republicans and Democrats had hardened. So had the divergence in worldviews. The split in perception was evident from a single phrase that Schiff quoted in his opening statement. His voice dripping with disdain, Schiff referred to an October 17 statement by the acting White House chief of staff, Mick Mulvaney, that an American president using US security assistance to get a political favor was nothing new. "His answer was breathtaking: 'We do that all the time with foreign policy,'" Schiff said. "He said, 'I have news for everybody. Get over it.'" Schiff argued that the president's pressure campaign was improper, illegal, and "odious." To this, the Republicans, many of them citing a belief inspired by Cheney and Barr that the president could act as he wished under their view of executive power, said there was absolutely nothing wrong with Trump's behavior. If Schiff and other Democrats hoped to sway public opinion, they needed to demonstrate that Trump's behavior was unprecedented, dangerous, and a corruption of American democracy.

.   .   .

The first two witnesses called before the committee were two career diplomats: George Kent, the deputy assistant secretary of state for European and Eurasian affairs, and William Taylor, the top US diplomat in Ukraine. Kent, in a three-piece suit and plaid bow tie, and Taylor, dressed in a dark suit and green tie, were the embodiment of State Department mandarins. Both said they were proud of their public service. Taylor said he had ignored his wife's advice and agreed to serve in Ukraine because he believed in its importance to American national security. Kent described his family's generations of military service, including a great uncle who survived the Bataan Death March in World War II. Trump mocked both men in a tweet as boring.

In their testimony, they described their shock when they learned of Trump's request that Zelensky announce an investigation of the Bidens. "As the Committee is aware," Taylor testified, "I wrote that withholding security assistance in exchange for help with a domestic political campaign in the United States would be 'crazy.' I believed that then, and I believe it now." Kent described the growing alarm he felt at the emergence of an "irregular" policy channel led by Trump's personal lawyer, Rudy Giuliani. But both men lacked firsthand knowledge of the president's direct role in what happened.

They also declined to be drawn into the partisan fight. When asked leading questions by Democrats that would embarrass Trump, they declined to go beyond what they knew. When asked leading questions by Republicans that would aid Trump, they declined to go beyond what they knew. Unlike the politicians who surrounded them, they focused on fact. They were the opposite of the "deep state" caricatures drawn by Trump. As millions of Americans watched their testimony, Taylor and Kent seemingly refuted "deep state" conspiracy theories.

Two days later, Marie Yovanovitch, the former US ambassador to Ukraine, proved to be an even more powerful witness. "Let me be clear on who we are and how we serve this country," she said. "We are professionals. We are public servants who, by vocation and training, pursue the policies of the President, regardless of who holds that office." Yovanovitch went on, "We take our oath seriously—the same oath that each one of you take, to support and defend the Constitution of the United States against all enemies, foreign and domestic, and to bear true faith and allegiance to same."

Yovanovitch spoke of her deep pride in her family and her country. She testified that her mother grew up "stateless" in Germany during Nazi rule; her father fled the Soviet Union. Yovanovitch was born in Canada, grew up in Connecticut, and became a naturalized citizen at eighteen. In her testimony, she laid out in plainspoken terms how she had been treated by President Trump. Her testimony—and Trump's reaction to it—was a window into how Trump conducted himself as president. Speaking in measured tones, Yovanovitch said that she had been "kneecapped" and "smeared" by the president that she was serving. She described her dismay and fear after she learned that Trump had called her "bad news" in a phone call with President Zelensky and promised that she was going to "go through some things." "I was shocked and devastated that I would feature in a phone call between two heads of state in such a manner," she said. "It was a terrible moment."

Yovanovitch—who spent more than three decades in the US Foreign Service, with assignments in Somalia, Kyrgyzstan, Armenia, and Moscow—described an extraordinary series of events. While she was enforcing the US government's stated policy of countering corruption in Ukraine, she was undermined by Giuliani, the president's personal lawyer. According to Yovanovitch, Giuliani worked with corrupt Ukrainians who were angered by Yovanovitch's crackdown to force her out of her position. "What continues to amaze me is that they found Americans willing to partner with them," she testified. "And working together, they apparently succeeded in orchestrating the removal of a US ambassador." Yovanovitch said she respected the president's right to remove her but questioned his means of doing so. "I obviously don't dispute that the President has the right to withdraw an ambassador at any time for any reason, but what I do wonder is why it was necessary to smear my reputation also?"

Then, in an extraordinary step, Trump attacked Yovanovitch on Twitter during her testimony. "Everywhere Marie Yovanovitch went turned bad. She started off in Somalia, how did that go?" he wrote. "Then fast forward to Ukraine, where the new Ukrainian President spoke unfavorably about her in my second phone call with him. It is a U.S. President's absolute right to appoint ambassadors."

Sensing a political opportunity, Schiff read the tweets aloud to Yovanovitch. "What effect do you think that has on other witnesses' willingness to come forward and expose wrongdoing?" he asked. Yovanovitch replied, "I can't speak to what the President is trying to do, but I think the effect is to be intimidating."

.   .   .

Five days later, the most anticipated witness of the hearings appeared before the committee. The US ambassador to the European Union, Gordon Sondland, initially delivered testimony that seemed to all but assure President Trump's impeachment. In his opening statement, Sondland explained that he and other senior officials worked with Giuliani, "at the express direction of the President of the United States," to secure an investigation of Biden in exchange for a White House visit. "We did not want to work with Mr. Giuliani. Simply put, we were playing the hand we were dealt," he testified. "We followed the President's orders."

Sondland said the efforts were known to Vice President Pence, Secretary of State Pompeo, former national security advisor John Bolton, and other senior members of the administration. He testified that Giuliani "was expressing the desire of the President of the United States, and we knew that these investigations were important to the President." Sondland read aloud from emails that he said confirmed that State Department officials and senior officials in the White House were "all informed about the Ukraine efforts" and that "everyone was in the loop."

Democrats appeared to have achieved their goal. The hearings were designed to prove that Trump explicitly conditioned the White House visit—a symbolic gesture that Zelensky believed would help deter further Russian expansionism in his country—on the announcement of a Biden investigation. Sondland left no doubt of that. "I know that members of this committee have frequently framed these complicated issues in the form of a simple question: Was there a 'quid pro quo?'" Sondland said. "As I testified previously, with regard to the requested White House call and White House meeting, the answer is yes."

Schiff declared that Sondland had described impeachable offenses. "If the president abused his power and invited foreign interference in our elections, if he sought to condition, coerce, extort, or bribe an ally into conducting investigations to aid his reelection campaign, and did so by withholding official acts, a White House meeting, or hundreds of millions of dollars of needed military aid," Schiff said, "it will be up to us to decide whether those acts are compatible with the office of the presidency."

Sondland's testimony also raised the possibility of an article of impeachment regarding obstruction of justice. Sondland said he had not had access to "all of my phone records, State Department emails, and other State Department documents" that would have helped him in preparing his testimony. "These documents are not classified," Sondland said. "They should have been made available."

Schiff ended the morning session with a direct warning to Trump that framed the withholding of State Department documents as comparable to the acts of obstruction that helped bring down Nixon. "We can see why Secretary Pompeo and President Trump have made such a concerted and across-the-board effort to obstruct this investigation and this impeachment inquiry," Schiff said. "And I will just say this: they do so at their own peril. I remind the president that Article Three of the impeachment articles drafted against President Nixon was his refusal to obey the subpoenas of Congress."

After Sondland returned for testimony in the afternoon, his demeanor and narrative changed. Under questioning from Republicans, Sondland said that the president had not personally told him to carry out a "quid pro quo" with the Ukrainians. Instead, Sondland said that was his "understanding" of the president's wishes. Republicans attacked Sondland's credibility and tried to downplay the importance of his testimony. Devin Nunes, the ranking Republican member of the House Intelligence Committee, dismissed the hearings as "story time" and "asinine."

The following day, Fiona Hill, the former top Russia official on the

National Security Council, concluded the hearings with pointed testimony. The daughter of an English coal miner, Hill had won a scholarship to Harvard, earned a PhD in Russian history there, became a naturalized US citizen, and served as the top Russia expert on the National Intelligence Council, an internal think tank for American intelligence agencies. Ignoring criticism from some liberal friends, Hill served in the Trump administration because she wanted to give the president the best expertise possible. Over the course of five hours, Hill refused to be drawn into partisan commentary.

In one rebuke to Trump, she delivered a stirring warning about continuing Russian efforts to exacerbate political divisions among Americans. Hill said that the claim made by Trump and some Republicans that Ukraine, not Russia, had interfered in the 2016 elections was propaganda produced by Russian intelligence services. "Some of you on this committee appear to believe that Russia and its security services did not conduct a campaign against our country and that perhaps, somehow, for some reason, Ukraine did," Hill said. "This is a fictional narrative that is being perpetrated and propagated by the Russian security services themselves."

Hill said that the goal of the Russian effort was to smear Ukraine, create doubt about Russia's role in 2016, and divide Americans. She said that one of the primary goals of the Russian disinformation in 2016 was to amplify divisive rhetoric and conspiracy theories, create confusion, and exacerbate political division in the United States. "President Putin and the Russian security services operate like a super PAC," Hill testified. "They deploy millions of dollars to weaponize our own political opposition research and false narratives. When we are consumed by partisan rancor, we cannot combat these external forces as they seek to divide us against each other, degrade our institutions, and destroy the faith of the American people in our democracy."

She warned that Russia was intent on doing the same in 2020. And the country's continued polarization made it easier for the Russians to succeed. "Right now, Russia's security services and their proxies have geared up to repeat their interference in the 2020 election. We are running out of time to stop them," she said. "In the course of this investigation, I would ask that you please not promote politically derivative falsehoods that so clearly advance Russian interests."

Will Hurd, the moderate Republican and former CIA officer from Texas, was still seen as persuadable. As Hill's testimony came to an end, it appeared that he might oblige them. "I disagree with this bumbling foreign policy," Hurd said. Then he declared that he did not believe impeachable offenses had been proven. "An impeachable offense should be compelling, overwhelmingly clear and unambiguous, and it's not something to be rushed or taken lightly. I have not heard evidence proving the president committed bribery or extortion."

In an interview several days later, Hurd said he had met Marie Yovanovitch in an American embassy while working for the CIA overseas. She had impressed him enormously. "She is a good representative of the diplomatic corps," Hurd said. "She is tough as nails and smart as hell." When I asked him about Republican claims that the diplomats were part of a conspiracy against Trump, he flatly rejected the claim. He said the diplomats were not members of a nefarious "deep state." He also said they weren't effete snobs who "sipped champagne" and attended cocktail parties. He praised their patriotism and commitment.

Hurd repeated the criticism that he had made during the hearing about Trump's phone call with Zelensky. "I would not have handled the phone call that way. It showed a lack of preparation," Hurd said. "These things are not freewheeling conversations with your friend."

When I asked him about the evidence against Trump, his tone shifted. He was dismissive of Gordon Sondland, the Republican donor who served as the US ambassador to the European Union. He felt that he "gave a lot of opinions about what he thought were facts." Hurd then criticized the fairness of Schiff's investigation and the hearings, and said he would have liked to have heard from more witnesses.

He criticized Democrats, not Trump, for deepening partisan division. "When we continue to have these fights," he said, referring to rising partisanship in Washington, "it's doing what the Russians want."

Hurd embraced the need for strong CIA oversight, and worried about the country's future. He also made it plain that he felt Schiff and other Democrats had twisted the truth as much as Republicans, feeding as many stories as possible about Trump-Russia collusion when no clear evidence of it had emerged. Hurd lamented Trump's excesses but resented what he felt was an overreaction to Trump in the media. Democrats saw Trump as an existential threat to American democracy. Hurd saw Trump as amateurish and misguided.

When I asked him about impeachment, Hurd sounded at ease with his decision. He didn't seem torn at all. He said an impeachable offense had not been proven. "That's why we have elections to decide whether we like what someone is doing," Hurd said. "Impeachment needs to be bipartisan. It needs to be overwhelmingly clear."

TWENTY

Deadlock

On December 9, the Justice Department inspector general, Michael Horowitz, released a long-awaited report on whether the FBI had properly conducted its 2016 Trump-Russia investigation. For months, Trump and Fox News commentators had predicted that Horowitz's report would find clear political bias. Instead, it concluded that Trump's allegations of an FBI "coup" were false.

The report—based on more than a hundred and seventy interviews and a million-plus pages of documents—did find misconduct, most of it involving applications to the FISA Court to conduct surveillance. During the campaign, low-level FBI officials had asked for permission to wiretap Carter Page, a former Trump foreign policy advisor. Later, in a request to renew the warrant, a lawyer falsified an email to make it appear that Page had never been a source for the CIA, when the opposite was true. Agents also withheld concerns about the reliability of allegations against Trump in the dossier compiled by the former British intelligence officer Christopher Steele.

Horowitz's work showed that the government's secretive surveillance process required significant reform. But the report found that the opening of the probe was legally justified, and said investigators found no evidence of political bias. "We did not find documentary or testimonial evidence that political bias or improper motivation influenced the decisions," Horowitz wrote. (A separate investigation into Peter Strzok, a senior counterintelligence agent who had sent scornful text messages about Trump, came to a similar conclusion.) James Baker, the former FBI general counsel, called the report vindication. He told me that the bureau began the investigation before receiving a copy of the Steele dossier and before the Page email was altered. At the time, Democratic Party communications stolen by Russia were circulating online, and Trump had publicly called for Russia to steal and release Hillary Clinton's emails; several of his campaign officials had been in contact with Russian officials and with suspected intelligence operatives. "We have an obligation to protect the United States from Russia," Baker said. "Presented with the same facts, I would open the investigation again."

Barr released a response to the report, disputing Horowitz's conclusions. Despite the core finding that the investigation was legally justified, Barr argued that the report "makes clear that the F.B.I. launched an intrusive investigation of a U.S. presidential campaign on the thinnest of suspicions." Durham, the federal prosecutor appointed to carry out a separate investigation, suggested that he and Barr had gathered evidence that contradicted Horowitz. "We advised the inspector general that we do not agree with some of the report's conclusions as to predication and how the F.B.I. case was opened," he said. This statement was contrary to a Justice Department practice of not commenting on investigations until they are finished.

Trump went further, suggesting that Horowitz was part of a cabal formed in the previous Administration. "Remember that I.G. Horowitz was appointed by Obama," he tweeted. "There was tremendous bias and guilt exposed, so obvious, but Horowitz couldn't get himself to say it. Big credibility loss. Obama knew everything!"

Christopher Wray, the FBI director, immediately admitted the bureau's errors and announced forty reforms designed to prevent improper surveillance. But, in a television interview, he pushed back about other false claims. When asked about Trump's calls for an investigation into Ukraine's meddling in the election, Wray replied, "We have no information that indicates that Ukraine interfered." Wray also urged Americans to vet their sources of information. "There's all kinds of people saying all kinds of things out there," he said. "And I think part of us being well protected against malign foreign influence is to build together an American public that's resilient, that has appropriate media literacy, and that takes its information with a grain of salt."

After Wray defended the FBI, Trump attacked him as well. "I don't know what report current Director of the FBI Christopher Wray was reading, but it sure wasn't the one given to me," he tweeted. "With that kind of attitude, he will never be able to fix the FBI, which is badly broken despite having some of the greatest men & women working there!"

Wray was not fired, but Trump's attacks were having an impact. Current and former law-enforcement and intelligence officials said that three years of Trump's Twitter attacks, conspiracy theories, and high-profile firings have left their leaders wary of speaking in public, testifying before Congress, or talking to reporters. They know that they will be asked about Trump's false claims. If they respond accurately, they risk being fired for contradicting the president.

The country's intelligence agencies continue to produce private assessments that counter Trump's specious assertions. They affirm that Russia, not Ukraine, interfered in the 2016 election and predict that it is likely to meddle again in 2020, according to members of the House and the Senate intelligence committees. The FBI and the CIA have also assessed that white nationalists and ISIS members represent continued threats, issues that Trump has downplayed. But agency directors believe that they can best protect their institutions by keeping such concerns private. "Survival is victory," the government official told me. "If you are able to go out on your own terms, or go out last, it's a victory for the institution."

If Barr's inquiry results in criminal charges, it would be a radical departure from past practice. When Durham investigated CIA officers for torture, he pressed no criminal charges. Previous investigations into intelligence failures that cost American lives—such as missing warning signs before the 9/11 attacks or wrongly concluding that Saddam Hussein had weapons of mass destruction—carried no possibility of criminal sanction. James Clapper, who was the director of national intelligence in 2016, cautioned that the election assessment is a work of analysis. "If a prosecuting attorney is investigating analysts for their intelligence judgments, that's not good," Clapper said. James Baker worried that Trump's intimidation of investigators would have consequences at the FBI. "It could reduce the willingness to give frank assessments or to pursue controversial cases," he said, adding, "I'm nervous about the institution."

.   .   .

On December 18, 2019, the House voted to impeach Trump for abuse of power and obstruction of Congress in party-line votes of 230 to 197 and 229 to 198. Every Republican member of the House sided with the president. In a speech on the House floor, Hurd repeated his earlier arguments against impeachment. "Throughout this process the American people have learned of bungling foreign policy decisions, but we have not heard evidence, beyond a reasonable doubt, of bribery or extortion. We have seen a rushed process divide our country," he said. "Today, accusations have been hurled at each other, questioning one another's integrity. Today, a dangerous precedent will be set in impeachment becoming a weaponized political tool. We know how this partisan process will end this evening. But what happens tomorrow?"

Public opinion polls showed that impeachment did not alter Americans' perceptions; it entrenched them. Democrats overwhelmingly believed that Trump had committed impeachable offenses, would try to cheat in the 2020 election, and should be removed from office. Republicans overwhelmingly believed that Trump had not committed impeachable offenses, was a victim of false Democratic claims, and should remain in office. His political base remained deeply committed to him.

As 2019 came to a close, Dr. James Veltmeyer, a physician based in La Jolla, California, who ran unsuccessfully for the Republican nomination for his local congressional seat in 2018, circulated an article online defending Trump. Veltmeyer claimed that Trump's impeachment was the latest effort to oust him by the "New World Order," "military-industrial complex," and "the media," who were bent on carrying out "the Carter-Bush-Clinton-Bush-Obama agendas of continuous war and the continuous looting of America's wealth and hollowing out of the American middle class." Veltmeyer vowed that average Americans who had been betrayed by both the Democratic and Republican parties would reelect Trump in a landslide in 2020. "Unlike other Republican presidents of the recent past, he can't be bought and has no price. Unlike them, he doesn't give in and he doesn't give up." Alex Jones, the conspiracy theorist who operates the Infowars website, devoted much of a radio program to attacking Fiona Hill. "I want her ass indicted," Jones said. "I want her indicted for perjury. Today. Indict that whore."

Steve Bannon, the Trump advisor who had called for the dismantling of the "administrative state" when Trump took office three years earlier, reveled in the reaction to Trump's impeachment. Bannon told the *Washington Post* that the president had defeated an effort by unelected bureaucrats to remove him from power. Republican attacks on those who "actively worked against [Trump's] policies on Ukraine" or defied his wishes on Ukraine, Bannon said, should serve as "a warning that if you go against the president, there is going to be a price to be paid."

The final report from Republicans on the House Intelligence Committee echoed Bannon's language. "The Democrats are trying to impeach a duly elected President based on the accusations and assumptions of unelected bureaucrats who disagreed with President

Trump's policy initiatives and processes," the report said. "They are trying to impeach President Trump because some unelected bureaucrats were discomforted by an elected President's telephone call with Ukrainian President Volodymyr Zelensky."

Bannon marveled at how rapidly Republican lawmakers opposed impeachment, according to the *Post*. Early in the scandal, Bannon said, few Republicans were willing to publicly support Trump's claim that his call with Ukraine's president was "perfect." "Today, look at House Judiciary, a hundred percent say it is a perfect call," Bannon said. "A hundred percent say there's nothing wrong."

After a three-week trial in the Senate, Trump was acquitted on February 5 of abuse of power and obstruction of Congress in nearly party-line votes that fell far short of the two-thirds majority needed for removal. All Democrats voted to convict Trump on both counts. In a surprise, Republican senator Mitt Romney voted to convict Trump of abuse of power, breaking ranks with his party—and infuriating the president. In an emotional speech, Romney said that Trump was "guilty of an appalling abuse of public trust." "With my vote I will tell my children and their children that I did my duty," Romney said. "What the president did was wrong. Grievously wrong."

As he did after the Mueller report, Trump claimed complete and total vindication. Forty years after the creation of a post-Watergate and post-Church reform order designed to prevent executive branch abuses of power, a president had subverted the system.

. . .

In private, current and former FBI agents and Justice Department officials say they are tired of Trump's attacks on the FBI. Recent retirees told me that they were surprised by how little they missed working at the bureau.

Some agents have embraced Wray's admonition to do their work and ignore the political brawl around them. After two and a half years on the job, Wray, a low-key former prosecutor and corporate lawyer, has inspired loyalty for handling a difficult situation gracefully.

The bureau, like the country, is deeply divided; even some agents who find Trump personally distasteful say that they support his policies. Comey was a popular director, but agents complain that his calls for people to vote against Trump play into conspiracy theories about the bureau. The clearest sentiment is disdain for the political class.

The political combat of the Trump era is breeding apathy and disgust. FBI and Justice Department officials said that if Trump was reelected there would be an exodus of employees. Some retired agents fear that the institution will not survive another four years.

Tom O'Connor, the former Massachusetts police officer turned FBI agent, retired from the FBI on September 11, 2019. Eighteen years after he and fellow FBI investigators collected human remains from the Pentagon, O'Connor ended his career. He declined to comment on Trump's impeachment but expressed deep pride in the FBI. "It is frustrating to hear people in power say things about a great organization that is nonpolitical," O'Connor said. "But the work of the FBI investigators will rule the day."

In his twenty-two years at the bureau, O'Connor investigated and helped prosecute Al Qaeda members, Blackwater Security Guards, and racially motivated violent extremists from the Aryan Nations and other American groups. He summed up his job as to "investigate evil in whatever form it takes." O'Connor said his future plans are unclear. The one thing he ruled out was running for elected office. "That is something I will not do," he said. "I want to do something with meaning." His aversion to politics reflects the growing alienation many Americans feel from their own democracy.

The "Deep State"

There is no "deep state"—not in the conspiratorial way that Donald Trump uses the term. The long history of abuse by the FBI and CIA should not be ignored, nor should the improper actions of the low-level FBI officials who wiretapped former Trump campaign advisor Carter Page. The FBI and CIA are both enormously powerful organizations whose conduct must be vigorously monitored by elected officials, the courts, and the press. But there is no evidence of a widespread, politically motivated "coup." President Trump, as he often does, is exaggerating.

In dozens of interviews, no current or former government officials told me they had seen evidence of a conspiracy by FBI and CIA officials to force an American president from power. Privately, current and former Trump administration officials admitted that the president's claims of a "deep state" are an exaggeration. Members of the Obama, Bush, and Clinton administrations have agreed that bias, caution, and turf consciousness exist among career civil servants, but that is different from an organized plot.

President Trump no longer deserves the benefit of the doubt when it comes to the vast conspiracies that he alleges. Three years after his taking office, the number of false or misleading claims that he has made reached 16,241, according to the *Washington Post*. The number of falsehoods has grown each year, from 1,999 in 2017, to 5,689 in 2018, to 8,155 in 2019. His false claims are growing. He averaged 6 per day in 2017, nearly 16 per day in 2018, and more than 22 per day in 2019.

In his criticisms of the FBI and CIA, President Trump has played on the fears many Americans have of the country's powerful intelligence and law enforcement agencies. Those suspicions are justified, and I share them. Both the CIA and FBI have long histories of abusing Americans' civil rights and privacy, and of targeting minorities, particularly African-Americans and, especially since 9/11, Muslims.

The performance of congressional oversight committees over the last forty years has been mixed at best. The Church, Iran-Contra, and 9/11 investigations produced broad, largely bipartisan findings. Since 9/11, though, congressional investigations have grown increasingly partisan. In the Trump era, relations between the two parties on the House Intelligence Committee broke down completely.

Spy chiefs have largely accepted the need for oversight but have also learned how to manage committee members. The FISA Court has proven to be the most problematic post-Church reform institution of all. It has been far too passive, failing to act decisively, for instance, when it was alerted to Bush administration warrantless mass surveillance. The court has produced few rulings that publicly take the Justice Department and FBI to task for their surveillance abuses. And the actions by FBI officials in Carter Page's case show that the culture surrounding FISA applications has become far too lax. FBI Director Wray's reforms are a positive step, but congressional hearings and more sweeping changes are needed. The FISA Court process should be more adversarial, like the rest of the American judicial system. The surveillance of members of political organizations should require higher levels of evidence than criminal or counterintelligence organizations. Most of all, the FISA Court's procedures, legal standards, and decision making should be more transparent to the public. American conservatives and liberals have both lost faith in the FISA process and court. Blanket secrecy fuels blanket suspicion.

.   .   .

The political dynamic that most threatens proper intelligence oversight is the rising call for a more powerful presidency. For decades, leaders of both parties have played a role in increasing the reach and influence of the chief executive. Each decade has brought a new test of the balance of power between the executive and the legislative branches.

In the 1980s, first Abscam and then the Iran-Contra scandal strained the relationship between the executive and legislative branches. During Abscam, FBI Director William Webster embraced congressional oversight rather than stonewalling it. His openness—as well as the convictions by juries of those who accepted bribes—helped solidify a consensus that joint oversight of the FBI by the executive, legislative, and judicial branches was most effective.

The Iran-Contra affair was a far graver breach of the constitutional order that tested the balance of power between the legislative and executive branches. White House aides flagrantly violated laws banning military aid to the Contras and weapons sales to Iran. They brazenly lied under oath to members of Congress. Unlike Webster, National Security Council aide Oliver North argued that presidents and their aides should be able to do whatever they deemed necessary to protect the country from threats. Dick Cheney, then a congressman, argued that North and his allies had done nothing improper, because foreign policy and national security should be controlled solely by the executive branch. But Democrats and a majority of Republicans said that Congress must be able to act as a check on a wayward president. Daniel Inouye, the Democratic chair of the Iran-Contra Committee, warned that a "cabal" of officials who believed they had a "monopoly on truth" was a recipe for "autocracy."

Over time, though, Cheney's argument that the executive branch had a right to conduct foreign policy on its own and that policy disputes were being criminalized gained support. After losing the 1992 presidential election, George H. W. Bush, with William Barr's full support, pardoned several of the men who flouted congressional oversight during Iran-Contra. As Bush's presidency came to a close, the legislative branch's power weakened.

The Clinton presidency produced three new dynamics: failed independent counsel investigations, growing partisanship abetted by the emergence of cable news networks, and the spread of conspiracy theories regarding the federal government. Clinton, who emerged from the impeachment with strong political support, showed that legislative branch overreach was possible. Independent counsel investigations of the Reagan, Bush, and Clinton administrations failed to produce evidence of major abuses. And the killings of civilians in federal law enforcement raids in Ruby Ridge and Waco fueled fears of federal law enforcement agencies.

One lesson of the Clinton era was that oversight and investigatory powers should be used carefully. Too many congressional hearings and too many independent counsels diluted the impact of investigations. By the late 1990s, the post-Watergate and post–Church reform consensus regarding the need to hold presidents, as well as the FBI and CIA, accountable, was gradually eroding. The invocation of Watergate and past FBI and CIA abuses was losing its political potency.

After the 9/11 attacks, public support for empowering the president, the CIA, and the FBI to protect the country soared. George W. Bush and Dick Cheney immediately took full advantage of it. Without the approval of the legislative or judicial branches, they secretly conducted mass surveillance. In their efforts to protect the country and expand executive power, they gave credence to the conspiracy theories of both the American left and right. An overzealous executive eavesdropped on its citizens without warrants, operated secret torture facilities abroad, and launched a costly war in Iraq based on faulty intelligence.

Barack Obama came to office promising to restrain the power of the presidency and respect the rule of law. Initially, he did. With time, though, Obama, like Bush, came to embrace covert action as a means to protect the country from terrorism. Three scandals—Clapper's answer to Wyden, Snowden's leaks, and Brennan's battles with Feinstein over torture—undermined Obama's claim of transparency. Liberal Democrats and libertarian Republicans grew more suspicious of the White House and the intelligence community. Aided by the emergence of social media, unregulated campaign spending, and gerrymandering, political polarization intensified. As Obama's tenure came to an end, Republicans and Democrats learned that energizing their party's political base could produce electoral wins at the ballot box.

As the 2016 election approached, Obama's executive orders and intelligence scandals became fodder for a new Republican narrative. Conservatives claimed that Obama's use of executive orders, drone strikes, and executive privilege were abuses of power. To Republicans, Obama and his top allies, particularly Hillary Clinton, were dangerous authoritarians. To Democrats, George W. Bush and Dick Cheney were.

.   .   .

In 2016, Donald Trump took full advantage of those fears. In an era of spiraling income inequality, he sensed the frustrations, grievances, and economic struggles of millions of Americans, and he promised solutions. He deftly played on Americans' historic distrust of Washington and the country's elite. He aggressively attacked whoever challenged him, from Republican primary opponents to the news media to Hillary Clinton.

In his three years in office, his administration has reshaped the country's legal system—appointing two Supreme Court justices and more than a hundred eighty other judges, most of whom can be counted on to rule against abortion and in favor of executive power. Trump has expanded executive power and weakened legislative oversight more than any other post-Watergate chief executive. After Democrats won control of the House in 2018, he rejected virtually all forms of congressional oversight.

One tactic that Trump has used to exert power is by acting in a new way on the adage that information is power. He has strictly limited the release of information about himself while attacking the credibility of information from rivals. "It's actually quite clever," said NYU legal ethicist Stephen Gillers. "The Congress needs information to do its job, and the president has frozen it out—especially in the impeachment investigation. Another check is the media, and the president's use of the term 'fake news' can cause people to lose faith in the media. What remains are the courts, which are slow and cumbersome."

Some analysts contend that Trump is overplaying his legal hand. Benjamin Wittes, of Lawfare, predicted that the Supreme Court would reject Trump's and Barr's extreme positions, creating precedents that ultimately reduce the power of the presidency. "The idea that the President gets to assert executive privilege over material that has already been made public is laughable," Wittes says. "I think they are very likely to lose a lot of this." Donald Ayer, the former Bush administration deputy attorney general, has warned that Trump's and Barr's interpretations of executive power could be validated. "The ultimate question is what happens when these reach the Supreme Court, which has two Trump appointees," he said. "There is a real danger that he succeeds."

Ayer fears that Barr and Trump have combined a Reagan-era drive to dismantle government with a Trump-era drive to politicize it. In the 2020 campaign, Trump will argue that he alone can protect the country from the dangers posed by the left, immigrants, and other enemies. And Barr's vision of presidential power will be the party's mainstream position. "Barr sought out the opportunity to be Donald Trump's Attorney General," Ayer says. "This, I believe, was his opportunity—the opportunity of a lifetime—to make major progress on advancing his vision of an all-powerful Chief Executive."

.   .   .

The Church Committee consensus, which has been unraveling since 2001, has broken down completely in the Trump era for multiple reasons. Our political class and a growing number of voters have embraced a "win at all costs" ethos of politics. Congressional oversight that was, in part, a fact-finding exercise in the past has been politically weaponized. After 9/11, both parties discovered that carrying out partisan investigations in Congress could rally their political bases.

Whatever the merits of the probes, Democrats found that investigating waste and abuse by military contractors in the Iraq war damaged George W. Bush and energized liberal voters; Republicans, in turn, found that investigating Benghazi and Hillary Clinton's emails damaged Clinton and energized conservatives. At the same time, news organizations searching for sustainable business models have found that partisan coverage draws large and loyal audiences. Online, controversy and conspiracy travel farther and faster than nuance.

Trump has exacerbated and taken advantage of all of these trends. His use of conspiracy theories has sowed division and confusion. His attacks on those who dare investigate him undermines Americans' faith in the criminal justice system. His administration's blanket rejection of House oversight diminishes Americans' faith in Congress. And his dark vision of public life, where he seemingly believes that everyone acts out of self-interest, transactions are zero-sum games, and everybody cuts corners, takes advantage, and lies, will drive Americans away from public service over time.

Since 9/11, the American presidency has grown ever more powerful, with both Republican and Democratic presidents embracing executive power when faced with national security threats or partisan gridlock. Trump has taken this to a new extreme, claiming far more executive branch power and privilege than any of his post-Watergate predecessors. American history shows that the concentration of power—combined with secrecy—is a recipe for abuse. The continued pursuit of executive power by presidents is a route to authoritarianism.

The institutional government has not significantly changed; the politics swirling around it have. A new consensus is required between politicians and voters, and among Americans who are more deeply divided politically than they have been in decades. Politicians have a vested interested in spreading conspiracy theories about their opponents. Politicians have a vested interest in dividing Americans. If the polarization continues, I increasingly fear it could spark political violence. Members of Congress from both parties told me that they are receiving growing numbers of death threats. A cycle of distrust, disdain, and conspiracy theory is fraying American democracy. In the midst of such rancor, the chances of a bipartisan consensus along the lines of the Church reforms are nonexistent. Confrontation, demonization, and conspiracy theories are too politically profitable.

Trump is following the playbook he has deftly used since entering politics—spreading conspiracy theories about his rivals while shrouding his own actions in secrecy. If a "deep state" is a group of officials who secretly wield government power with little accountability or transparency, Trump and his loyalists increasingly fit that definition. Rudy Giuliani has served as a private envoy of the president who carries out a secret foreign policy outside government channels. He is not a government official, nor subject to government ethics rules, nor subject to questioning by Congress. Fox News host Sean Hannity has served as a private communications arm of the White House, holding late-night phone conversations with the president, acting as one of his informal advisors, and passionately promoting him on-air. The president, after consulting with unidentified aides and supporters, demands that the Justice Department investigate officials and corporations he views as enemies and aid those he considers allies. Top White House aides defy congressional subpoenas and refuse to answer questions under oath. Past presidents claimed that some White House communications were subject to executive privilege, but not all of them.

Under the guise of stopping a "coup" that does not exist, Trump is upending the checks and balances that are the foundation of American democracy. He is politicizing the Justice Department and other government agencies and using them to attack his enemies. Whether out of fear or calculation, Trump is creating a parallel, shadow government filled with like-minded loyalists, without transparency, democratic norms, or public processes — a "deep state" of his own.

ACKNOWLEDGMENTS

Three groups of people made this book possible. The first are the dozens of current and former government officials who agreed to speak with me. Some are whistleblowers who face potential prosecution for leaking information. Others risked jobs (and security clearances) that support their families by speaking out. Others are comfortably elected or retired and face few professional, political, or financial risks in speaking with me. Some support President Trump. Others disdain him. I'm grateful to each of them for engaging with me in one of the most politically polarized periods in the country's history. I owe the deepest thanks to those who agreed to serve as this book's central characters: Richard Blee, Tom O'Connor, Joan Dempsey, James Baker, Will Hurd, and James Clapper. There are many others who spent long hours with me whom I cannot name. I thank them all.

The second group who made this possible are the journalists who have covered the FBI, CIA, Congress, and the White House for the last forty years. Their journalism—from daily news stories to investigative pieces to in-depth books—has created a rich body of work. Their chronicling of decades of scandal, reform, and scandal again are the foundation on which this book is built. The endnotes cite the specific works that aided me the most, but I'm deeply indebted to all of them for their work. Their work made me proud, yet again, to be a journalist.

The third group are the wide array of friends who provided guidance, support, and encouragement over the last several years. Some directly aided me with this book. Others were patient when it pulled me away. They include Steve Adler, Tim Aeppel, Gary Bass, John Bastian, Yara Bayoumy, Emma Beals, Barry Bearak, John Blanton, Julian Borger, Joel Brand, Elisabet Cantenys, Lauretta Charlton, Leigh Cheng, Susan Chira, Reg Chua, Helen Coster, Steve Engelberg, Lisa Ferrari, Diane and John Foley, Alix Friedman, Tim Golden, Gail Gove, Paul Haven, Katya Jestin, Christine Kay, Bill Keller, Shailesh Lal, Jonathan Landay, Jim Ledbetter, Tahir Luddin, Marcus Mabry, Rob Mahoney, Asad Mangal, David McCraw, Katie and Charlie and Jonathan Moore, Michael Scott Moore, George Packer, Ned Parker, Matt Purdy, Barbara Quinn, Jason Rezaian, Kit Roane, Jon and Kem Sawyer, Laura Secor, Allison Silver, Joel Simon, Warren Strobel, Kanna Sundaram, Eric Umansky, John Walcott, Ben Ward, Mike Williams, and Eric Wold.

The New America Foundation kindly chose me as a National Security Fellow and supported my reporting and research. My deepest thanks to Awista Ayub, Sarah Baline, Peter Bergen, Celina Daniel, Tyra A. Mariani, Daniel Rothenberg, and Anne Marie Slaughter. I thank Oren Depp for his research assistance at ASU and my fellow 2020 New America fellows for their encouragement and help.

At *The New Yorker*, myriad colleagues helped me with this project, gave me encouragement and guidance, or put up with the time the book pulled me away from work there. My deepest thanks to Fabio Bertoni, Jon Blitzer, Carla Blumenkranz, Nathan Burstein, Virginia Cannon, Andrew DenHoed, Nimal Eames-Scott, Adam Entous, Lainna Fader, Ronan Farrow, Dexter Filkins, Rob Fischer, Deirdre Foley-Mendelssohn, Susan Glasser, Philip Gourevitch, David Haglund, Soo-jeong Kang, Raffi Khatchadourian, Eric Lach, Larissa MacFarquhar, Jane Mayer, Pam McCarthy, Joanna Milter, Evan Osnos, Natalie Raabe, Patrick Radden-Keefe, Josh Rothman, Emily Stokes, Ben Taub, Maraithe Thomas, Nick Trautwein, Dorothy Wickenden, Paige Williams, Jessica Winter, Robin Wright, and Daniel Zalewski. Mike Luo generously and patiently supported this book throughout an astonishingly busy news year, giving me leaves, encouragement, and support when it complicated his own plans, goals, and ambitions. David Remnick, in a gesture that still amazes me, read every word of this book, provided elegant edits, and encouraged me to find my own voice.

My editor at Norton, John Glusman, championed this book, deftly edited it, and pushed me from beginning to end. John made me a better reporter, clearer analyst, and more lucid writer. More than anyone, he believed in me and this book. For that, I will be forever grateful. He and Helen Thomaides displayed extraordinary patience and grace when events repeatedly changed the book's editing and ending. I thank Jodi Beder, Rebecca Homiski, Anna Oler, Kyle Radler, and Don Rifkin for their help at Norton as well. My literary agents, Sarah Chalfant and Rebecca Nagel, helped me every step of the way. Sean Lavery, my friend and colleague at *The New Yorker*, rigorously fact-checked it. Andrea Bernstein read the book and provided invaluable guidance. All mistakes, errors, and omissions are solely my own.

Most of all, my family supported me. My parents Carol, Harvey, Andrea, and George, my siblings Lee, Laura, Erik, Joel, and Dan, and my in-laws Mary Jane, Jim, Chris, Chrissy, Christie, Howard, Jason, Karen, Leilani, and Rachel encouraged me in more ways than they know. My nephews and nieces Steven, Ben, Grace, and Brooke inspired me, and my niece Kristen and her husband Sam reminded me of the sacrifices of those who serve in the military. My wife Kristen has endured, shared, and lived through every step of this process. She has faced more challenges than should ever be asked of a spouse. Yet, together, we have overcome each one of them. I could not ask for a more extraordinary partner. Her unwavering love, support, and fortitude sustains me as it always has. Finally, my daughters, Ella and Julia, are too young to fully grasp the contents of this book but waited patiently through the mornings, nights, and weekends it took to complete it. I wrote this book because of my love for this country, for Kristen, and for Ella and Julia.

NOTES

PROLOGUE: WHISTLEBLOWERS

xi **Published by Reuters:** Jonathan Landay and David Rohde, "Exclusive: In Call with Putin, Trump Denounced Obama-Era Nuclear Arms Treaty—Sources," Reuters, February 9, 2017, https://www.reuters.com/article/us-usa-trump-putin/exclusive-in-call-with-putin-trump-denounced-obama-era-nuclear-arms-treaty-sources-idUSKBN15O2A5.

xi **Other, more damaging accounts:** Greg Miller and Philip Rucker, "'This Was the Worst Call by Far': Trump Badgered, Bragged and Abruptly Ended Phone Call with Australian Leader," *Washington Post*, February 2, 2017, https://www.washingtonpost.com/world/national-security/no-gday-mate-on-call-with-australian-pm-trump-badgers-and-brags/2017/02/01/88a3bfb0-e8bf-11e6-80c2-30e57e57e05d_story.html.

xiii **warrantless eavesdropping program:** Philip Shenon, "Leak Inquiry Said to Focus on Calls with Times," *New York Times*, April 12, 2008, https://www.nytimes.com/2008/04/12/washington/12leak.html.

xiii **politically motivated attack:** Peter Hermann, "Gunman Cased Baseball Field for Weeks before Opening Fire at June Congressional Baseball Practice," *Washington Post*, October 6, 2017, https://www.washingtonpost.com/local/public-safety/gunman-cased-baseball-field-for-weeks-before-opening-fire-at-june-congressional-baseball-practice/2017/10/06/fe51cc96-aab8-11e7-b3aa-c0e2e1d41e38_story.html.

xiv **"the president, conservatives":** Ian Schwartz, "Hannity Rips 'Deep State': 'Unelected Fourth Branch of Government Looking for Retribution.'" *RealClear Politics*, June 17, 2017, https://www.realclearpolitics.com/video/2017/06/17/hannity_rips_deep_state_unelected_fourth_branch_of_government_looking_for_retribution.html.

xiv **twice the number he did in 2018:** Peter Baker and Laura Jakes, "Trump's War on the 'Deep State' Turns against Him," *New York Times*, Oct. 23, 2019, https://www.nytimes.com/2019/10/23/us/politics/trump-deep-state-impeachment.html?action=click&module=Top%20Stories&pgtype=Homepage.

xv **Scott told me:** Peter Dale Scott, interview with the author, June 21, 2019.

xv **a 4,000-word article in Breitbart News:** Virgil, "The Deep State vs. Donald

Trump," Breitbart, December 12, 2016, https://www.breitbart.com/politics/2016/12/12/virgil-the-deep-state-vs-donald-trump/.

xvi   **73 percent of Republicans agreed:** Chris Kahn, "Most Republicans Believe FBI, Justice Dept. Trying to 'Delegitimize' Trump: Reuters/Ipsos Poll," Reuters, February 5, 2018, https://www.reuters.com/article/us-usa-trump-russia-poll/most-republicans-believe-fbi-justice-dept-trying-to-delegitimize-trump-reuters-ipsos-poll-idUSKBN1FP2UH.

xvi   **positive view of the bureau has declined:** Mohamed Younis, "FBI's Positive Job Ratings Steady among Americans," Gallup, May 10, 2019, https://news.gallup.com/poll/257489/fbi-positive-job-ratings-steady-among-americans.aspx.

xvii   **more Democrats than Republicans said they trust:** Victoria Balara, "Fox News Poll: Majorities Have Confidence in CIA, FBI, and SCOTUS," Fox News, October 16, 2019, https://www.foxnews.com/politics/fox-news-poll-majorities-have-confidence-in-cia-fbi-and-scotus.

xvii   **Since 1939, the Hatch Act had barred:** Amber Phillips, "What Is the Hatch Act, and Why Did Kellyanne Conway Get Accused of Violating It So Egregiously?" *Washington Post*, June 13, 2019, https://www.washingtonpost.com/politics/2019/06/13/what-is-hatch-act-why-did-kellyanne-conway-get-accused-violating-it-so-egregiously/.

xvii   **civil servants take an oath of office:** Legal Information Institute, "5 U.S. Code § 3331. Oath of Office," Cornell Law School, https://www.law.cornell.edu/uscode/text/5/3331.

xix   **nine million Americans work for the federal government:** Neil Gordon, "Contractors and the True Size of Government," *Project on Government Oversight*, October 5, 2017, https://www.pogo.org/analysis/2017/10/contractors-and-true-size-of-government/.

xix   **make up roughly five percent:** Bureau of Labor Statistics, "Labor Force Statistics from the Current Population Survey," Department of Labor, https://data.bls.gov/pdq/SurveyOutputServlet?graph_name=LN_cpsbref1&request_action=wh.

xix   **has remained largely constant since the 1950s:** "Sizing Up the Executive Branch," US Office of Personnel Management, https://www.opm.gov/policy-data-oversight/data-analysis-documentation/federal-employment-reports/reports-publications/sizing-up-the-executive-branch-2016.pdf.

xix   **A British prime minister appoints only a few hundred:** Andrew Blick and Professor George Jones, "The Institution of Prime Minister," The National Archives, January 1, 2012, https://history.blog.gov.uk/2012/01/01/the-institution-of-prime-minister/.

CHAPTER ONE: THE CHURCH COMMITTEE

3   **implicated both Democrats and Republicans:** Senate Select Committee to Study Governmental Operations with Respect to Intelligence Activities, Final Report, "Intelligence Activities and the Rights of Americans," (94th Cong., 2nd sess., 1976), Book I, https://archive.org/details/ChurchCommittee.

3   **John Steinbeck, Hubert Humphrey, and Richard Nixon:** Walter F. Mondale, *The Good Fight* (New York: Scribner, 2010), 147.

3   **Agency operatives had secretly funded:** "Essay: How to Care for the CIA Orphans," *Time,* May 19, 1967, http://content.time.com/time/magazine/article/0,9171,840898,00.html.

4   **more than one million Americans:** Mondale, *Good Fight*, 147.

4   **and the writer Norman Mailer:** Senate Select Committee, "Intelligence Activities and the Rights of Americans," Book II, 55–56, https://www.intelligence.senate.gov/sites/default/files/94755_II.pdf.

4   **NSA had opened intelligence files:** Walter Pincus, "This NSA History Has a Familiar Ring to It," *Washington Post*, May 19, 2014, https://www.washington post.com/world/national-security/this-nsa-history-has-a-familiar-ring-to-it/2014/05/19/32369f4c-ddca-11e3-8009-71de85b9c527_story.html.

4   **The IRS was also implicated:** Senate Select Committee, II:6, https://www.intelligence.senate.gov/sites/default/files/94755_II.pdf.

4   **US Supreme Court justices:** "F.B.I. Kept a File on Supreme Court," *New York Times*, August 21, 1988, https://www.nytimes.com/1988/08/21/us/fbi-kept-a-file-on-supreme-court.html.

4   **Chief executives from both parties received it:** Senate Select Committee, II:8–10, 106–7, https://www.intelligence.senate.gov/sites/default/files/94755_II.pdf.

6   **Nixon's 1972 reelection campaign:** Carl Bernstein and Bob Woodward, "FBI Finds Nixon Aides Sabotaged Democrats," *Washington Post,* October 10, 1972, https://www.washingtonpost.com/wp-srv/national/longterm/watergate/articles/101072-1.htm.

6   **Mitchell was convicted of conspiracy:** "John N. Mitchell Dies at 75; Major Figure in Watergate," *New York Times*, November 10, 1988, https://www.nytimes.com/1988/11/10/obituaries/john-n-mitchell-dies-at-75-major-figure-in-watergate.html.

6   **"black bag jobs":** Mondale, *Good Fight*, 148.

7   **"a soul sister":** "Church Committee Hearing on FBI Intelligence Activities," C-SPAN, November 18, 1975, video, 13:50, https://www.c-span.org/video/?409760-1/church-committee-hearing-fbi-intelligence-activities.

7   **"Never once did I hear":** Mondale, *Good Fight*, 148.

8   **"the impact of those abuses":** "Church Committee Hearing on FBI Intelligence Activities," C-SPAN video, 16:27.

8   **Church chastised presidents and members of Congress:** "Church Committee Hearing on FBI Intelligence Activities," C-SPAN video, 00:28.

8   **neglecting to lead it:** Mondale, *Good Fight*, 137.

8   **the "Family Jewels":** Thomas Blanton, "The CIA's Family Jewels," The National Security Archive, June 26, 2007, https://nsarchive2.gwu.edu/NSA EBB/NSAEBB222/index.htm.

9   **the CIA's own cables:** Mondale, *Good Fight*, 145–46.

9   **Angleton and his aides:** By Stephen Engelberg, "James Angleton, Counterin-
    telligence Figure, Dies," *New York Times*, May 12, 1987, https://www.nytimes
    .com/1987/05/12/obituaries/james-angleton-counterintelligence-figure-dies.html.

9   **Colby, who removed Angleton:** Tim Weiner, "William E. Colby, 76, Head
    of C.I.A. in a Time of Upheaval," *New York Times*, May 7, 1996, https://www
    .nytimes.com/1996/05/07/us/william-e-colby-76-head-of-cia-in-a-time-of
    -upheaval.html.

9   **was given 150 staffers:** US Senate, "Select Committee to Study Governmen-
    tal Operations with Respect to Intelligence Activities," https://www.senate.gov/
    artandhistory/history/common/investigations/ChurchCommittee.htm.

9   **Fritz Schwarz, the Church Committee's chief counsel:** Fritz Schwarz, inter-
    view with the author, January 21, 2019.

10 **It was my assumption:** Senate Select Committee, II:14, https://www.intelligence
    .senate.gov/sites/default/files/94755_II.pdf.

10 **In a prescient interview on *Meet the Press*:** Nate Anderson, "How a 30-Year-
    Old Lawyer Exposed NSA Mass Surveillance of Americans—in 1975," Ars
    Technica, June 30, 2013, https://arstechnica.com/tech-policy/2013/06/how-a
    -30-year-old-lawyer-exposed-nsa-mass-surveillance-of-americans-in-1975/2/.

11 **The Foreign Intelligence Surveillance Act:** US Department of Justice, Office of
    Justice Programs, Bureau of Justice Assistance, "The Foreign Intelligence Sur-
    veillance Act of 1978," September 19, 2013, https://it.ojp.gov/PrivacyLiberty/
    authorities/statutes/1286.

11 **damaging information about John F. Kennedy and other officials:** Mondale,
    Good Fight, 137.

CHAPTER TWO: FORD, CHENEY, AND RUMSFELD

12 **Scalia's allies included Donald Rumsfeld:** Scott Shane, "Recent Flexing of
    Presidential Powers Had Personal Roots in Ford White House," *New York Times*,
    December 30, 2006, https://www.nytimes.com/2006/12/30/washington/30roots
    .html.

13 **"A feeble executive":** The Avalon Project, "The Executive Department Further
    Considered, The Federalist Papers: No. 70," Yale Law School, https://avalon
    .law.yale.edu/18th_century/fed70.asp.

13 **The decision would doom Ford's election:** Joseph Carroll, "Americans Grew
    to Accept Nixon's Pardon," Gallup, May 21, 2001, https://news.gallup.com/
    poll/3157/americans-grew-accept-nixons-pardon.aspx.

14 **Democrats in Congress overrode Ford's veto:** Shane, "Recent Flexing of Pres-
    idential Powers."

14 **Edward Levi, the president of the University of Chicago:** Neil A Lewis,
    "Edward H. Levi, Attorney General Credited with Restoring Order after
    Watergate, Dies at 88," *New York Times*, March 8, 2000, https://www.nytimes
    .com/2000/03/08/us/edward-h-levi-attorney-general-credited-with-restoring
    -order-after-watergate.html.

16   **Church and other Democrats opposed Bush's nomination:** James Risen, "How George H. W. Bush Rode a Fake National Security Scandal to the Top of the CIA," *The Intercept*, December 8, 2018, https://theintercept.com/2018/12/08/george-hw-bush-cia-director/.

16   **In his confirmation hearing, Bush:** US Senate, Committee on Armed Services, "Nomination of George Bush to Be Director of Central Intelligence," December 15 and 16, 1975 (Washington, DC: US Government Printing Office, 1975), 8.

16   **Richard Welch, the CIA station chief:** US Central Intelligence Agency, "Remembering CIA's Heroes: Richard S. Welch," Dec 22, 2015, https://www.cia.gov/news-information/featured-story-archive/2011-featured-story-archive/heroes-richard-s-welch.html.

17   **the Senate debated Bush's nomination:** Loch K. Johnson, *A Season of Inquiry* (Lexington: University Press of Kentucky, 1974), 180.

17   **Daniel Schorr, who gave a copy to the *Village Voice*:** N. R. Kleinfield, "Otis G. Pike, 92, Dies; Long Island Congressman Took On C.I.A.," *New York Times*, January 20, 2014, https://www.nytimes.com/2014/01/21/nyregion/otis-pike-congressman-who-took-on-cia-dies-at-92.html.

17   **"foot-dragging, stone-walling, and careful deception":** John Prados and Arturo Jimenez-Bacardi, "The CIA's Constitutional Crisis," National Security Archive, June 2, 2017, https://nsarchive.gwu.edu/briefing-book/intelligence/2017–06–02/white-house-cia-pike-committee-1975.

18   **Barr's mother, Mary, taught at Columbia:** Marie Brenner, " 'I Had No Problem Being Politically Different': Young William Barr among the Manhattan Liberals," *Vanity Fair*, October 7, 2019, https://www.vanityfair.com/news/2019/10/the-untold-tale-of-young-william-barr.

18   **he was forced out:** Gene I. Maeroff, "Barr Quits Dalton School Post, Charging Trustees' Interference," *New York Times*, February 20, 1974, https://www.nytimes.com/1974/02/20/archives/barr-quits-dalton-school-post-charging-trustees-interference.html.

18   **a nun promised to pray for him:** Judith Miller, "What Trump's Attorney General nominee Bill Barr's Commitment to Family, Faith, Service Tell Us," Fox News, January 13, 2019, https://www.foxnews.com/opinion/judith-miller-why-bill-barr-trumps-attorney-general-nominee-has-little-to-gain-but-much-to-lose.

19   **received a master's degree in government and Chinese studies:** US Senate, Committee on Judiciary, "Questionnaire of Non-Judicial Nominees, William Pelham Barr," https://www.judiciary.senate.gov/imo/media/doc/William%20Barr%20Senate%20Questionnaire%20(PUBLIC).pdf.

19   **"body blows":** Byron Tau and Sadie Gurman, "Attorney General Nominee Barr Helped Navigate CIA through Rocky Times with Congress," *Wall Street Journal*, Feb. 12, 2019, https://www.wsj.com/articles/attorney-general-nominee-barr-helped-navigate-cia-through-rocky-times-with-congress-11549974600.

19   **Bella Abzug, a liberal Democrat:** John J. Goldman, "Former N.Y. Rep. Bella

Abzug Dies at 77," *Los Angeles Times*, April 1, 1998, https://www.latimes.com/archives/la-xpm-1998-apr-01-mn-34960-story.html.

19 **opening her mail:** John M. Crewdson, "C.I.A. Opened Bella Abzug's Mail, Kept 20-Year File," *New York Times*, March 6, 1975, https://www.nytimes.com/1975/03/06/archives/cia-opened-bella-abzugs-mail-kept-20year-file-angry-congresswoman.html.

19 **"I went up" ... a 2001 oral history of the Bush:** The Miller Center, "William P. Barr Oral History," University of Virginia, April 5, 2001, https://millercenter.org/the-presidency/presidential-oral-histories/william-p-barr-oral-history.

20 **a lifelong war that Barr would wage against congressional oversight:** Brad Miller, "The 40-Year War: William Barr's Long Struggle against Congressional Oversight," *American Prospect*, September 9, 2019, https://prospect.org/power/40-year-war-bill-barr-oversight/.

20 **James R. Clapper Jr., an Air Force intelligence officer:** James R. Clapper, *Facts and Fears* (New York: Viking, 2018), 5–8.

22 **"To be honest, I was resentful":** James R. Clapper, interview with the author, April 2, 2019.

CHAPTER THREE: CARTER STRENGTHENS OVERSIGHT

23 **Jimmy Carter, the leading Democratic presidential candidate:** Tim Weiner, *Legacy of Ashes* (New York: Anchor, 2008), 405.

23 **a series of limited briefings by Bush and CIA experts:** John L. Helgerson, "Getting to Know the President, Second Edition: Intelligence Briefings of Presidential Candidates, 1952–2004," Central Intelligence Agency, 87, https://www.cia.gov/library/center-for-the-study-of-intelligence/csi-publications/books-and-monographs/getting-to-know-the-president/pdfs/U-%20Chapter%204-Carter.pdf.

24 **"The conversation ranged over virtually the entire field of intelligence":** Helgerson, "Getting to Know the President," 88.

24 **"The embarrassment of the CIA revelations":** Jimmy Carter, " 'Our Nation's Past and Future' ": Address Accepting the Presidential Nomination at the Democratic National Convention in New York City," The American Presidency Project, https://www.presidency.ucsb.edu/node/244286.

24 **"Peterson Field":** Helgerson, "Getting to Know the President," 88–89.

26 **Bush offered to continue to serve as CIA director:** Helgerson, "Getting to Know the President," 97–98.

26 **CIA's funding of various dictators:** Weiner, *Legacy of Ashes*, 407.

26 **former Kennedy administration aide Ted Sorensen:** "The Rejection of Sorensen: A Drama of Human Failing," *New York Times*, February 2, 1977, https://www.nytimes.com/1977/02/02/archives/the-rejection-of-sorensen-a-drama-of-human-failing-in-rare-defeat.html.

27 **Daniel Inouye, a Democratic senator from Hawaii:** Robert McFadden "Daniel

Inouye, Hawaii's Quiet Voice of Conscience in Senate, Dies at 88," *New York Times*, December 17, 2012, https://www.nytimes.com/2012/12/18/us/daniel -inouye-hawaiis-quiet-voice-of-conscience-in-senate-dies-at-88.html.

28   **the new House Intelligence Committee:** Britt Snider, "The Agency and the Hill: The CIA's Relationship with Congress, 1946–2004," 51–54, The Center for the Study of Intelligence, https://www.cia.gov/library/center-for-the-study-of -intelligence/csi-publications/books-and-monographs/agency-and-the-hill/05 -The%20Agency%20and%20the%20Hill_PartI-Chapter2.pdf.

28   **a college student named Richard Blee:** Richard Blee, interview with the author, May 24, 2019.

28   **David Blee, the CIA's chief of counterintelligence:** James Risen, "David H. Blee, 83, C.I.A. Spy Who Revised Defector Policy," *New York Times*, August 17, 2000, https://www.nytimes.com/2000/08/17/us/david-h-blee-83-cia-spy-who -revised-defector-policy.html.

30   **Turner and Carter both ranked:** "Stansfield Turner, Who Led Major CIA Reforms, Dies," Associated Press, January 18, 2018, https://apnews.com/693a dc636e714907a9fb05c61e1c4230.

31   **"We were aware that some of the unqualified":** Tim Weiner, "Stansfield Turner, C.I.A. Director Who Confronted Communism under Carter, Dies at 94," *New York Times*, January 18, 2018, https://www.nytimes.com/2018/01/18/ obituaries/stansfield-turner-dead.html.

31   **allowed CIA analysts to see which topics most engaged the president:** Helgerson, "Getting to Know the President," 107.

31   **Carter approved a new covert action campaign:** Weiner, "Stansfield Turner."

32   **William Webster, a 53-year-old St. Louis federal appeals court judge:** Charles R. Babcock, "Carter Chooses St. Louis Judge as FBI Director," *Washington Post*, January 19, 1978, https://www.washingtonpost.com/archive/politics/1978/01/19/carter -chooses-st-louis-judge-as-fbi-director/210fdbed-f067-45e5-88e4-b58db7b6420b/.

33   **Webster asked that his swearing-in ceremony be held at the FBI headquarters:** The Miller Center, "William H. Webster Oral History," University of Virginia, August 21, 2002, https://millercenter.org/the-presidency/presidential -oral-histories/william-h-webster-oral-history.

33   **Mondale, a former member of the Church Committee, gave Webster a copy:** Mondale, *The Good Fight*, 153.

33   **Bell indicted three former FBI executives:** Charles R. Babcock, "FBI Fires 2 for Weatherman Break-Ins," *Washington Post*, December 6, 1978, https://www .washingtonpost.com/archive/politics/1978/12/06/fbi-fires-2-for-weatherman -break-ins/9d0adfe4-5220-423c-b52a-35758a29a78b/.

34   **the convictions of two former senior FBI officials:** Robert Pear, "President Reagan Pardons 2 Ex-F.B.I. Officials in 1970's Break-Ins," *New York Times*, April 16, 1981, https://www.nytimes.com/1981/04/16/us/president-reagan-pardons-2 -ex-fbi-officials-in-1970-s-break-ins.html.

34   **Bell criminally investigated Carter's relatives and aides:** "Attorney General

Bell Departs," *Washington Post*, August 6, 1979, https://www.washingtonpost .com/archive/politics/1979/08/06/attorney-general-bell-departs/2abfd382-2d46-4fdf-9f02-bf608e329a1c/.

34   **Billy Carter settled the lawsuit:** "Billy Carter Dies at 51," Associated Press, September 25, 1988, https://apnews.com/a102292adce731e2a8177c8a49ea0cea.

34   **Lance was acquitted of all charges:** Matt Schudel, "Bert Lance, Banker and Carter Budget Director," *Washington Post*, August 16, 2013, https://www .washingtonpost.com/politics/bert-lance-banker-and-carter-budget-director/ 2013/08/16/a200f4f8-0689-11e3-9259-e2aafe5a5f84_story.html.

34   **Civil Service Reform Act:** Adam Clymer, "Political Scientists See Little Impact of 1978 Civil Service Law," *New York Times*, May 3, 1982, https://www.nytimes .com/1982/05/03/us/political-scientists-see-little-impact-of-1978-civil-service -law.html.

35   **Ethics in Government Act:** Linda Greenhouse, "Blank Check; Ethics in Government: The Price of Good Intentions," *New York Times*, February 1, 1998, https://www.nytimes.com/1998/02/01/weekinreview/blank-check-ethics-in -government-the-price-of-good-intentions.html?scp=7&sq=ethics%20in%20 government%20act&st=nyt.

35   **Inspector General Act:** Michael E. Horowitz, "Give Inspectors General Access to the Records They Need to Do Their Jobs," *Washington Post*, October 18, 2015, https://www.washingtonpost.com/opinions/give-inspectors-general-access-to -the-records-they-need-to-do-their-jobs/2015/10/18/54942f30-738a-11e5-9cbb -790369643cf9_story.html.

35   **freedom of information laws:** Malak Monir, "Explaining the White House FOIA Rule Repeal," *USA Today*, March 17, 2015, https://www.usatoday.com/ story/news/nation-now/2015/03/17/white-house-office-of-administration -freedom-of-information-act-foia/24906463/.

CHAPTER FOUR: REAGAN, MEESE, AND IRAN-CONTRA

37   **Melvin Weinberg, a shrewd New York grifter:** Harrison Smith, "Mel Weinberg, Con Artist at Center of Abscam Sting, Dies at 93," *Washington Post*, June 7, 2018, https://www.washingtonpost.com/local/obituaries/mel-weinberg-con -artist-at-center-of-abscam-sting-dies-at-93/2018/06/07/6ed689ac-6a5d-11e8-9e38-24e693b38637_story.html?utm_term=.11534ccaa074.

37   **tried to swindle Yaqui Indians:** Robert McFadden, "Mel Weinberg, 93, the F.B.I.'s Lure in the Abscam Sting, Dies," *New York Times*, June 6, 2018, https:// www.nytimes.com/2018/06/06/obituaries/mel-weinberg-dead-abscam-informant .html.

38   **"the salad dressing, the schmaltz":** Robert W. Greene, *The Sting Man: Inside Abscam* (New York: E. P. Dutton, 1981).

38   **"When a guy is in a jam":** Leslie Maitland, "At the Heart of the Abscam Debate," *New York Times Magazine*, July 25, 1982. https://www.nytimes.com/1982/07/25/ magazine/at-the-heart-of-the-abscam-debate.html.

38 **John Good, an ambitious FBI agent:** Alex Hannaford, "American Hustle: The Man behind the Scam," *Daily Telegraph,* December 16, 2013, https://www .telegraph.co.uk/culture/film/10513778/American-Hustle-the-man-behind-the -scam.html.

38 **two missing seventeenth-century paintings:** Robert McFadden, "Williams Trial Is the Last of 8 Major Abscam Cases," *New York Times,* May 3, 1981, https://www.nytimes.com/1981/05/03/nyregion/williams-s-trial-is-the-last-of-8 -major-abscam-cases.html.

39 **John Murtha, a Pennsylvania Democrat, turned down a bribe:** Jimmy So, "The Real Lessons of the Abscam Sting in 'American Hustle,'" *Daily Beast,* December 17, 2013. https://www.thedailybeast.com/the-real-story-and-lesson -of-the-abscam-sting-in-american-hustle.

40 **"Money talks in this business and bullshit walks":** Charles R. Babcock, "Rep. Myers Is Convicted of Bribery," *Washington Post,* August 30, 1980, https://www.washingtonpost.com/archive/politics/1980/08/30/rep-myers-is -convicted-of-bribery/5626a409-adae-4ce3-b7e7-ec847f5214b6/?utm_term= .2ad24a8ff8b0.

40 **Harrison "Pete" Williams Jr., a Democrat from New Jersey:** Adam Bernstein, "Harrison A. Williams Jr. Dies," *Washington Post,* November 20, 2001, https:// www.washingtonpost.com/archive/local/2001/11/20/harrison-a-williams-jr -dies/4699b70e-632a-480b-b63d-85c469b37c67/?utm_term=.00520040cb2a.

40 **The number-three official in the department at the time, Rudolph Giuliani:** Maitland, "Abscam Debate."

41 **William Webster, in his third year as FBI director:** Mary Thornton, "FBI Unscathed in Aftermath of Abscam 'Sting,' Webster Believes," *Washington Post,* October 18, 1982, https://www.washingtonpost.com/archive/politics/1982/10/18/ fbi-unscathed-in-aftermath-of-abscam-sting-webster-believes/69e17cb8-47e9- 4de4-a11f-790ff3bd9a7a/?utm_term=.93f722abbd57.

41 **"I said 'if they're corrupt, they'll come back'":** Miller Center, "William H. Webster Oral History."

41 **Robert Hanssen, an FBI counterintelligence agent:** Michael Ellison, FBI Agent 'Sent Spies to Their Death' for Cash and Diamonds," *Guardian,* February 20, 2001, https://www.theguardian.com/world/2001/feb/21/michaelellison.

41 **"possibly the worst intelligence disaster in U.S. history":** Commission for Review of FBI Security Programs, "A Review of FBI Security Programs," US Department of Justice, March 2002, https://fas.org/irp/agency/doj/fbi/webster report.html.

42 **His estranged wife, Cynthia Marie Weinberg, insisted that he had accepted a payoff:** Gregory Jaynes, "Wife of Key Abscam Figure Is Found Hanged in Florida," *New York Times,* January 29, 1982, https://www.nytimes.com/1982/01/29/ us/wife-of-key-abscam-figure-is-found-hanged-in-florida.html.

42 **fake designer handbags and clothing:** Smith, "Weinberg."

42 **Reagan pardoned the two former senior FBI officials:** Pear, "Reagan Pardons."

43   **"The Carter administration would have people:** Miller Center, "William H. Webster Oral History."

43   **"I think that at times":** Godfrey Sperling Jr., *Christian Science Monitor*, "Gerald Ford on Reagan, Watergate, and State of the Presidency," October 11, 1983, https://www.csmonitor.com/1983/1011/101143.html.

43   **secrecy oaths:** Richard D. Lyons, "William French Smith Dies at 73; Reagan's First Attorney General," *New York Times*, October 30, 1990, https://www.nytimes.com/1990/10/30/obituaries/william-french-smith-dies-at-73-reagan-s-first-attorney-general.html.

44   **a dissenting appeals court decision:** "Judges Rule 5–2," *New York Times*, October 13, 1973, https://www.nytimes.com/1973/10/13/archives/judges-rule-52-historic-decision-finds-president-not-above-laws.html.

44   **according to friends:** Chuck Cooper, interview with the author, November 29, 2019.

45   **Members of Congress had accused Olson:** "Special Prosecutor Drops E.P.A. Case without Indictment," *New York Times*, August 27, 1988, https://www.nytimes.com/1988/08/27/us/special-prosecutor-drops-epa-case-without-indictment.html.

46   **Joan Dempsey had no idea:** Joan Dempsey, interview with the author, May 21, 2019.

48   **Reagan, meanwhile, delegated near-absolute authority to Casey:** Weiner, *Legacy of Ashes*, 434–77.

48   **Reagan was engaged, friendly, and raised largely factual questions:** Helgerson, "Getting to Know the President," 116.

49   **Instead, he asked questions to Casey, his CIA director:** Weiner, *Legacy of Ashes*, 434–35.

50   **"in a global and totalitarian war":** Louis Menand, "Wild Thing: Did the O.S.S. Help Win the War against Hitler?" *The New Yorker*, March 14, 2011, https://www.newyorker.com/magazine/2011/03/14/wild-thing-louis-menand.

50   **Nancy Reagan had reportedly blocked him:** Eric Pace, "William Casey, Ex-C.I.A. Head, Is Dead at 74," *New York Times*, May 7, 1987, https://www.nytimes.com/1987/05/07/obituaries/william-casey-ex-cia-head-is-dead-at-74.html.

50   **"Casey was an inappropriate choice":** Helgerson, "Getting to Know the President," 183–84.

50   **"simply Bill Casey's ideology":** Weiner, *Legacy of Ashes*, 439, 442.

50   **Casey expanded the covert operations that Carter had initiated in Afghanistan:** Steve Coll, *Ghost Wars* (New York: Penguin Press, 2004), 125–29.

51   **"Burdened by years of bureaucratic encrustation":** Robert Gates, *From the Shadows: The Ultimate Insider's Story of Five Presidents and How They Won the Cold War* (New York: Simon & Schuster, 2007), 110.

51   **Reagan also issued Executive Order 12333:** Snider, "The Agency and the Hill," 239–40.

52   **Casey stonewalled the House and Senate:** Gates, *From the Shadows*, 213, 246–47.

52   **Casey insisted he had informed:** Snider, "The Agency and the Hill," 61.

52   **National Security Council aide Oliver North:** Ross Cheit, "Understanding the Iran-Contra Affair," Brown University, https://www.brown.edu/Research/ Understanding_the_Iran_Contra_Affair/n-contrasus.php/.

53   **Casey died in a New York hospital:** Pace, "Casey."

54   **Reagan denied any knowledge:** Andrew Glass, "Bush Pardons Iran-Contra Felons, December 24, 1992," *Politico*, December 24, 2018, https://www.politico .com/story/2018/12/24/bush-pardons-iran-contra-felons-dec-24-1992-1072042.

55   **"The buck stops here":** Joe Pichirallo, "Poindexter Gets 6 Months in Prison," *Washington Post*, June 12, 1990, https://www.washingtonpost.com/archive/ politics/1990/06/12/poindexter-gets-6-months-in-prison/6458a92c-7b72- 49d4-91a8-049b2db93d57/.

55   **Senator Inouye cautioned that a "cabal" of officials:** "Daniel Inouye Iran Contra Closing Remarks," C-SPAN, August 3, 1987, https://www.c-span.org/ video/?c4593554/user-clip-daniel-inouye-iran-contra-closing-remarks.

55   **a minority report that dismissed the majority report as "hysterical":** Sean Wilentz, "Mr. Cheney's Minority Report," *New York Times*, July 9, 2007, https:// www.nytimes.com/2007/07/09/opinion/09wilentz.html.

56   **"The power of the purse":** "The Dark Side: Cheney in His Own Words," *Frontline*, June 20, 2006, https://www.pbs.org/wgbh/pages/frontline/darkside/ themes/ownwords.html#2.

CHAPTER FIVE: BUSH, BARR, AND THE
POWER OF THE PRESIDENCY

57   **Reagan's average approval rating:** Frank Newport, Jeffrey M. Jones, and Lydia Saad, "Ronald Reagan from the People's Perspective: A Gallup Poll Review," Gallup, June 7, 2004, https://news.gallup.com/poll/11887/ronald-reagan-from -peoples-perspective-gallup-poll-review.aspx.

58   **"At no point along the way":** David Hoffman, "Questions Dog Vice President," *Washington Post,* January 7, 1988, https://www.washingtonpost.com/archive/ politics/1988/01/07/questions-dog-vice-president/3b7d389a-e266-407e-8745- 3fc0d792ee1f/?utm_term=.e5ca1ec013c9.

59   **Presidential Covert Action finding:** Hoffman, "Questions Dog Vice President."

59   **"Lay it out there":** Michael Oreskes, "Bush and Dole Attack Each Other as Iowa Race Takes Negative Turn," *New York Times*, January 10, 1988, https:// www.nytimes.com/1988/01/10/us/bush-and-dole-attack-each-other-as -iowa-race-takes-negative-turn.html.

59   **Dole decisively won the Iowa caucuses:** E. J. Dionne Jr., "Dole Wins in Iowa, with Robertson Next," *New York Times,* February 9, 1988, https://www.nytimes .com/1988/02/09/us/dole-wins-in-iowa-with-robertson-next.html.

59   **campaign manager Lee Atwater and communications advisor Roger Ailes:**

David Von Drehle, "George Herbert Walker Bush, the 41st President of the United States and the Father of the 43rd, Dies at 94," *Time*, December 1, 2018, https://time.com/longform/president-george-hw-bush-dead/.

59   **They attacked Dole:** Jack Nelson, "Robertson Did Avoid Combat, Friend Concurs," *Los Angeles Times*, September 25, 1986, https://www.latimes.com/archives/la-xpm-1986-09-25-mn-10039-story.html.

60   **"You cannot make concessions to terrorists":** E. J. Dionne Jr., "Bush and Dukakis, with Anger, Debate Leadership and Issues from Abortion to Iran-Contra: The Presidential Debate," *New York Times*, Sept. 26, 1988, https://www.nytimes.com/1988/09/26/us/bush-dukakis-with-anger-debate-leadership-issues-abortion-iran-contra.html.

61   **Barr, who was only 39, hesitated:** Miller Center, "William P. Barr Oral History."

61   **an unsolicited memo:** William P. Barr, "Common Legislative Encroachments on Executive Branch Authority," Justice Department, July 27, 1989, https://www.justice.gov/file/24286/download.

61   **a legal call-to-arms:** Tom Hamburger, "How William Barr, Now Serving as a Powerful Ally for Trump, Has Championed Presidential Powers," *Washington Post*, May 16, 2019, https://www.washingtonpost.com/politics/how-william-barr-now-serving-as-a-powerful-ally-for-trump-has-championed-presidential-powers/2019/05/14/418fe6d4-727f-11e9-9eb4-0828f5389013_story.html.

62   **"We set up some things because of Boyden's and my own interest in the powers of the Presidency":** Miller Center, "William P. Barr Oral History."

62   **21,000 US troops to invade Panama:** Andrew Glass, "United States Invades Panama, Dec. 20, 1989," *Politico*, December 20, 2018, https://www.politico.com/story/2018/12/20/united-states-invades-panama-1989-1067072.

63   **take people into custody in foreign countries:** Hamburger, "How William Barr Has Championed Presidential Powers."

64   **Secretary of Defense Dick Cheney objected to Barr giving Bush political advice:** Miller Center, "William P. Barr Oral History."

64   **After Bush and his aides convinced Congress:** Robert Chesney, "Bill Barr on War Powers: Insights from His 2001 Oral History Interview," *Lawfare*, December 12, 2018, https://www.lawfareblog.com/bill-barr-war-powers-insights-his-2001-oral-history-interview.

65   **increased drug-related prison sentences:** Miller Center, "William P. Barr Oral History."

65   **his staunch opposition to *Roe v. Wade*:** David Shortell, "What Barr's Work under Bush 41 Tells Us about How He'll Handle His New Job," CNN, March 7, 2019, https://www.cnn.com/2019/03/02/politics/william-barr-george-hw-bush/index.html.

66   **"There's no other power like it":** Miller Center, "William P. Barr Oral History."

66   **"Coverup-General Barr":** William Safire, "Essay: 1st Global Political Scandal," *New York Times*, November 12, 1992, https://www.nytimes.com/1992/11/12/opinion/essay-1st-global-political-scandal.html.

66 **found no wrongdoing by Barr:** "Bush Administration Cleared in Iraqgate Probe," *Los Angeles Times*, January 24, 1995, https://www.sfgate.com/news/article/Bush-Administration-Cleared-in-Iraqgate-Probe-3047804.php.

67 **The diary entry from Weinberger:** Lyle Denniston, "Weinberger Note Contradicts Bush on Iran-Contra Diary Made Public after New Indictment," *Baltimore Sun*, October 31, 1992, https://www.baltimoresun.com/news/bs-xpm-1992-10-31-1992305001-story.html.

68 **In a statement accompanying the pardons:** George Bush, "Proclamation 6518—Grant of Executive Clemency," The American Presidency Project, https://www.presidency.ucsb.edu/node/268672.

69 **The pardons infuriated Walsh:** Neil A. Lewis, "Lawrence E. Walsh, Prosecutor in Iran-Contra Scandal, Dies at 102," *New York Times,* March 20, 2014, https://www.nytimes.com/2014/03/21/us/politics/lawrence-e-walsh-iran-contra-prosecutor-dies-at-102.html.

70 **"The other big problem is this notion":** Miller Center, "William P. Barr Oral History."

CHAPTER SIX: CLINTON, RENO, AND IMPEACHMENT

71 **In his inaugural address:** Jack Germond and Jules Witcover, "Inaugural Speech Shows Clinton's Determination on Politics," *Baltimore Sun*, January 21, 1993, https://www.baltimoresun.com/news/bs-xpm-1993-01-21-1993021167-story.html.

72 **Miami prosecutor named Janet Reno:** Ruth Marcus, "Clinton Nominates Reno at Justice," *Washington Post*, February 12, 1993, https://www.washingtonpost.com/wp-srv/politics/govt/admin/stories/reno021293.htm.

73 **Randy Weaver:** David Johnston, "Director of F.B.I. Demotes Deputy," *New York Times*, July 15, 1995, https://www.nytimes.com/1995/07/15/us/director-of-fbi-demotes-deputy.html.

73 **the FBI's Hostage Recovery Unit took over the operation:** Staff, "The Echoes of Ruby Ridge," *Newsweek*, August 27, 1995, https://www.newsweek.com/echoes-ruby-ridge-182402.

75 **"obviously wrong":** Susan J. Douglas, "Remembering Janet Reno," *Politico Magazine*, December 31, 2016, https://www.politico.com/magazine/story/2016/12/janet-reno-obit-214567 and https://www.justice.gov/archive/ag/speeches/1993/04-19-1993c.pdf.

75 **"This is a profound disgrace":** Greg Henderson, "Emotional Reno Describes Ill-Fated Waco Decisions," UPI, April 28, 1993, https://www.upi.com/Archives/1993/04/28/Emotional-Reno-describes-ill-fated-Waco-decisions/8341735969600/.

75 **An undercover agent warned his superiors:** Tim Weiner, "Agent Says His Warnings over Waco Were Ignored," *New York Times,* July 25, 1995, https://www.nytimes.com/1995/07/25/us/agent-says-his-warnings-over-waco-were-ignored.html.

76 **no evidence that Koresh was molesting children:** Stephen Labaton, "Report on Assault on Waco Cult Contradicts Reno's Explanations," *New York Times*,

October 9, 1993, https://www.nytimes.com/1993/10/09/us/report-on-assault-on
-waco-cult-contradicts-reno-s-explanations.html.

76   **calling the ATF "armed terrorists":** John Mintz, "Bush Resigns from NRA,
Citing Broadside on Agents," *Washington Post*, May 11, 1995, https://www
.washingtonpost.com/archive/politics/1995/05/11/bush-resigns-from-nra-citing
-broadside-on-agents/22f449e9-9e19-4bba-951e-9cc92135b89c/.

76   **Steve Stockman, a Republican congressman from Texas:** Steven A. Holmes,
"Congressman Calls Raid near Waco a Clinton Plot," *New York Times,* May 13,
1995, https://www.nytimes.com/1995/05/13/us/terror-in-oklahoma-in-congress
-congressman-calls-raid-near-waco-a-clinton-plot.html.

76   **Stockman would be sentenced to a decade:** Emma Platoff, "Steve Stockman,
Former Texas Congressman, Sentenced to 10 Years in Federal Prison," *Texas
Tribune*, November 7, 2018, https://www.texastribune.org/2018/11/07/Steve
-stockman-former-congressman-sentenced-10-years-houston/.

76   **Linda Thompson, a militia member and Clinton critic:** Jason Vest, "The
Spooky World of Linda Thompson," *Washington Post*, May 11, 1995, https://
www.washingtonpost.com/archive/lifestyle/1995/05/11/the-spooky-world-of
-linda-thompson/d09e85b3-a789-47b0-bb66-fb21d95bc712/.

77   **"witch hunt":** Darren Samuelsohn, "Trump's War against Mueller Borrows
from Bill Clinton's Playbook," *Politico,* June 21, 2018, https://www.politico
.com/story/2018/06/21/trump-mueller-clinton-independent-counsel-660491.

78   **Clinton asked Reno to appoint a special counsel:** Gwen Ifill, "Clinton Asks
Reno to Name a Counsel on His Land Deals," *New York Times,* January 13,
1994, https://www.nytimes.com/1994/01/13/us/the-whitewater-inquiry-clinton
-asks-reno-to-name-a-counsel-on-his-land-deals.html.

78   **"has been in the past and is today":** Mokhibar, "Independent Counsel Law."

79   **"Women and kids were killed at Waco and Ruby Ridge":** Rodger Doyle,
"The American Terrorist," *Scientific American*, June 2001, https://www
.scientificamerican.com/article/the-american-terrorist/.

80   **"To attack Secret Service agents":** "Letter of Resignation Sent by Bush to
Rifle Association," *New York Times,* May 11, 1995, https://www.nytimes.com/
1995/05/11/us/letter-of-resignation-sent-by-bush-to-rifle-association.html.

80   **Republicans argued that Clinton had secretly ordered the tear gas assault:**
Neil A Lewis: "In Waco Hearings, Parties Undergo a Role Reversal," *New York
Times*, August 3, 1995, https://www.nytimes.com/1995/08/03/us/in-waco-hear
ings-parties-undergo-a-role-reversal.html.

81   **Sessions had alienated FBI agents:** Michael Isikoff and Ruth Marcus, "Clinton
Fires Sessions as FBI Director," *Washington Post*, July 20, 1993, https://www
.washingtonpost.com/archive/politics/1993/07/20/clinton-fires-sessions-as-fbi
-director/1c1b437e-a695-48d0-bc9e-afa5f0f69b79/.

81   **Agents who refused to cooperate were demoted:** Terry Atlas, "FBI Director's
Mistakes Slowly Come to Light," *Chicago Tribune*, October 27, 1992, https://
www.chicagotribune.com/news/ct-xpm-1992-10-2--9204070439-story.html.

82   **"does not even pass the red face test":** "Excerpts from Barr's Memorandum to Sessions," *New York Times*, Jan. 20, 1993, https://www.nytimes.com/1993/01/20/us/excerpts-from-barr-s-memorandum-to-sessions.html.

82   **the two men would come to loathe one another:** David Johnston, "F.B.I. Director to Retire," *New York Times*, May 1, 2001, https://www.nytimes.com/2001/05/01/national/fbi-director-to-retire.html.

83   **criticized the director as sanctimonious:** John F. Harris and David A. Vise, "With Freeh, Mistrust Was Mutual," *Washington Post*, January 10, 2001, https://www.washingtonpost.com/archive/politics/2001/01/10/with-freeh-mistrust-was-mutual/37ede22a-2229-46c8-9a73-7859bd54b85f/.

85   **a primary character in Tracy Kidder's book:** Tracy Kidder, *Home Town* (New York: Washington Square Press, 1999).

85   **"I had a great gig":** Tom O'Connor, interview with the author, May 30, 2019.

86   **glaring mistakes by the FBI:** Edward Walsh and David A. Vise, "Louis Freeh to Resign as Director of the FBI," *Washington Post*, May 2, 2001, https://www.washingtonpost.com/archive/politics/2001/05/02/louis-freeh-to-resign-as-director-of-the-fbi/106f0bfa-ace7-4c79-baaf-c758e98f0252/?utm_term=.29e19fa0dce2.

86   **Freeh regretted taking the appointment:** Tim Weiner, *Enemies* (New York: Random House, 2012), 382, 405, 409–12.

87   **In a *Washington Post* article assessing the vexed relationship:** Harris and Vise, "With Freeh, Mistrust Was Mutual."

88   **most Americans agreed with Democrats:** Keating Holland, "A Year after Clinton Impeachment, Public Approval Grows of House Decision," CNN, December 16, 1999, http://archives.cnn.com/1999/ALLPOLITICS/stories/12/16/impeach.poll/.

88   **saw his $75 million investigation as a witch hunt:** Nancy LeTourneau, "Let's Put the Cost of the Mueller Investigation in Perspective," *Washington Monthly*, June 1, 2018, https://washingtonmonthly.com/2018/06/01/lets-put-the-cost-of-the-mueller-investigation-in-perspective/.

CHAPTER SEVEN: GEORGE W. BUSH, 9/11, AND THE RETURN OF THE IMPERIAL PRESIDENCY

90   **Richard Blee arrived at the White House:** Richard Blee, interview with the author, May 24, 2019.

90   **his weekly meeting with Rice:** Thomas H. Kean and Lee H. Hamilton, *The 9/11 Commission Report* (Washington, DC: National Commission on Terrorist Attacks, 2004), 204, https://www.9-11commission.gov/report/911Report.pdf.

91   **Clinton named George Tenet CIA director in 1996:** "The Dark Side: George Tenet," *Frontline*, June 20, 2006, https://www.pbs.org/wgbh/pages/frontline/darkside/themes/tenet.html.

92   **"Let's go distract":** Richard Blee, interview with the author, September 9, 2018.

92   **Rice asked the officials to develop a range of options:** Keane and Hamilton, *9/11 Commission Report*, 204–5.

92   **"Look, . . . a plane hit the World Trade Center":** Blee, interview, September 9, 2018.

93   **Tom O'Connor, the FBI agent who had investigated the bombing of the USS** *Cole***:** Tom O'Connor, interview with the author, May 30, 2019.

95   **6,000 American soldiers and hundreds of thousands of Iraqis and Afghans:** Neta C. Crawford and Catherine Lutz, "Human Costs of Post-9/11 Wars," Brown University Watson Institute, November 13, 2019, https://watson.brown .edu/costsofwar/figures/2019/direct-war-death-toll-2001–801000.

95   **"were almost immediately misunderstood":** Keane and Hamilton, *9/11 Commission Report*, 79, 82–83, 260–62, 277.

96   **public support for Bush, the CIA, and the FBI soared:** Humphrey Taylor, "Big Improvement in Rating of Several Government Agencies since Last Fall," The Harris Poll, October 17, 2001, https://theharrispoll.com/wp-content/ uploads/2017/12/Harris-Interactive-Poll-Research-BIG-IMPROVEMENT -IN-RATING-OF-SEVERAL-GOVERNMENT-AGENCIES-SINCE-LAST -FALL-2001–10.pdf.

97   **His vice president, Dick Cheney, seized the moment:** Charlie Savage, *Takeover* (New York, Little, Brown and Company, 2007).

97   **passed the USA PATRIOT Act:** Frank Davies, "'USA Patriot Act' Seen as Both Eye-Catching, Tough to Criticize," Knight-Ridder Newspapers, March 3, 2005, https://www.mcclatchydc.com/latest-news/article24446458.html.

97   **"sneak and peek" searches:** Dan Eggen, "Ashcroft Defends Anti-Terrorism Law," *Washington Post*, August 20, 2003, https://www.washingtonpost.com/ archive/politics/2003/08/20/ashcroft-defends-anti-terrorism-law/fa62dbf7- 00d0-4cff-8b14-9f434342ce32/.

98   **Jihadist propaganda, advertisements for flight schools in the United States, and bomb-making manuals:** David Rohde, "In 2 Abandoned Kabul Houses, Some Hints of Al Qaeda Presence," *New York Times,* Nov. 17, 2001, https://www .nytimes.com/2001/11/17/world/nation-challenged-kabul-2-abandoned-kabul -houses-some-hints-al-qaeda-presence.html. And David Rohde and C. J. Chivers, "Qaeda's Grocery Lists and Manuals of Killing," *New York Times,* March 17, 2002, https://www.nytimes.com/2002/03/17/world/a-nation-challenged-qaeda -s-grocery-lists-and-manuals-of-killing.html.

99   **James Baker, a senior Justice Department lawyer:** James Baker, interview with the author, May 30, 2019.

99   **"There is something spooky going on":** US Department of Justice, Office of the Inspector General, "A Review of the Department of Justice's Involvement with the President's Surveillance Program," July 2009, 71–88, https://oig.justice.gov/ reports/2015/PSPVol.III.pdf.

106   **"I did not see anything nefarious":** Joan Dempsey, interview with the author, November 4, 2019.

106   **"mobile production facilities" . . . "Curveball":** Clapper, *Facts and Fears*, 86–88, 98–99.

108   **given no reason for their dismissal:** "Fired U.S. Attorneys: A Who's Who," National Public Radio, April 15, 2007, https://www.npr.org/templates/story/story.php?storyId=7777925.

108   **a series of emails:** Ari Shapiro, "Timeline: Behind the Firing of Eight U.S. Attorneys," National Public Radio, April 15, 2007, https://www.npr.org/templates/story/story.php?storyId=8901997.

109   **Tom O'Connor . . . arrived in Baghdad:** Thomas O'Connor, interview with the author, October 22, 2019.

111   **cost over $800 billion:** "Iraq War in Figures," BBC, December 14, 2011, https://www.bbc.com/news/world-middle-east-11107739.

CHAPTER EIGHT: OBAMA, SNOWDEN, AND DRONES

112   **executive orders designed to reverse Bush-era counterterrorism policies:** Scott Shane, Mark Mazzetti, and Helene Cooper, "Obama Reverses Key Bush Security Policies," *New York Times*, January 22, 2009, https://www.nytimes.com/2009/01/23/us/politics/23obama.html.

114   **John Brennan, a little-known retired career CIA analyst:** Mattathias Schwartz, "John Brennan, Former C.I.A. Spymaster, Steps out of the Shadows," *New York Times Magazine*, June 27, 2018, https://www.nytimes.com/2018/06/27/magazine/john-brennan-president-trump-national-security-state.html.

114   **"ambivalence and institutional moral cowardice":** Andrew Sullivan, "No Way. No How. No Brennan," *Atlantic*, November 21, 2008, https://www.theatlantic.com/daily-dish/archive/2008/11/no-way-no-how-no-brennan/208302/.

116   **Obama began to employ, with greater frequency, CIA drone strikes and NSA surveillance:** Peter Baker and Mark Mazzetti, "Brennan Draws on Bond with Obama in Backing C.I.A.," *New York Times*, December 14, 2014, https://www.nytimes.com/2014/12/15/us/politics/cia-chief-and-president-walk-fine-line.html.

117   **the attacks killed 2,372 to 2,581 people in 2016:** Scott Shane, "Drone Strike Statistics Answer Few Questions, and Raise Many," *New York Times,* July 3, 2016, https://www.nytimes.com/2016/07/04/world/middleeast/drone-strike-statistics-answer-few-questions-and-raise-many.html.

117   **In a series of interviews in 2016, Brennan said:** David Rohde, "John Brennan's Attempt to Lead America's Spies into the Age of Cyberwar," Reuters, November 2, 2016, https://www.reuters.com/investigates/special-report/usa-cia-brennan/.

118   **"But that belief was was mistaken":** "Obama's Drone War Is a Shameful Part of His Legacy," *Washington Post,* May 5, 2016, https://www.washingtonpost.com/opinions/obamas-drone-war-is-a-shameful-part-of-his-legacy/2016/05/05/a727eea8-12ea-11e6-8967-7ac733c56f12_story.html.

118   **James Clapper, now a retired Air Force general, had a private fifteen-minute job interview:** Clapper, *Facts and Fears*, 128–33.

119   **the single greatest intelligence triumph in its history:** Steve Coll, *Directorate S* (New York, Penguin Press, 2018).

120   **The Marine general who oversaw Guantánamo, General John Kelly:** Charles Levinson and David Rohde, "Pentagon Thwarts Obama Effort to Close Guantanamo," Reuters, December 29, 2015, https://www.reuters.com/article/us-usa-gitmo-release-special-report-idUSKBN0UB1B020151229.

122   **the FBI informed Clapper of the Petraeus affair:** Clapper, *Facts and Fears,* 195–97.

124   **Later, Clapper said that he had misunderstood Wyden's question:** James Clapper, interview with the author, July 1, 2019; Clapper, *Facts and Fears,* 207–10.

126   **highest levels of American public suspicion of US intelligence agencies since the Church reforms:** W. Geiger, "How Americans Have Viewed Government Surveillance and Privacy since Snowden Leaks," Pew Research Center, June 4, 2018, https://www.pewresearch.org/fact-tank/2018/06/04/how-americans-have-viewed-government-surveillance-and-privacy-since-snowden-leaks/.

127   **"He's playing to his constituency":** Clapper, interview, July 1, 2019.

127   **"Regardless of what was going through":** Ron Wyden, interview with the author, January 10, 2019, and "Wyden Statement on Director Clapper's Resignation," November 17, 2016, https://www.wyden.senate.gov/news/press-releases/-wyden-statement-on-director-clappers-resignation.

128   **O'Connor was delighted:** Thomas O'Connor, interview with the author, October 22, 2019.

131   **Obama, like so many presidents before him, came to embrace covert action:** Charlie Savage, *Power Wars* (New York: Little Brown and Company, 2015).

CHAPTER NINE: THE 2016 CAMPAIGN

136   **Olsen later said that he had tried:** Matthew Olsen, interview with the author, January 24, 2019.

140   **Deputy CIA Director Morell, who had become the focus of a bitter Republican attack:** Michael Morell, interview with the author, April 16, 2019.

142   **When the *Post* examined the accuracy of a sampling of 92 of Trump's statements:** Glenn Kessler, "All of Donald Trump's Four-Pinocchio Ratings, in One Place," *Washington Post*, March 22, 2016, https://www.washingtonpost.com/news/fact-checker/wp/2016/03/22/all-of-donald-trumps-four-pinocchio-ratings-in-one-place/.

143   **Clapper and other American intelligence officials viewed the activity:** Clapper, interview, July 1, 2019; Clapper, *Facts and Fears,* 314–15.

145   **One of the worried FBI officials was James Baker:** James Baker, interview with the author, April 9, 2019.

151   **McDonough said he had two theories:** Denis McDonough, interview with the author, January 25, 2019.

151   **when the *New York Times* asked McConnell:** Charles Homans, "Mitch

McConnell Got Everything He Wanted. But at What Cost?" *New York Times Magazine*, January 22, 2019, https://www.nytimes.com/2019/01/22/magazine/mcconnell-senate-trump.html.

151 **Baker faced one of the most difficult decisions:** Baker, interview, April 9, 2019.

153 **Only a few thousand of the 650,000 emails:** Adam Goldman and Matt Apuzzo, "How the F.B.I. Reviewed Thousands of Emails in One Week," November 7, 2016, https://www.nytimes.com/2016/11/08/us/politics/hillary-clinton-donald-trump-fbi-emails.html.

153 **The pollster and pundit Nate Silver argued:** Nate Silver, "The Comey Letter Probably Cost Clinton the Election," *FiveThirtyEight*, May 3, 2017, https://fivethirtyeight.com/features/the-comey-letter-probably-cost-clinton-the-election/.

CHAPTER TEN: THE PRESIDENT-ELECT
AND THE "DEEP STATE"

155 **Comey and Baker were stunned by Trump's win:** James Baker, interview with the author, April 16, 2019.

155 **Career Justice Department officials privately criticized Comey and Baker's decision:** Former Justice Department official, interview with the author.

156 **Clapper and other senior American intelligence officials were surprised by Trump's win as well:** James Clapper, interview with the author, February 18, 2019.

157 **As planned, aides shredded the note to Clinton:** James Clapper, *Facts and Fears*, 358, 361, 362.

158 **Four days later, the *Washington Post* broke the story:** Adam Entous, Ellen Nakashima, and Greg Miller, "Secret CIA Assessment Says Russia Was Trying to Help Trump Win White House, *Washington Post*, December 9, 2016, https://www.washingtonpost.com/world/national-security/obama-orders-review-of-russian-hacking-during-presidential-campaign/2016/12/09/31d6b300-be2a-11e6-94ac-3d324840106c_story.html.

158 **Republicans saw the leak of the CIA's finding:** Former Republican official, interview with the author.

161 **Flynn was one of Trump's most bombastic advisors:** James Kitfield, "How Mike Flynn Became America's Angriest General," *Politico Magazine*, October 16, 2016, https://www.politico.com/magazine/story/2016/10/how-mike-flynn-became-americas-angriest-general-214362.

161 **Flynn alienated DIA employees:** James Clapper, *Facts and Fears*, 330–31.

162 **In a blistering 2016 interview with the *New York Times*:** Matthew Rosenberg, "Michael Flynn Is Harsh Judge of C.I.A.'s Role," *New York Times*, December 12, 2016, https://www.nytimes.com/2016/12/12/us/politics/donald-trump-cia-michael-flynn.html.

163 **In 2015, Flynn sat next to Vladimir Putin:** Dana Priest, "Trump Adviser Michael T. Flynn on His Dinner with Putin and Why Russia Today Is Just Like CNN," *Washington Post*, August 15, 2016, https://www.washingtonpost.com/

news/checkpoint/wp/2016/08/15/trump-adviser-michael-t-flynn-on-his-dinner
-with-putin-and-why-russia-today-is-just-like-cnn/.

163   **He received a $33,750 speaking fee:** Ken Dilanian, "Russians Paid Mike
Flynn $45K for Moscow Speech, Documents Show," NBC News, March 16,
2017, https://www.nbcnews.com/news/us-news/russians-paid-mike-flynn-45k
-moscow-speech-documents-show-n734506.

164   **"We expected retaliation":** Clapper, interview, February 18, 2019.

164   **"The logical question is 'what's going on here?' ":** Clapper, *Facts and Fears*,
366.

164   **"There was a general concern about violating the principle of having one
president at a time":** Clapper, interview, February 18, 2019.

165   **Clapper intentionally made the "key judgments" section:** Clapper, interview,
February 18, 2019.

165   **"It was chaos":** Clapper, *Facts and Fears*, 373–74.

166   **Pence, in particular, impressed Clapper:** Clapper, interview, February 18, 2019.

166   **Clapper said that US intelligence agencies didn't have the authority:** Clapper,
Facts and Fears, 374–75.

167   **"Jim felt strongly that he needed to try":** Clapper, interview, February 18,
2019.

168   **Comey decided it was better to inform Trump:** Clapper, interview, February
18, 2019; James Baker, interview with the author, April 16, 2019.

168   **"The way they all struck me was no exposure, or outright ignorance":** Clapper, interview, February 18, 2019.

169   **Brennan urged me to not report them:** John Brennan, interview with the
author, October 2016.

170   **the intelligence community made mistakes in their initial interactions with
Trump:** Michael Morell, interview with the author, April 16, 2019.

CHAPTER ELEVEN: THE TRANSFER OF POWER

172   **one of the most ominous inaugural addresses in American history:** Michael C.
Bender, "Donald Trump Strikes Nationalistic Tone in Inaugural Speech," *Wall
Street Journal*, January 20, 2017, https://www.wsj.com/articles/donald-trump
-strikes-nationalistic-tone-in-inaugural-speech-1484957527?tesla=y&mod=e2tw.

173   **standing in front of a wall of stars representing the 117 agents who had died
serving their country:** Robin Wright, "Trump's Vainglorious Affront to the
C.I.A.," *The New Yorker*, January 22, 2017, https://www.newyorker.com/news/
news-desk/trumps-vainglorious-affront-to-the-c-i-a.

173   **speech unlike any address ever given to the CIA by an American president:**
The White House, "Remarks by President Trump and Vice President Pence at
CIA Headquarters," January 21, 2017, https://www.whitehouse.gov/briefings
-statements/remarks-president-trump-vice-president-pence-cia-headquarters/.

173   **Preelection polls showed that members of the military had supported**

Trump: George R. Altman and Leo Shane III, "Military Times Survey: Troops Prefer Trump to Clinton by a Huge Margin," *Military Times*, May 9, 2016, https://www.militarytimes.com/news/2016/05/09/military-times-survey-troops -prefer-trump-to-clinton-by-a-huge-margin/.

174 **John Brennan, Obama's outgoing director, was very controlling:** Former intelligence official, interview with the author.

175 **Joan Dempsey, the Arkansas native who rose to be the number-three official at the CIA:** Joan Dempsey, interview with the author, January 23, 2019.

176 **"It creates a perception in the public that the intelligence community is political":** Morell, interview, April 16, 2019.

CHAPTER TWELVE: LOYALTY

177 **no FBI director had dined alone with a president since the days of J. Edgar Hoover:** James Comey, *A Higher Loyalty* (New York: Flatiron Books, 2018) 233–44.

177 **Trump told Comey, "I need loyalty, I expect loyalty":** Robert S. Mueller III, *Report on the Investigation into Russian Interference in the 2016 Presidential Election* (Washington, DC: US Department of Justice, 2019), vol. II, 34–35, https://www.justice.gov/storage/report.pdf.

177 **"You will get that from me":** Mueller, *Report*, II:34–35.

177 **Trump did not understand that the bureau had spent forty years trying to distance itself from the abuses:** Comey, *A Higher Loyalty*, 234.

178 **Flynn also falsely stated that he did not remember a follow-up conversation:** Comey, *A Higher Loyalty*, 237–38; Mueller, *Report,* II:30.

178 **Flynn had lied to Spicer, the White House spokesman, Vice President Mike Pence, and other officials:** Greg Miller, Adam Entous, and Ellen Nakashima, "National Security Adviser Flynn Discussed Sanctions with Russian Ambassador Despite Denials, Officials Say," *Washington Post*, February 9, 2017, https://www.washingtonpost.com/world/national-security/national-security-adviser -flynn-discussed-sanctions-with-russian-ambassador-despite-denials-officials -say/2017/02/09/f85b29d6-ee11-11e6-b4ff-ac2cf509efe5_story.html.

178 **Deputy Attorney General Sally Yates and Mary McCord, a senior Justice Department official:** Mary McCord, interview with the author, January 23, 2019.

178 **On February 13, Flynn resigned:** Greg Miller, Adam Entous, and Ellen Nakashima, "Flynn's Swift Downfall: From a Phone Call in the Dominican Republic to a Forced Resignation at the White House," *Washington Post*, February 14, 2017, https://www.washingtonpost.com/world/national-security/ flynns-swift-downfall-from-a-phone-call-in-the-dominican-republic-to-a -forced-resignation-at-the-white-house/2017/02/14/17b0d8e6-f2f2-11e6-b9c9 -e83fce42fb61_story.html

179 **"I hope you can see your way clear to letting this go, to letting Flynn go":** Mueller, *Report*, II:39–40.

179   **and gave copies to Baker and his other senior staff:** James Baker, interview with the author, April 16, 2019.

181   **Trump asked the country's top two intelligence officials:** Mueller, *Report*, II:55–57.

183   **Coats recalled that Trump brought up the Russia investigation so many times:** Mueller, *Report*, II:57.

184   **on April 11, 2017, Trump called Comey again:** Mueller, *Report*, II:58–59.

185   **a counterintelligence inquiry into whether the president himself had been working on behalf of Russia:** Adam Goldman, Michael S. Schmidt, Nicholas Fandos, "F.B.I. Opened Inquiry into Whether Trump Was Secretly Working on Behalf of Russia," *New York Times*, January 11, 2019, https://www.nytimes .com/2019/01/11/us/politics/fbi-trump-russia-inquiry.html.

185   **Rosenstein appointed Mueller as special counsel:** Philip Rucker, Ashley Parker, Sari Horwitz, and Robert Costa, "Inside Trump's Anger and Impatience— and His Sudden Decision to Fire Comey," *Washington Post*, May 10, 2017, https://www.washingtonpost.com/politics/how-trumps-anger-and-impatience -prompted-him-to-fire-the-fbi-director/2017/05/10/d9642334-359c-11e7-b373- 418f6849a004_story.html?utm_term=.46cc4291f12a.

CHAPTER THIRTEEN: OBSTRUCTING THE MUELLER INVESTIGATION

188   **White House Chief of Staff Reince Priebus and Chief Strategist Steve Bannon learned that Trump:** Mueller, *Report*, II:79–80.

190   **Trump instructed Priebus to get Sessions to resign immediately:** Mueller, *Report*, II:95.

190   **Trump was exaggerating his powers as president:** Jordyn Phelps, "What Is a Recess Appointment, and Is It a Feasible Option for Trump If Sessions Goes?" ABC News, July 27, 2017, https://abcnews.go.com/Politics/recess-appointment -feasible-option-trump-sessions/story?id=48859976.

191   **McGahn and Priebus discussed the possibility that they would both have to resign:** Mueller, *Report*, II:95–96.

192   **Trump called the attorney general at home:** Mueller, *Report*, II:107.

CHAPTER FOURTEEN: THE COLLAPSE OF CONGRESSIONAL OVERSIGHT

193   **Former Justice Department colleagues saw Wray as well intentioned but weak:** Former Justice Department official, interview with the author.

194   **the average age of a US senator had steadily risen since the 1980s and was now 62:** Jennifer E. Manning, "Membership of the 115th Congress: A Profile," Congressional Research Service, December 20, 2018, https://www.senate.gov/ CRSpubs/b8f6293e-c235-40fd-b895-6474d0f8e809.pdf.

194   **The average age of Americans of all professions is 42:** "Labor Force Statistics

from the Current Population Survey," Bureau of Labor Statistics, January 18, 2019, https://www.bls.gov/cps/cpsaat18b.htm.

195 **Some called him more impressive than the members of Congress:** Benjamin Wittes, "Wray Does Well; the Senate Judiciary Committee Does Not," *Lawfare,* July 12, 2017, https://www.lawfareblog.com/wray-does-well-senate-judiciary-committee-does-not.

195 **Will Hurd, a Republican congressman from West Texas:** Will Hurd, interview with the author, September 11, 2019.

196 **he mounted a long-shot bid for class president:** Tim Alberta, "Will Hurd Is the Future of the GOP*," *Politico Magazine,* May 5, 2017, https://www.politico.com/magazine/story/2017/05/05/congressman-will-hurd-texas-republican-profile-215102.

196 **"When I think of chaos and carnage":** Will Hurd, interview with the author, October 18, 2019.

197 **The fury of one official, in particular, struck him:** Hurd, interview, October 18, 2019.

198 **Hurd distanced himself from Trump:** Bill Lambrecht, "Hurd Is Staying out of Trump's Shadow: Congressman Distances Self from Potential GOP Nominee," *San Antonio Express-News,* March 20, 2016, 1, A24.

199 **Hurd went a step further and said he would not vote for Trump:** John W. Gonzalez, "Hurd, Gallego Battle Grinds On," *San Antonio Express-News,* October 9, 2016, 1, A18.

200 **Nunes held an impromptu press conference:** Derek Hawkins and Kyle Swenson, "Adam Schiff and Devin Nunes: From 'Bromance' to Bitter Adversaries," *Washington Post,* February 1, 2018, https://www.washingtonpost.com/news/morning-mix/wp/2018/02/01/adam-b-schiff-and-devin-nunes-from-bromance-to-bitter-adversaries/.

201 **"I wouldn't have done it that way":** Hurd, interview with the author, September 14, 2019.

CHAPTER FIFTEEN: THE DISINFORMATION PRESIDENCY

203 **he continued to use his Twitter feed and to a lesser extent, his public comments:** Mike McIntire, Karen Yourish, and Larry Buchanan, "In Trump's Twitter Feed: Conspiracy-Mongers, Racists and Spies," *New York Times,* Nov. 2, 2019, https://www.nytimes.com/interactive/2019/11/02/us/politics/trump-twitter-disinformation.html.

203 **Trump also took pride in dismissing the advice of experts:** Patrick Radden Keefe, "McMaster and Commander," *The New Yorker,* April 30, 2018, https://www.newyorker.com/magazine/2018/04/30/mcmaster-and-commander.

204 **"He's very engaging":** Former White House official, interview with the author.

204 **One former senior official singled out Steve Bannon for criticism:** Former senior White House official, interview with the author.

204   **while Trump's public rhetoric toward Iran and North Korea was bombastic:** A current senior White House official, interview with the author.

205   **the failure of the Clinton, George W. Bush, and Obama administrations:** Another current official, interview with the author.

206   **After he took office, Trump received his briefing as he sat behind the "Resolute" desk:** Philip Rucker and Ashley Parker, "How President Trump Consumes—or Does Not Consume—Top Secret Intelligence," *Washington Post*, May 29, 2017, https://www.washingtonpost.com/politics/how-president-trump -consumes—or-does-not-consume—top-secret-intelligence/2017/05/29/1caaca 3e-39ae-11e7-a058-ddbb23c75d82_story.html.

207   **"two or three points, with the syntactical complexity of 'See Jane run'":** Radden Keefe, "McMaster and Commander."

207   **"Pompeo can be the president's best friend":** Former White House official, interview with the author.

207   **They accused him of self-aggrandizement:** Current administration official, interview with the author.

208   **Pompeo even pitched covert CIA operations to Trump without being asked to prepare them:** Adam Entous, "Mike Pompeo, the Spymaster Who Couldn't Stay in His Lane," *The New Yorker*, March 15, 2018, https://www.newyorker.com/ news/news-desk/mike-pompeo-the-spymaster-who-couldnt-stay-in-his-lane.

208   **a July 19, 2017, National Security Council meeting regarding Afghanistan:** Carol E. Lee and Courtney Kube, "Trump Says U.S. 'Losing' Afghan War in Tense Meeting with Generals," NBC News, https://www.nbcnews.com/news/us -news/trump-says-u-s-losing-afghan-war-tense-meeting-generals-n789006.

209   **The restaurant had, in fact, closed for only two months:** Frank J. Prial, "'21' And El Morocco: 2 Legends Reopen," *New York Times*, April 29, 1987, https:// www.nytimes.com/1987/04/29/nyregion/21-and-el-morocco-2-legends-reopen .html.

209   **"An American company will do this cheaper and better":** A former nation security official, interview with the author.

209   **In January 2018, Trump's appetite for conspiracy theories sparked chaos:** David Rohde, "How Disinformation Reaches Donald Trump," *The New Yorker*, October 3, 2019, https://www.newyorker.com/news/news-desk/how -disinformation-reaches-donald-trump.

CHAPTER SIXTEEN: THE LOUDEST VOICE

213   **a debunked, three-year-old conspiracy theory circulated during the 2016 campaign:** Glenn Kessler, "The Repeated, Incorrect Claim that Russia Obtained '20 Percent of Our Uranium,'" *Washington Post*, October 31, 2017, https://www .washingtonpost.com/news/fact-checker/wp/2017/10/31/the-repeated-incorrect -claim-that-russia-obtained-20-percent-of-our-uranium/.

213   **sale of a Canadian company that controlled twenty percent of the US ura- nium:** Michelle Ye Hee Lee, "The Facts behind Trump's Repeated Claim about

Hillary Clinton's Role in the Russian Uranium Deal," *Washington Post*, October 26, 2016, https://www.washingtonpost.com/news/fact-checker/wp/2016/10/26/the-facts-behind-trumps-repeated-claim-about-hillary-clintons-role-in-the-russian-uranium-deal/.

216   **Hannity then commented, "This is not hyperbole":** Samantha Schmidt, "A Coup in America? Fox News Escalates Anti-Mueller Rhetoric," *Washington Post*, December 18, 2017, https://www.washingtonpost.com/news/morning-mix/wp/2017/12/18/a-coup-in-america-fox-news-escalates-anti-mueller-rhetoric/.

218   **He pressured the FBI to conduct a cursory review of sexual abuse allegations:** David Rohde, "Does the Kavanaugh Investigation Show How Trump Will Use the F.B.I. in the Future?" *The New Yorker,* October 12, 2018, https://www.newyorker.com/news/daily-comment/does-the-kavanaugh-investigation-show-how-trump-will-use-the-fbi-in-the-future.

CHAPTER SEVENTEEN: TRUMP, BARR, AND THE GUTTING OF CONGRESSIONAL POWER

223   **O'Connor did not want to blame either side in the dispute:** David Rohde, "For a Besieged F.B.I., the Shutdown Is the Latest Trump-Era Assault," *The New Yorker,* January 19, 2019, https://www.newyorker.com/news/daily-comment/for-a-besieged-fbi-the-shutdown-is-the-latest-trump-era-assault.

232   **Tom O'Connor arrived on Capitol Hill to attend a hearing:** Thomas O'Connor, interview with the author, October 23, 2019.

232   **One was Luis Alvarez, a New York City Police detective:** "Luis Alvarez and Jon Stewart Plead with Congress to Reauthorize 9/11 Victims Compensation Fund," CSPAN, June 11, 2019, https://www.c-span.org/video/?c4801983/luis-alvarez-jon-stewart-plead-congress-reauthorize-911-victims-compensation-fund

234   **He was 53:** Sam Roberts, "Luis Alvarez, Champion of 9/11 Responders, Dies at 53," *New York Times*, June 29, 2019, https://www.nytimes.com/2019/06/29/obituaries/luis-alvarez-dead.html.

235   **"The president was not exculpated":** David Rohde, "Mueller Testimony: 'The President Was Not Exculpated,'" *The New Yorker*, July 24, 2019, https://www.newyorker.com/news/current/mueller-testimony-the-president-was-not-exculpated.

236   **Distrust was the defining dynamic:** David Rohde, "Mueller Revealed the Conspiracy-Theory-Driven State of American Politics," *The New Yorker*, July 24th, 2019, https://www.newyorker.com/news/current/the-competing-partisan-plot-lines-of-robert-muellers-testimony.

236   **Trump nominated Ratcliffe:** David Rohde, "Trump's Message to U.S. Intelligence Officials: Be Loyal or Leave," *The New Yorker*, July 29, 2019, https://www.newyorker.com/news/daily-comment/trumps-message-to-us-intelligence-officials-be-loyal-or-leave.

237   **Senator Angus King, a Maine Independent:** Angus King, interview with the author, July 29, 2019.

CHAPTER EIGHTEEN: CHECKS AND BALANCES

239   **A meticulous nine-page whistleblower complaint:** "Document: Read the Whistle-Blower Complaint," *New York Times*, September 26, 2019, https://www.nytimes.com/interactive/2019/09/26/us/politics/whistle-blower-complaint.html.

240   **"The Hatch Act is singularly important":** Joan Dempsey, interview with the author, November 4, 2019.

241   **the whistleblower complaint was leaked to the *Washington Post*:** Greg Miller, Ellen Nakashima, and Shane Harris, "Trump's Communications with Foreign Leader Are Part of Whistleblower Complaint That Spurred Stand-off between Spy Chief and Congress, Former Officials Say," *Washington Post*, September 18, 2019, https://www.washingtonpost.com/national-security/trumps-communications-with-foreign-leader-are-part-of-whistleblower-complaint-that-spurred-standoff-between-spy-chief-and-congress-former-officials-say/2019/09/18/df651aa2-da60-11e9-bfb1-849887369476_story.html.

243   **The reaction to the whistleblower complaint:** David Rohde, "Public Servants Are Starting to Respond to Donald Trump's False Attacks," *The New Yorker*, October 14, 2019, https://www.newyorker.com/news/daily-comment/public-servants-versus-donald-trump.

248   **"They are saying that they have a smoking gun":** Will Hurd, interview with the author, October 18, 2019.

CHAPTER NINETEEN: IMPEACHMENT

253   **"What continues to amaze me":** David Rohde, "The President's Attempt to Intimidate Marie Yovanovitch Backfires," *The New Yorker*, November 15, 2019, https://www.newyorker.com/news/news-desk/trump-impeachment-hearings-the-presidents-attempt-to-intimidate-marie-yovanovitch-backfires.

257   **"We are running out of time to stop them":** Joseph Marks, "Fiona Hill Warns Republicans That Claims of Ukraine Interference Could Help Russia in 2020," *Washington Post*, November 22, 2019, https://www.washingtonpost.com/news/powerpost/paloma/the-cybersecurity-202/2019/11/22/the-cybersecurity-202-fiona-hill-warns-republicans-that-claims-of-ukraine-interference-could-help-russia-in-2020/5dd71a26602ff1181f264013/.

CHAPTER TWENTY: DEADLOCK

259   **the Justice Department inspector general, Michael Horowitz, released a long-awaited report:** Office of the Inspector General, "Review of Four FISA Applications and Other Aspects of the FBI's Crossfire Hurricane Investigation," US Department of Justice, December 9, 2019, https://www.justice.gov/storage/120919-examination.pdf, pp. viii–ix.

263   **Veltmeyer claimed that Trump's impeachment was the latest effort:** James Veltmeyer, "Trump: Existential Threat to the New World Order," December

27, 2019, https://myzipmail.com/enote/Details/Trump__Existential_Threat_to_The_New_World_Order_e0c5bafa-3500-4f86-9490-1e5fd904c4ff.

263   **Bannon told the *Washington Post*:** Greg Miller and Greg Jaffe, "In Aftermath of Ukraine Crisis, a Climate of Mistrust and Threats," *Washington Post*, December 24, 2019, https://www.washingtonpost.com/national-security/in-aftermath-of-ukraine-crisis-a-climate-of-mistrust-and-threats/2019/12/24/03831e3e-2359-11ea-a153-dce4b94e4249_story.html.

EPILOGUE: THE "DEEP STATE"

267   **the number of false or misleading claims:** Glenn Kessler, Salvador Rizzo, and Meg Kelly, "President Trump Has Made 16,241 False or Misleading Claims in His First Three Years," *Washington Post*, January 20, 2019, https://www.washingtonpost.com/politics/2020/01/20/president-trump-made-16241-false-or-misleading-claims-his-first-three-years/.

INDEX